Praise for *Brainstorm*

'A much-needed guide to the perils—and *promise!*—of adolescence, *Brainstorm* is full of practical tips for fostering happiness and success throughout the teen years. A must read for all those with adolescents in their lives.'
— **Christine Carter, PhD**, author of *Raising Happiness* and director of Greater Good Parents at the Greater Good Science Center, University of California, Berkeley

'Siegel gives us a fresh and insightful examination of adolescence from his point of view as an expert on the brain. The book also shows him to be a thoughtful parent, a compassionate guide, and a very fine writer. I strongly recommend *Brainstorm* to teens and to those who care about them.'
— **Mary Pipher, PhD**, author of *Reviving Ophelia* and *The Green Boat*

'*Brainstorm* recognises the power, courage, and creativity of the next generation of change makers and invites us on a reflective and experiential journey of living life to the fullest, through adolescence and beyond. It is essential reading for all those interested in creating a better world for themselves and others.'
— **Craig Kielburger**, co-founder of Me to We and Free The Children

'*Brainstorm* is eye-opening and inspiring, a great gift to us all—teens, parents of teens, and anyone who wants a full and rich life on this planet. Daniel J. Siegel shows how the supposed downsides of the teen years all have upsides, and that the lessons for living that await teens are lessons any of us, at any age, can learn from. Teens and their parents stand to benefit immensely from reading this book, separately or together.'
— **Daniel Goleman, PhD**, author of *Emotional Intelligence*

'Dr Siegel aptly characterises the teen years as the most powerful life phase for activating courage, purpose, and creativity. With his usual personal and compassionate delivery, he illustrates how we can all become more aware, empathetic, and understanding of teenagers and ourselves. A visionary and a guide, Siegel knows that if we treat teenagers with the respect and understanding they deserve, they are more likely to live up to their greatest capacities.'
— **Laura S. Kastner, PhD**, clinical professor of psychiatry and behavioural sciences, University of Washington, and author of *Wise-Minded Parenting*

'At last a book that really explains adolescence! "You just don't get me" is a common refrain from teenagers to their parents and teachers. Adolescents who read this book will discover that Daniel J. Siegel gets them. My favourite thing about this book is that Siegel sees adolescence not as a problem to be solved or a hardship to be endured, but rather as a wellspring of courage and creativity. This respectfulness is why the book works so well as a manual for adolescents, as well as their parents and mentors.'

— **Lawrence J. Cohen, PhD**, author of *The Opposite of Worry*

'This book is filled with validation, vision, and clarity to help us navigate the seas of an often overwhelming time in life—the teenage years. Dan Siegel illuminates where there was mystery, empowers where there was fear, and inspires where there was trepidation. I am indebted to Dan for his deep kindness and ability to so articulately share his scientific, psychological, and social intelligence. This book is chock-full of cutting-edge knowledge as well as a deep compassion for teenagers, the adults they will become, and the teenagers in all of us.'

— **Alanis Morissette**, Grammy Award–winning singer and songwriter

'A positively refreshing twist on the age-old topic of adolescent behaviour. In a captivating conversational tone suited to teens (or those who work with or care for them), author Dan Siegel debunks myths of "hormone-crazed teenagers" and replaces them with a more constructive narrative about age-related "remodelling in the brain". This book offers mind-opening brain science alongside practical tools that teens can use to navigate the emotions and relationships they encounter each day.'

— **Barbara L. Fredrickson**, Kenan Distinguished Professor of Psychology, University of North Carolina, Chapel Hill, and author of *Positivity* and *Love 2.0*

'*Brainstorm* is a necessary look at why adolescents do what they do that can put parents in an emotional frenzy. The information that Dr Siegel shares not only is invaluable for understanding your growing child's brain, but helps build more compassion and patience. A gift for us all.'

— **Goldie Hawn**, Academy Award–winning actress, producer, director, and founder of MindUP™

'The teen years don't have to be filled with turmoil! In *Brainstorm*, Dan Siegel serves up a rich blend of smart insights and nitty-gritty tips to guide teens and the adults who care for them through this amazing period of creativity, conflict, and love.'

— **Harvey Karp, MD, FAAP**, author of *The Happiest Toddler on the Block*

Scribe Publications
BRAINSTORM

Daniel J. Siegel, MD, received his medical degree from Harvard University and completed his postgraduate medical education at UCLA, where he is currently a clinical professor. He is the executive director of the Mindsight Institute, and the author of numerous books, including the acclaimed bestsellers *Mindsight: change your brain and your life*, *The Whole-Brain Child* (co-authored with Tina Payne Bryson), and *Parenting from the Inside Out* (co-authored with Mary Hartzell). He lives in Los Angeles with his wife and occasionally with his launched adolescents.

BRAINSTORM

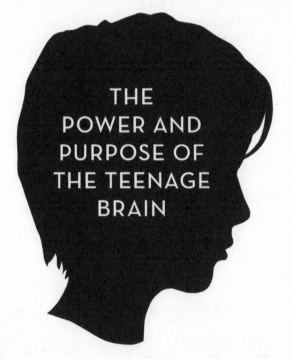

THE
POWER AND
PURPOSE OF
THE TEENAGE
BRAIN

DANIEL J. SIEGEL, MD

SCRIBE

Melbourne • London

Scribe Publications Pty Ltd
18–20 Edward St, Brunswick, Victoria 3056, Australia
2 John St, Clerkenwell, London, WC1N 2ES, United Kingdom

First published in the United States by Jeremy P. Tarcher/Penguin, 2013

Published by Scribe 2014, reprinted 2015 (three times)

This edition published 2014

Book design by Ellen Cipriano
Printed and bound in the UK by CPI Group (UK) Ltd, Croydon CR0 4YY

National Library of Australia Cataloguing-in-Publication entry

Siegel, Daniel J., author.

Brainstorm: the power and purpose of the teenage brain / Daniel J. Siegel.

9781922070944 (Australian paperback)
9781922247452 (UK paperback)
9781925113075 (e-book)

1. Adolescent psychology 2. Brain 3. Cognition in adolescence

155.5

A CIP record for this title is available from the British Library

scribepublications.com.au
scribepublications.co.uk

To Madeleine and Alexander,
for illuminating the vital essence of adolescence.

To Caroline,
for being a compassionate companion along this wild and
wonder-filled journey.

And to my mom,
for keeping your inner adolescent alive and well and being an
inspiration to us all.

Contents

Part II. Your Brain ▪ 65

PART I

■

The Essence of Adolescence

Adolescence is as much a perplexing time of life as it is an amazing one. Running roughly between the ages of twelve and twenty-four (yes, into our mid-twenties!), adolescence is known across cultures as a time of great challenge for both adolescents and the adults who support them. Because it can be so challenging for everyone involved, I hope to offer support to both sides of the generational divide. If you are an adolescent reading this book, it is my hope that it will help you make your way through the at times painful, at other times thrilling personal journey that is adolescence. If you are the parent of an adolescent, or a teacher, a counselor, an athletic coach, or a mentor who works with adolescents, my hope is that these explorations will help you help the adolescent in your life not just survive but thrive through this incredibly formative time.

Let me say from the very start that there are a lot of myths surrounding adolescence that science now clearly shows us are simply not true. And even worse than being wrong, these false beliefs can actually make life more difficult for adolescents and adults alike. So let's bust these myths right now.

One of the most powerful myths surrounding adolescence is that raging hormones cause teenagers to "go mad" or "lose their minds." That's simply false. Hormones do increase during this period, but it is not the hormones that determine what goes on in adolescence. We now know that what adolescents experience is primarily the result of changes in the development of the brain. Knowing about these changes can help life flow more smoothly for you as an adolescent or for you as an adult with adolescents in your world.

Another myth is that adolescence is simply a time of immaturity and teens just need to "grow up." With such a restricted view of the situation, it's no surprise that adolescence is seen as something that everyone just needs to endure, to somehow survive and leave behind with as few battle scars as possible. Yes, being an adolescent can be confusing and terrifying, as so many things during this time are new and often intense. And for adults, what adolescents do may seem confounding and even senseless. Believe me, as the father of two adolescents, I know. The view that adolescence is something we all just need to endure is very limiting. To the contrary, adolescents don't just need to survive adolescence; they can thrive *because* of this important period of their lives. What do I mean by this? A central idea that we'll discuss is that, in very key ways, the "work" of adolescence—the testing of boundaries, the passion to explore what is unknown and exciting—can set the stage for the development of core character traits that will enable adolescents to go on to lead great lives of adventure and purpose.

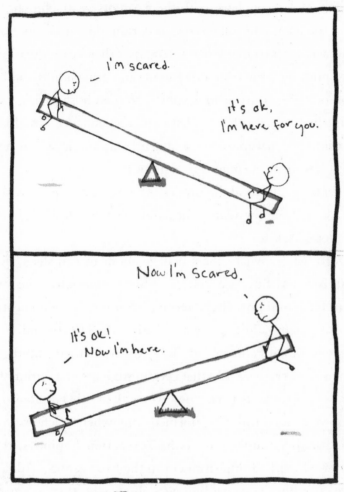

Taking turns.

A third myth is that growing up during adolescence requires moving from dependence on adults to total independence from them. While there *is* a natural and necessary push toward independence from the adults who raised us, adolescents still benefit from relationships with adults. The healthy move to adulthood is toward interdependence, not complete "do-it-yourself" isolation. The nature of the bonds that adolescents have with their parents as attachment figures changes, and friends become more important during this period. Ultimately, we learn to move from needing others' care during childhood, to pushing away from our parents and other adults and leaning more on our peers during adolescence, to then both giving care and receiving help from others. That's interdependence. In this book we'll explore the nature of these attachments and how our need for close relationships continues throughout the life span.

When we get beyond the myths, we are able to see the real truths they mask, and life for adolescents, and the adults in their lives, gets a whole lot better.

Unfortunately, what others believe about us can shape how we see ourselves and how we behave. This is especially true when it comes to teens and how they "receive" commonly held negative attitudes that many adults project (whether directly or indirectly)— that teens are "out of control" or "lazy" or "unfocused." Studies show that when teachers were told that certain students had "limited intelligence," these students performed worse than other students whose teachers were not similarly informed. But when teachers were informed that these same students had exceptional abilities, the students showed marked improvement in their test scores. Adolescents who are absorbing negative messages about who they are and what is expected of them may sink to that level instead of realizing their true potential. As Johann Wolfgang von Goethe wrote, "Treat people as if they were what they ought to be and you help them become what they are capable of being." Adolescence is not a period of being "crazy" or "immature." It is an essential time of emotional intensity, social engagement, and creativity. This is the essence of how we "ought" to be, of what we are capable of, and of what we need as individuals and as a human family.

Brainstorm is set up as follows: The first part examines the essence of adolescence and how understanding its important dimensions can create vitality now and throughout the life span. The second part explores the way the brain grows during adolescence so that we can make the most of the opportunities this period of life creates for us. The third part explores how relationships shape our sense of identity and what we can do to create stronger connections with others and with ourselves. In the fourth part, we dive into the ways in which the changes and challenges of adolescence can be best navigated by being present, by being receptive to what is happening so that we can be fully aware of the inner and interpersonal aspects of these experiences. I'll also provide practical steps along the way, in the Mindsight Tools sections, which offer science-proven ways to strengthen our brains and our relationships.

Because we each learn most effectively in different ways, you may want to experience this book in whatever approach is best for you after reading Part I. If you enjoy learning by blending concepts and facts with science and stories, reading the book from front to back might be best. If instead you learn best by doing, by actual practice, then the four Mindsight Tools sections would be a useful place to start; you can explore the science and stories later. I wrote the book in such a way that if you want to dive into a particular topic, you can do so by reading that part first—for relationships that would be Part III, while for the brain that would be Part II. If you learn best by story-driven discussions, you might read Part IV first, and the earlier sections and practice entries later. Mix it up and find what works best for you. The parts and the Tools sections fit together as a whole; it's up to you how to sample them in a way that meets your needs.

This book is all about understanding and nurturing the essential features of adolescence to bring the most health and happiness into the world regardless of what age we are.

The Benefits and Challenges of Adolescence

The essential features of adolescence emerge because of healthy, natural changes in the brain. Since the brain influences both our minds and our relationships, knowing about the brain can help us with our inner experience and our social connections. In our journey I'll show how this understanding, and learning the steps to strengthen the brain in practical ways, can help us build a more resilient mind and more rewarding relationships with others.

During the teen years, our minds change in the way we remember, think, reason, focus attention, make decisions, and relate to others. From around age twelve to age twenty-four, there is a burst of growth and maturation taking place as never before in our lives. Understanding the nature of these changes can help us create a more positive and productive life journey.

I'm the father of two adolescents. I also work as a physician in the practice of child, adolescent, and adult psychiatry, helping kids, teens, adults, couples, and families make sense of this exciting time in life. In addition to working as a psychotherapist, I also teach about mental health. What has struck me in each of these roles is that there is no book available that reveals the view that the adolescent period of life is in reality the one with the most power for courage and creativity. Life is on fire when we hit our teens. And these changes are not something to avoid or just get through, but to encourage. *Brainstorm* was born from the need to focus on the positive essence of this period of life for adolescents and for adults.

While the adolescent years may be challenging, the changes in the brain that help support the unique emergence of the adolescent mind can create qualities in us that help not only during our adolescent years, if used wisely, but also as we enter adulthood and live fully as an adult. How we navigate the adolescent years has a direct impact on how we'll live the rest of our lives. Those creative qualities also can help our larger world, offering new insights and innovations that naturally emerge from the push back against the status quo and from the energy of the teen years.

For every new way of thinking and feeling and behaving with its positive potential, there is also a possible downside. Yet there *is* a way to learn how to make the most of the important positive qualities of the teenage mind during adolescence and to use those qualities well in the adult years that come later.

Brain changes during the early teen years set up four qualities of our minds during adolescence: novelty seeking, social engagement, increased emotional intensity, and creative exploration. There are changes in the fundamental circuits of the brain that make the adolescent period different from childhood. These changes affect how teens seek rewards in trying new things, connect with their peers in different ways, feel more intense emotions, and push back on the existing ways of doing things to create new ways of being in the world. Each of these changes is necessary to create the important shifts that happen in our thinking, feeling, interacting, and decision making during our adolescence. Yes, these positive changes have negative possibilities, too. Let's see how each of these four features of the adolescent brain's growth has both upsides and downsides, and how they fill our lives with both benefits and risks.

1. *Novelty seeking* emerges from an increased drive for rewards in the circuits of the adolescent brain that creates the

inner motivation to try something new and feel life more fully, creating more engagement in life. **Downside:** Sensation seeking and risk taking that overemphasize the thrill and downplay the risk result in dangerous behaviors and injury. Impulsivity can turn an idea into an action without a pause to reflect on the consequences. **Upside:** Being open to change and living passionately emerge, as the exploration of novelty is honed into a fascination for life and a drive to design new ways of doing things and living with a sense of adventure.

2. *Social engagement* enhances peer connectedness and creates new friendships. **Downside:** Teens isolated from adults and surrounded only by other teens have increased-risk behavior, and the total rejection of adults and adult knowledge and reasoning increases those risks. **Upside:** The drive for social connection leads to the creation of supportive relationships that are the research-proven best predictors of well-being, longevity, and happiness throughout the life span.

3. *Increased emotional intensity* gives an enhanced vitality to life. **Downside:** Intense emotion may rule the day, leading to impulsivity, moodiness, and extreme, sometimes unhelpful, reactivity. **Upside:** Life lived with emotional intensity can be filled with energy and a sense of vital drive that give an exuberance and zest for being alive on the planet.

4. *Creative exploration* with an expanded sense of consciousness. An adolescent's new conceptual thinking and abstract reasoning allow questioning of the status quo, approaching problems with "out of the box" strategies, the creation of

new ideas, and the emergence of innovation. **Downside:** Searching for the meaning of life during the teen years can lead to a crisis of identity, vulnerability to peer pressure, and a lack of direction and purpose. **Upside:** If the mind can hold on to thinking and imagining and perceiving the world in new ways within consciousness, of creatively exploring the spectrum of experiences that are possible, the sense of being in a rut that can sometimes pervade adult life can be minimized and instead an experience of the "ordinary being extraordinary" can be cultivated. Not a bad strategy for living a full life!

While we can brainstorm lots of new ideas inside us that we can share collaboratively during the creative explorations and novelty seeking of adolescence, we can also enter another kind of brainstorm as we lose our coordination and balance and our emotions act like a tsunami, flooding us with feelings. That's when we get filled with not only mental excitement but also with mental confusion. Adolescence involves both types of brainstorms.

In a nutshell, the brain changes of adolescence offer both risk and opportunity. How we navigate the waters of adolescence—as young individuals on the journey or as adults walking with them—can help guide the ship that is our life into treacherous places or into exciting adventures. The decision is ours.

Maintaining the Power and Purpose of the Adolescent Mind into Adulthood

Too often I hear adults in my practice say that their life is in a rut. They feel "stuck" or "empty," have lost their novelty-seeking drive, and are filled with the boredom of just doing the same old things over and over again. They also find their lives filled with a lack of social connectedness—they feel isolated and alone. And for many, life has lost its emotional intensity, things feel lackluster, even boring. This ennui can lead to apathy or even depression and despair. Nothing seems to matter; nothing seems to feel alive or vital. When adults stop using their potential for creative exploration, the way they reason and approach life's problems becomes simply a repeated familiar routine and imagination goes out the window. Life can become, well, lifeless. When adults lose the creative power of the adolescent mind, their lives can lose vitality and become meaningless.

The playfulness and humor that emerge from the creation of new combinations of things are essential to keep our lives full of vitality. Hang out with teens and you'll often hear laughter and hysterics. And sometimes you'll hear a lot of crying. So emotional intensity can bring joy, and it can bring tears, for sure. Hang out with many adults, and you'll often hear predominantly serious talk. Yes, life is serious. But we can bring joy and humor to these lives we lead. We need to live with humor and zest, not in spite of the world's problems but because of them.

Yet when adults lose the four distinguishing features of adolescence, when they stop cultivating the power of novelty seeking, social engagement, emotional intensity, and creative exploration, life can become boring, isolating, dull, and routinized. Who would intentionally choose to live like that? Most likely no one. But it happens all the time. It seems we adults are prone to just cruise on auto pilot. Why? It can be difficult coping with life's circumstances, to face the world's stresses. Sometimes it's easier to just shut down these essential aspects of a vital life that come during adolescence and instead try and stay in "survival mode" as we develop a routine we can rely on to function. But allowing ourselves to lose our vitality will only make life harder—and it also can lead to not keeping the brain as strong as it could be as we age.

So I'm suggesting that what adolescents have going for them that is both a challenge and a gift is actually what adults need in order to maintain vitality in their lives. Here's another myth. People tend to assume that the brain stops growing after childhood. But that's not true. The brain not only grows and changes during childhood and adolescence, but continues to grow throughout the life span. My proposal to you is that the four features of adolescence are exactly what we need to not only live a vital life as teens, but also to keep our brains growing throughout our lives.

Here's a way to remember this "essence" of the brain changes in adolescence. I love acronyms, much to my students' either delight or dismay. So if this acronym is helpful for you, great. Here it is: The essence of the adolescent brain changes that are the essence of healthy ways of living throughout the life span spell the word *essence* itself:

ES: *Emotional Spark*—honoring these important internal sensations that are more intense during adolescence but serve to create meaning and vitality throughout our lives.

SE: *Social Engagement*—the important connections we have with others that support our journeys through life with meaningful, mutually rewarding relationships.

N: *Novelty*—how we seek out and create new experiences that engage us fully, stimulating our senses, emotions, thinking, and bodies in new and challenging ways.

CE: *Creative Explorations*—the conceptual thinking, abstract reasoning, and expanded consciousness that create a gateway to seeing the world through new lenses.

This is the essence of living well during adolescence and during the adult years: *Emotional Spark—Social Engagement—Novelty—Creative Explorations*. Adol-ESSENCE. Or: *Adolescence is Adult-ESSENCE.*

hey, you remind me of someone.

I wonder if some of the tension that I see in parents as a reaction toward adolescents is at times a deep longing for these very features they themselves may have lost. Not having an emotional spark can make a teen's exuberance threatening. Not being socially engaged can make an adult feel disconnected in the face of a teen's social life. How many new friends did we make at ages thirty, forty, or fifty? All the drive for new things in an adolescent's life can make an adult's daily routines seem dull. And the creative explorations that drive a teen into all sorts of new ways of thinking and behaving can make the humdrum and predictability of adult life at times seem too con-trolled and too limiting.

Perhaps if adults could recapture some of this vital essence the gap between the generations would lessen. What I mean by this is that sometimes what we see in others can remind us of what we are

missing in ourselves, and this reminder makes us
pointed, angry, or sad. As a therapist, I see this all t(
for instance, parents cannot stand some aspect of their
ality because it reminds them of something that bugs
their own life. If we take a deep breath and realize we are   .ong
learners, then an adult's intense emotional reaction to a teen, for example, can serve as a reminder for us to explore our own inner lives
and not simply react outwardly.

Adults have things to learn from adolescence as a period we went
through and from adolescents as the ones going through that developmental period right now. Adolescents can remind us of what we
have a right to experience in our lives. Similarly, as adolescents we
have things to learn from adults, as adults share with us their experiences as they support our development toward independence.

Learning to use the power of the adolescent mind can help us
have a positive experience as it emerges during this period of intense
change. When navigated well, these brain changes can lead to positive outcomes later on. Holding on to the essential power of the
teenage mind into later adolescence and beyond, into the adult years,
can enable us to continue lifelong learning and recognize the important life-affirming sense of adventure, vitality, and courage that adolescence brings. Learning to use the power of the emerging adolescent
mind well is as important for us as adolescents as it is for us as adults!

Adolescence from the Inside Out

We'll be exploring the essence of adolescence from an "inside out"
approach. What this means is that we can learn how understanding
our own or others' inner workings can help us understand the outer

ьehaviors of ourselves and of others. This inside-out understanding can help us create the life we want, not simply settle for what we are given. To take on this inside-out approach, we'll learn about how the brain, self-awareness, and relating to others all help create the experience of who we are—how they help create our minds—so that we can be better equipped for this period of life.

We'll also explore important and relevant scientific ideas and reveal how to apply science in helpful ways. This book is written so that it feels like a conversation between me as author and you as reader. My hope is that reading it will make you feel as if we are actually talking together, in person, about this important period of life.

I'm excited to invite you to join with me in this conversation-like exploration to put yourself in the experience, to reflect on what is going on in your own life. With two adolescents in my personal life now, one in his early twenties and the other in her late teens, I am presented every day with the opportunities and challenges of being a parent of two individuals going through this period of life. And being their father also recalls the memories and meanings of my own adolescent years. I'll share with you as we go along some of these inside-out reflections that are directly relevant to the topics we'll be focusing on.

For you as an adolescent, these discussions can invite you to think about your own life now. If you are an adult reading this, you may find yourself reflecting on what is going on now or what went on in your own adolescence. Your reading experience—like my writing experience—is intended as an invitation for us to become actively involved in a conversation with each other and for you to reflect on your own experiences with me. You may find it helpful to keep a personal journal to capture your own reflections, a process that may feel good and also one that has been shown to support the ability to

make sense of things. If you are looking for a journey of discovery where what you learn and what you reflect on can help you travel through the adolescent years and harness the creative power of this period and hold on to its essence with more knowledge, insight, and understanding, you've come to the right place.

We never stop discovering who we are or what has meaning in life. Our minds continually emerge in ways that can support a healthy, exuberant life as we grow and develop throughout our lives. So this is truly an exploration I am asking you to join me in, not some download of facts and figures, not just a bunch of opinions and mandates on what you should do. And whether you are in adolescence or adult years, this exploration can help your mind emerge in helpful ways. Since this is a conversation, it means we'll be asking questions, basic questions, that we'll wrestle with as we attempt to answer them. The fact is that we don't know the final answers to a lot of questions about the brain or the mind, but asking them and searching for the answers are essential steps for us to take.

My own kids ask me why I like teaching so much, and I say it is because I am always learning when I connect with people in educational experiences. I feel it's an important stance to take—that we are lifelong learners. To have an understanding of where another person is coming from during this developmental period helps everyone navigate it well and continue to grow.

During childhood, parents are often seen as the be-all and end-all of role models. In fact, adolescence is a time when we begin to see our parents as actual people, not heroes, who have their own flaws and limitations. Perhaps seeing parents in this way helps us leave them and go out into the world. As Mark Twain once said, "When I was a boy of fourteen, my father was so ignorant I could hardly stand to have the old man around. But when I got to be twenty-one, I was astonished at how much the old man had learned in seven years."

Naturally, pushing away from the status quo is a fundamental way to create novel experiences. And novelty seeking is both a part of the push back and inherently rewarding. Adolescence is also a time filled with new ideas. In many ways, seeking novelty is rewarding as it fills experiences, behaviors, perceptions, thoughts, ideas, intentions, and beliefs with the spirit of adventure.

This striving for novelty is a creative power that can be harnessed for the benefit of everyone, *if* we see this move toward new things and independence in a positive way. On the other hand, if adults fight against these fundamental features of adolescence, it's like fighting against the natural push of a waterfall. The force of adolescence

Øur bra1n5 ar3 prøgramma[l]

...and w3 ar3 th3 prøgramm3r5.

will find some way to manifest itself in a teen's external actions and internal mental shifts. You cannot stop a waterfall, but you can learn to direct its course and harness its power.

The good news is that the developmental state of adolescence does not have to be experienced as a war between the generations. If adults try to block the flow of adolescence, it is likely that communication, so important to relationships, will be tainted with tension and disrespect. Disconnection, secrecy, isolation, and many other negative and hurtful social responses can emerge. The key is for the adolescent and the adult-who-once-was-an-adolescent to recognize these important brain changes and learn to navigate these years constructively and collaboratively in order to keep communication open between them, to optimize life for everyone, and to avoid tragic endings of risky behaviors. The challenge is not easy, but it at least should be made clear.

This is our balancing act, for adolescents and adults alike: making push toward independence, the drive for reward, and the passion for novelty result in positive outcomes in life.

The brain is our enabler—our control center—and the good news is that when we understand the brain, we can harness its powerful drives to make positive choices and constructive changes in our lives. Understanding how the brain links its different circuits, how it becomes integrated with development, is a useful way of seeing how we can help promote optimal functioning in our lives during adolescence and beyond. This integration is altering the linkage of different areas in the brain, and even between people, that can help us understand and optimize the important changes in adolescence.

Here is the powerful finding from science: You can learn the steps to make your brain more integrated and to strengthen it. You can learn how to improve the way your mind functions and make your brain healthier and your relationships more rewarding. These are the basic things we'll explore in the pages ahead. You'll learn through stories and science about these important aspects of your life; and you'll be offered practices to create more integration in your life. And if you learn these things, they can make the rest of your life better. No kidding.

Risk and Reward

While most measurable aspects of our lives are improving during adolescence, such as physical strength, immune function, resistance to heat and cold, and the speed and agility of how we respond, we are three times more likely to suffer serious injury or death during this time than we were in childhood or than we will be in adulthood. This increase in risk is not "by chance"—scientists believe it comes from the innate changes in how the brain develops during this period.

The question is whether we can support the exploration of new things while we also minimize the chance of permanent harm. That's the issue, and that's one of the challenges we'll address in the pages ahead.

Just before my son's first birthday, he and I were walking around the block near our apartment, gathering stones we could toss around (a favorite pastime of his), when I noticed a line of cars jammed along what was usually a pretty quiet street. When we got home, I heard from some neighbors who had been stuck in the traffic that there had been a terrible accident just a mile from our apartment.

That evening I was horrified to find out what had happened.

My favorite teacher during my psychiatric training program was pulling out of his driveway with his wife that late afternoon, headed for a Friday night dinner and a movie. I'll call my teacher Bill. (As in all the true stories you'll read about, I've changed the names and identifying features of the people in these nonfiction narratives to honor their privacy and protect the confidentiality of all concerned—except, naturally, I've left my own details and those of my family members.) As Bill and his wife left for the evening, his wife later told me, they were excited to go out together. Bill drove his car to the corner of their residential street, looked both ways, and when the coast was clear carefully drove his car across the westbound lanes to head east toward the restaurant, a trip he and his wife had been taking for nearly a half century. But this time was different. In that brief time crossing over the lanes, a car suddenly appeared headed west and barreled into them. Before they knew it, their car was hit head-on, split in half, and Bill was killed instantly. Amazingly, Bill's wife and the driver of the speeding car were unharmed, physically at least.

The driver was a nineteen-year-old young man in a brand-new sports car. Two months earlier, after crashing into a tree, he had been arrested for speeding down that same twisty boulevard. His parents replaced that wrecked sports car with another. Bill's wife told me that the investigators at the scene later estimated that the teenager had been driving at least ninety-five miles an hour. I traced the path of that teen's car in my mind over and over again, trying to make sense of this senseless accident. At that speed and with those curves, Bill could never have seen the car approach before crossing those westbound lanes to head east, and the oncoming teenage driver at that speed would never have seen Bill's car crossing his path until it was too late.

I did whatever I could to support Bill's family, friends, and colleagues in the memorial services at the university and at the clinical institutions where Bill had taught for so many years. I reflected on what he had taught me as an expert in development and the mind—how our early experiences shape who we are, shape who we become; how so much of our behavior is driven by mental processes outside our awareness. Just a few weeks before his tragic death, Bill and I had met to talk about some of the research I was starting to do on attachment and memory. "That's so fascinating!" Bill said. "Tell me more!" He was such an inspiring teacher, someone who would listen closely to what was going on inside me, support my interests, encourage me to pursue my passions. And at that meeting I told him so. "Thanks, Dan, but you know I think of you more as a peer now, a colleague." I thanked him, and felt honored to be connected to him however he defined our relationship. I wondered how Bill's life devotion to exploring why people do what they do might help all of us comprehend this reckless and fatal accident.

When I began to look into the facts about the adolescent period, I was shocked to find that though teenagers are more physically fit and healthier than children or adults, they actually make up the largest group with avoidable causes of death. By avoidable I mean that risky or dangerous behaviors lead to permanent injuries or fatalities. With accidents, drug use, wounding from weapons, suicide, and

Pushing boundaries.

murder, the period from twelve to twenty-four is the most dangerous time of our lives. Bill's death fit with well-established statistics.
The reality is that many teenagers—like this nineteen-year-old—act
in extreme ways that risk life and limb, harming their own and others' lives in irreversible ways.

Why do such risk-taking, limit-testing, sensation-seeking behaviors happen? With my one-year-old son there by my side around the
time of Bill's death, I wondered if there was anything I could do as
his father to prevent him from participating in such destructive behavior. If that was possible, I wanted to figure it out and share it with
my patients and the mental health community so that tragedies like
the one that ended Bill's life might be avoided.

Adolescence is a time of great boundary pushing that can be
challenging and create catastrophes; but this pushing-back propensity can also be a remarkably positive, essential part of our lives. Our
challenge is to engage and explore ways to push at life's boundaries
without driving a hundred miles an hour down a public street and
killing someone in our path. For males especially, who seem to bio-
logically need to court danger, in some fashion to "come of age" as
young men, to test limits and face risk to prove they can come out
alive, there must be some culturally sanctioned rites of passage we
can reinvent that don't involve a two-ton weapon barreling down
the road with innocent victims in its wake. When an adolescent ga-
zelle runs up close to a cheetah to inspect its potential predator, it is
risking its own life, not the life of its fellow gazelles, adolescents or
adults. As modern human beings who share with other mammals
this adolescent drive toward danger, cars and alcohol make accidents
one of the top killers in this otherwise healthy period of life.

In the twenty years since Bill's death, the tragic school shootings
and public explosions we bear witness to have often been carried out
by males in their adolescence. There is an increasing disconnect in

today's world and we need to do something to help teens so that such destructive behavior can be understood and made less likely to happen.

Rather than simply wondering what is going on, it would be much more productive to explore the nature of adolescence with individuals in their teens and twenties and with the adults who help support them in such a way that maybe, just maybe, the chances of these destructive actions occurring might be lessened, even if in some small but personally significant way. I think Bill would be happy if understanding the adolescent processes leading to his tragic death could help avoid such tragedies for others in the future.

Pushing Away

In broad terms, the adolescent push against what is known, safe, and familiar is a two-sided coin. Yes, that adolescent pushing away from adults seems to be built into our genes. It's what gets us to drive outrageously fast down a public street. That is the destructive side of the adolescent coin, a side we should try to control so the adolescent can grow well and stretch his or her wings but minimize damage to self or to others.

Yet there is a constructive side that can be used, too.

With awareness, the power of the adolescent mind can be utilized to benefit oneself and others. It is this constructive side that has led to so many innovations that have transformed our modern world in art, in technology, in music. This period of the teenage years and early twenties is a time of great potential and of great constructive power. The push against traditional ways of doing things and of thinking about reality can yield ways of thinking outside the box that enable new and creative ways of doing things to emerge.

With the problems our world faces today—the energy crisis, changes in the environment, overpopulation, war, poverty, and threats to the availability of healthy food, water, and air—never before have we so desperately needed a way to think beyond our usual strategies to create innovative ways of sustainable living on our precious planet. My suggestion to you is that the power of the adolescent mind has just that spark of emotion and social drive, just that push to explore new solutions to old ways of doing things, that may save life on our planet.

The key is how to discover these hidden positive aspects of adolescence and work together as adolescents and adults to make them work for us rather than against us.

Even if we don't buy into the idea that adolescents will save the world, at least understanding brain science may help explain how we can encourage a teen to decide to call home or come in by one in the morning instead of three. We may be more open to the notion that brain science shows how the very essence of adolescence can help individuals be healthier and happier. But the truth, too, is that these essential features also can help improve our planet.

Let me say here that if you as an adolescent begin to grasp the science behind the changes in your brain during your teenage years, your adolescence and your adulthood will be better. And if adults can gain insight into these same fundamental aspects of the adolescent mind, they, too, will have healthier and happier lives. We have a lot to learn from the adolescent mind as it emerges in these years and about how we can hold on to its essence throughout our lives. Whether you are a teenager or an older adolescent, or you are an adult making sense of adolescents in your life now or wondering what happened to you when you were this age, these essential features are an important part of the unfolding of your individual life history.

The Timing of Puberty, Sexuality, and Adolescence

Two changes happen universally in our human adolescence. One is that as puberty hits we begin to experience changes in the body and changes in our emotions. The second is that we push away from our parents, hanging out with our peers more and trying to do things in new ways.

With puberty, our sexual organs develop and create changes in hormone levels and in our secondary sexual characteristics, such as breasts in girls and facial hair in boys. For many of us after puberty, our feelings of sexuality begin to emerge. We become attracted to others in new ways that can be intense, wonderful, and frightening all at once. Puberty and sexual maturation often mark the onset of adolescence. For some individuals, the brain changes of adolescence may occur even before puberty, in cases, for example, of delayed sexual maturation.

Whenever puberty occurs, the new emerging sexuality gives rise to fertility—the ability to reproduce. A hundred years ago, the time between the onset of adolescence and the taking on of adult responsibilities of working and having and raising children was very short, a couple of years. In those days, puberty in girls happened around age fifteen or sixteen, and just a few years later teens would create a new family home. What has changed is that now there is a longer duration between puberty and the "end of adolescence," a transition that has no clear end point. The time for setting up a new family and becoming employed in many modern cultures can be a decade or two. With the onset of puberty now at a younger age than ever before—in girls, often before the teen years—and the later timing of setting up a home and assuming other adult responsibilities, adolescence is now quite extended.

While pushing away from adults is universal, what also may be unique to modern life is the increasing number of adolescents who respond to these challenges by completely excluding adults from their lives. For both adolescent and adult, keeping the lines of communication open is the most basic principle of navigating these years well.

In all cultures throughout the world the years that fall between childhood and adulthood are considered a distinct period of life. Interestingly, scientists have noted that it is a marked period in the animal kingdom as well—dogs and cheetahs, parrots and finches all experience adolescence as a distinct life stage. It's possible that this adolescent period, then, is something encoded in our genetic material; it's in our genes.

If we continued to do things just like they did in previous generations, we would be using the same old-world strategies that may not work in a new environment created by a constantly changing world. By pushing away from adults and hanging out more with peers during our adolescence, we can find new ways of dealing with the world and create new strategies for living. In the "adapt or die" realities of evolution, adolescents are our adaptive force.

Yet adults sometimes forget their own adolescence and settle into the status quo, feeling more comfortable with the way things are. While that sense of familiarity in a stressed life of adult responsibilities is understandable, as we've seen, it may also be a reason why the adult-adolescent relationship is filled at times with tension. Adults desire things to stay the same; adolescents are driven to create a new world. This is part of the source of what can become intense friction, sometimes destructively so, that can create pain in everyone, adolescent and adult alike.

We'll explore in great detail how our relationships shape our identity as we move from the important attachment relationships with our parents to the relationships we begin to cultivate more with our peers during adolescence. As we push away from adults during adolescence we begin to associate much more with peers. Associating with our peers during this time is vital for our survival. There is safety in numbers as we "leave the nest" and help one another brave this new world. This increased social engagement also helps us collaborate with our peers, with whom we'll set up a whole new world.

Throughout human history, we stayed together as communities, with adolescents exploring and establishing independence while maintaining a range of important and instructive interactions with their adult elders. Those strands of connectedness are being stretched in today's world, sometimes severing them with negative consequences of isolation and alienation. We are meant to live in a community, meant to live in connection with others. So if the pushing away from adults leads a teen to become isolated even from his or her peer group, then that total disconnection can be quite disorienting. Remember, adolescents pushing away from others is natural; shutting others out totally is not helpful (nor is it natural) for anyone. An important take-home message is that it is vital to keep the lines of connection and communication open and to remember that we all—adolescents and adults—need to be members of a connected community.

The Stress and Distress of Our Extended Adolescence

I sat recently with a group of older adolescents and young and older adults to brainstorm some new approaches to education and the Internet. In order to get the conversation going, we focused on what our teenage years were like and took on a group exercise to offer one word that captured a sense of those years. Here are the words these individuals offered to the group: *isolated, crazed, confused, a mess, alone, terrified, wild, out of control, lost, seeking,* and *frightened.*

I myself offered the word *disconnected*, which I felt, and right away I wondered if the word was too abstract, too intellectual, too disconnected itself from my own emotional experience or theirs. Such doubt, as we'll see later on, may be a part of our temperament, as it is with me. But the adolescent years are also filled with a sense of uncertainty by nature. Why? Because this is a time of great transition. We move from the relative safety and familiarity of the home nest to a temporary period—one that may last decades—of having no real home base. So right there we have two reasons for distress: losing the familiar and safe, and gaining the unfamiliar and dangerous. You never know what lurks in the world outside the home nest, do you?

In facing such newness, adolescence is a tough time. It can be disorienting, disturbing, discombobulating, and distressing. We can become disengaged, disenchanted, and discouraged. Maybe you can think of some other terms that describe these "dis-" states, like the feeling you've disappeared or are dissolving. These are the distasteful aspects of the transition from dependency and the nest-home life of childhood to the come-what-may years that lie ahead in the outside world before the more settled interdependency of adult life.

One source of not just comfort but basic survival is to identify more with your peers than with your parents, to connect with other adolescents and push away from adults. By being a part of an adolescent group, you get companionship on this transitional trek, as well as safety in numbers: Predators will be intimidated by a large group, and you can lose yourself in the group mass. That is one reason why for many but not all teens, fitting in can feel so important—it's an evolutionary holdover of life or death. You can feel comforted by membership in the group, strengthened by membership in the group, and even more creative in the collective intelligence of the group.

While group collaboration can certainly be a source of collective intelligence, it can also get you to jump off a cliff or drive too fast. And that's probably why some form of continued connection to the adults and their adult perspectives still exists in traditional cultures, and even in our animal cousins. Without adults around, young adolescents can literally go wild.

In many cultures the period of adolescence is marked by a culturally sanctioned rite of passage. For boys, there is often a sense of danger and actual risk taking, with the successful completion marked by a ceremony welcoming the youth into the adult world of responsibility. For girls, adolescence is a time of acknowledgment of fertility, the ability to bear children and care for them, so girls are welcomed into the community as new members ready to become a part of the adult generation. These rites of passage are formal acknowledgments of this important transition in life.

In modern culture, our rites of passage are often missing or minimized in importance. We seem to have lost many of our communal and sanctioned ways of taking risks and acknowledging the transition from childhood to adulthood. Human adolescents—and even adolescents of many other mammal species—leave the home and move away from those to whom they are genetically related. Some argue that the biological benefits of such geographical migration make commingling similar genes among our relatives less likely. From a group point of view for humans, there needs to be a clear separation of the dependency of the child and the responsibility of the adult.

With a lack of jobs and a great deal of uncertainty about participating in contemporary society, however, the adolescent period may in many ways be even further prolonged. Because modern cultural practices do not offer transitional relationships with non-parental adults to help acknowledge and facilitate the adolescent period, we have some major challenges as adolescents in our modern times. This might be something we may want to change in the future in our evolving cultural practices.

With this perspective, perhaps collectively we can create a cultural rite of passage, a way in which adolescents are connected to new adults who can help support them in risk-taking and novelty-creating experiences that minimize danger yet optimize the essence of adolescence. There is a lot of power in the emotional spark of this period. And with some adult involvement, the social engagement during this important time can fuel the drive for novelty and the creative explorations that emerge. The key is how we can all work together, across the generations, to honor this essence of adolescence, to discover and cultivate the hidden power and purpose of the adolescent mind.

Adolescent Transitions and the Centrality of Our Relationships

As I embark upon this conversation with you, I am also living these transitions in my own life. The weight of it all, but also the beauty, hit me recently on the morning my daughter was preparing to leave us to go off to college. I want to share this experience with you, as I hope it will speak to your own experiences as both adolescents and parents going through these changes.

The sun is rising slowly on an overcast day here in this desert city by the sea. Los Angeles is where I grew up, and this is where my wife and I have raised our two kids—now twenty-two and eighteen years of age. Clothes are folded in piles along the walls in the hallway outside our daughter's room. I wake early this morning, restless in bed, tumble out in the hazy light, and step into the hall that for eighteen years has been our passage to her room.

She was born four and a half years after her brother, whose room, empty since he moved away to college, has long become the repository of boxes of things to be sorted out and stored in his closet like memories of years now past. A lot has been happening all at once in our family in the past few months.

My father's recent passing, the first death in our immediate family in decades, marks the unfolding of the generations with a finality that underlines the flow of this life we call being human. Life is constantly changing, continually moving forward in time, no matter how much we may want things to simply stay as they are. This is the last day in our home before our daughter will take all those piled clothes, pack them up in boxes and suitcases, put them in her brother's car, and then drive off to college.

So much is happening, all at once, that I can't seem to grasp and hold on to it all. I think of a dear family friend, an Irish poet named John O'Donohue, who died suddenly just after he turned fifty-two. John was an accomplished, insightful author and philosopher, who left behind magnificent books on life and love. In an interview shortly before his death, he was asked if there was anything that still bothered him, something he could not deal with. John said that no matter how much he thought, no matter how much he wrote, he had a nagging feeling that time was like fine sand that he could not hold on to, however tightly he tried to grasp it—it just ran through his fingers.

And that's how I feel now. So much happening, so much life and death and change, and no matter what I do, I can't hold on to any of it. It just slips onward, ever forward.

To be aware, to awaken to the momentous time of it all, to feel its weight, to sense the inevitability of these tides of life, this flow of birth, childhood, adolescence, emergence into adulthood, transition, illness, death. To be aware of our dependence on one another, on our individual development from the earliest days into maturity— whenever that actually is—to a life filled with discovery, connection, growth, and then dissolution. When John and I would teach together, he'd always laugh and say that the "pain level is dropping now" and that the "joy level is rising rapidly" when we'd greet each other after a long time apart. Love fills these moments with laughter and light even in the face of this transience of our being.

When I was a teen, I first started wrestling with some of these notions of life and death, trying to make sense of how we could live lightly in life while knowing the heaviness of its finality. The streets of this city were my playground, where I'd ride my bike for hours, reflecting on this wild journey and how we should be aware of the reality of what it means to be awake, to be human. I came back here after leaving for my own education, returning to these streets and to this coastal city where the shore meets the sand, letting the waves of the sea be my companion all these years later.

Our own children have walked those same sandy paths, their footprints as light and temporary as mine decades ago. The waves washing away our steps through life, the tides moving in and out with the cycle of our days. Their childhood joys, and sorrows, as real and alive for them as they were then for me, as they are for each of us now. No matter our age, we are on this life journey together.

I feel the weight of time here and now. Is this the sadness of her leaving? The sadness of my father's dying? Is this some sense of helplessness at the uncertainty of it all, of the only certainty in life being change itself? I, too, cannot grasp the sand in my hands, cannot stop time from moving forever forward. I sit here, now, filled with it all.

I look at my daughter's clothes and I also see in my mind's eye a young toddler's toys strewn in this same hallway. I feel the rhythm of the music she and I would play in her preschool years, when on Wednesdays I'd take the afternoon off from work to pick her up from school and then we'd dance the afternoon away. We'd twirl in tempo, her feet dancing in air, my toes clinging to carpet as I swung her round and round. "More . . . More . . . More!" she'd cry out, and round and round we'd go, collapsing on the couch, exhausted, exhilarated, giggling, together.

I can see, too, an excited kindergarten kid holding her sweater as she carried her shoes downstairs, tied her laces just so, and picked up her lunch box as she bounded out the front door. If patients' appointments permitted, I'd run home for her arrival at the end of the day and see that boundless energy of excitement as she recounted the day's events. I'd head back to work, seeing people in therapy whose attachment to their own parents was often filled with strife. We'd work to make sense of their lives, their histories, their struggles. And I'd be working to make sense of my own, to embrace the profound importance of our relationships with one another.

How do we find a balance between our adolescents' personal decisions and our parental regulation, our concerns? Structure with empowerment is how my wife and I would think of our strategy of parenting. How could we support our adolescents while also allowing them to find their own voices? And how at the same time could we set the limits and cautions our own years of living had taught us?

Science would call this "authoritative parenting," a helpful approach that is filled with warmth, limit setting, and honoring of autonomy in age-appropriate ways. Such a stance is also the balanced approach of secure attachment: lending support while supporting separation. In fact, attachment is all about this way in which we provide a safe haven while also encouraging exploration. Attachment is all about both security at home and security in the world. We did our best to supply the basic S's of attachment, letting our kids be *seen*, be *safe*, be *soothed*, and feel *secure*. It is from this foundation of secure attachment that adolescents can then ride the white-water rapids of this tumultuous journey with the best hopes of balance and agility.

Since those earliest days raising our son, after my teacher Bill had been killed by that need-for-speed racing teen, I always thought in the back of my mind that providing secure attachment would be the best we could do as parents to create the kind of self-awareness in our son and daughter that would minimize the chances for such prevent-able destructive behaviors. Challenging to create in a busy life but crucial. As our kids each grew into their own adolescence, that security of childhood seemed to disappear, on the surface, and was re-placed with emotional tension, quick reactivity, and sense of disrespect and disregard. When the studies came out that many adolescents ex-perience more distress and negative emotional states, it made sense for how our own kids' experiences were unfolding during those early teen years. And as a young adult student once said to me about what he learned from his own adolescence, we need to remember that teens are changing a lot, and sometimes they'll be one way, with one kind of identity, feeling a lot and feeling intensely, and sometimes they'll be another way, feeling nothing and not interacting much. "Just let them be who they are at the time, not who you expect they should be" was his great advice.

Fortunately, the tectonic shifts in emotion and identity of those early adolescent years give rise to a more stable state for many teens as they leave the middle school years.

High school is the ultimate testing ground for such balancing acts of relationships, tests of attachment to us and new attachments to friends. Parenting adolescents is an emotionally challenging task when facing the decision to speak or not speak, to constrain or permit, to hold close in times of uncertainty, to give comfort when things don't go right. Finding a network of supportive relationships for parents seems crucial in giving us the reflective space to move through adolescence. When we realize that in our evolutionary past we raised children collaboratively and close family or friends or other designated and trusted individuals in our tribe cared for our offspring, we realize how unnatural being isolated as a parent, or as a family, truly is. When it comes to village life for the teen, during the time he or she is pushing against parents, there would be other adults in the tribe to whom the teen could turn for security and connection. But when the only close adult is your parent, the natural way to go in adolescence is entirely toward other adolescents.

As we grow through development, our needs for attachment do not end when our childhood emerges into adolescence; we transfer those needs for supportive connections with others to our friends and life partners. We need to be seen by our friends who serve as important attachment figures in our lives; we need to be safe with them; we need to be soothed by them; and we need to feel secure with them. My wife is my secure attachment figure, and I am hers. We seek comfort from the other at times of stress and internalize the sense of the other to bring an internal sense of security throughout the day.

The last three years of our daughter's adolescence has been a test, for her and for us, in patience. As with her brother's development, this middle period of adolescence feels like a preparation for physical departure and emotional separation. From fifteen to eighteen years old, our daughter, like other teens during this period, has found her way from experiencing life's moments of decision as struggles for clarity to sensing them as moments of expressing her identity. She, and we, have moved from eye rolls and intense emotional wrestling over issues of what she wears, how long she stays out, and what movies she can see and with whom, to finding a mutual space of respect where we can say what we are concerned about and she can state what she needs, what she wants, and what her thinking is regarding these day-to-day decisions as well as major life choices.

It took a while, but after a lot of tearful conflicts on all sides, we learned that by saying what was going on inside our own minds—what each of us was feeling, thinking, hoping for, how we were seeing things, and what we were hearing—we could then listen closely to the other's inner life and the intention behind what often had become simply proclamations of action, if not outright declarations of war. That's reflection, that's reflective conversation. Without such reflective dialogues with one another, the experience of these years would have been so different.

Our daughter's clothes are neatly folded along the wall of the hallway; her plans for these next twenty-four hours before her brother drives her and the packed car up to school, where we'll fly north to meet them, are laid out and include time spent mostly with her friends; and I stand here, feet heavy on the floor, eyes glued to her door, my heart in awe of her, of her growth, and of who she has become. She is ready to go. But like so many parents at this moment, I am not so sure if I am ready to see her leave.

As parents we can only do the best we can. It is helpful to realize that sometimes, in more than a third of us at least, there is active, intentional reflective and relational work to be done to move from a history of insecurity to a present life of security. Such a conscious presence on our part can help bring integration into our children's lives, to bring security to them as they push away and push on into their adolescence, so they'll carry the best intentions and connections from us that we can offer. That is a gift we can give to our children, and one we can offer to ourselves as well.

The intention, all the effort to live and to learn and to love from the inside out, that parents cultivate in their home lives will indeed provide the formative experiences to help our children thrive as they live their adolescence well and hold on to its essence as they emerge into their adult years. If you are an adolescent preparing to leave home or are already out on your own, I hope you will know that there is the possibility of having a secure home for you to return to any time you wish, or you will find your way to creating one that will serve as a home base for you in the future. This inside-out approach is what this book is all about: creating the secure base that enables us as families to turn the changes and challenges of the adolescent period into strengths we will draw on together as we navigate this journey that is our life.

MINDSIGHT TOOLS #1

■

Seeing and Shaping the Sea Inside

In the Mindsight Tools sections we'll explore practical ways you can strengthen your mind, make your brain more flexible and resilient, and improve your relationships. As we've seen in Part I, the changes during adolescence are not something to just get through; they are qualities we actually need to hold on to in order to live a full and meaningful life in adulthood. The practices we'll dive into will strengthen these essential qualities of living well throughout our lives.

In this first practice entry, we'll focus on what I refer to as "mindsight." Mindsight is the ability to truly "see" or know the mind. It's a word I created years ago in medical school when I found that many of my professors lacked this ability— or at least didn't exercise it well with their patients, or their students. I needed some word to remind me that seeing the mind, being empathic, compassionate, and kind, were important in all relationships, especially the one between a physician and a patient. It turns out that the greater our ability to understand the workings of our minds, the healthier our internal worlds become. This is because when we focus our attention on the mind, it's possible to build specific circuits in our brains. The mind is truly "plastic"—changeable through experience—and it is possible at any age to move it toward greater health and harmony.

Mindsight includes three fundamental skills.

The first is *insight*, the ability to sense your own inner mental life. Insight lets you know who you are now, who you've been in the past, and who you'd like to be in the near future. Insight connects past, present, and future and so it includes a mental time-travel ability that can give you a full and clear sense of who you are.

The second aspect of mindsight is *empathy*, or the ability to sense the inner mental life of another person. Empathy enables us to "see" from the other person's perspective, and to imagine what it's like to walk in their mental shoes. Empathy is a gateway to compassion and kindness, and it is also a key to social intelligence, as it allows us to understand others' intentions and needs so we can interact in a mutually satisfying way.

The third component of mindsight is *integration*, the ability to link different parts of something into an interconnected whole. Integration enables us to make our relationships rewarding as we honor differences and promote compassionate connections in how we communicate. Integration inside ourselves helps us link the different aspects of memory together connecting our past, present, and future in a coherent way so that we have a life story that makes sense of who we are. Integration also helps us link different aspects of the brain and body so that we are healthy and function well. Integration creates coordination and balance in our inner and interpersonal worlds. Integration is the basis for living a healthy life, and so the skill of mindsight with its insight, empathy, and integration enables us to create health in our bodies, our relationships, and our minds.

The highest region of the brain, the cortex, makes "maps" or patterns of firing neurons—the basic cells of the nervous system—that create an image or representation of various things. The back of the cortex makes maps of what we see, and the side areas make maps of what we hear. In the frontal area we make many kinds of maps, including a map of past events and a map of possible future experiences. The most forward part of this frontal area, the prefrontal cortex, makes a map of the mind itself. This is how we sense and imagine another person's feelings, thoughts, and memories, among the many aspects of our mental life. I call these "mindsight maps" because they enable us to perceive that others have a mind just as we do. When we sense the mind of another person, we are making a map in our brains of what we imagine that person's internal mental experience is at that moment. It is this ability to make maps of one's mind and of the minds of others that I refer to as mindsight, an important skill that powerfully changes how we understand ourselves. Mindsight is the key ability at the core of both emotional and social intelligence. And mindsight is something that we can learn, and learn well, to make our lives stronger.

Every person has feelings and thoughts and memories. But having mindsight empowers us to have a picture, a map of the mind so that we can use those feelings, thoughts, and memories in new and helpful ways. For example, mindsight enables us to go beyond "being sad" or "being angry" and to recognize that we have these feelings of sadness or anger, see that they are not the totality of who we are, accept them for what they are, and then allow them to transform so they do not lead to depression or anger and rage.

A mindsight map is a kind of picture inside ourselves of our inner mental life—the feelings and thoughts and perspectives—of others, or of ourselves.

Three Basic Kinds of Mindsight Maps

We have mindsight maps of *me* for insight, sometimes called self-awareness or self-knowing awareness. We have mindsight maps of *you* for empathy or other-knowing. We even have a mindsight map of *we* for the way we think, imagine, reason, and behave knowing we are a part of a larger whole, a part of a "we." This mindsight map of we enables us to live with morality as we consider the larger social good. Insight, empathy, and morality emerge from mindsight mapping in our brains.

As teens we can make these maps in new and evolving ways. The more we grow our ability to make these mindsight maps of me, you, and we, the freer, fuller, and more flexible our lives will be. An important aspect of our journey during adolescence is developing a more intricate way of understanding ourselves and others.

Mindsight is a skill. But we don't need to go to a training camp to start building this important integrative ability in our lives. We can simply start the regular practice of reflection and reflective conversations that we'll explore throughout the mindsight tools sections. One of the most exciting things to remember as we set out to learn these skills is that science suggests that such training of a skill grows connections among our neurons that help create a more integrated set of circuits in the brain. And these integrated circuits support how we balance our emotions, focus our attention, understand others and ourselves, approach problems, and interact with others. This is why integration is so helpful to create. Mindsight skills build integration in your brain.

As we've seen, learning mindsight skills means three things. One is seeing the mind of oneself for insight. The second is seeing the minds of others for empathy. And the third means moving our own minds and those of others toward integration. That's mindsight in a nutshell.

Seeing Inside the Sea Inside

When we reflect on things going on inside us, in our inner subjective mental life, we develop the mindsight mapmaking circuits of the brain. That's right. As we practice mindsight skills, we activate those prefrontal circuits and help them grow stronger. Since this region in the brain helps coordinate and balance our inner and interpersonal life, developing mindsight skills can help you understand what is going on and help you make what is going on work best.

But how does what we do with our mind's awareness, how we become conscious of our own subjective mental life and then make mindsight maps of our sea inside, change the physical structure of our brains? This happens because of a process called neuroplasticity, the way the brain changes its connections in response to experience. And experience here means how you focus your attention. When we pay attention to our inner mental life, we grow those important fibers that help us understand ourselves and others. That's what mindsight maps can do for us. They help illuminate the sea inside ourselves and others.

But what is this inner mental sea?

This rich inner world includes your feelings, thoughts, perceptions, memories, images, and sensations, as well as your intentions, attitudes, beliefs, hopes, dreams, and desires. Even though that's a long list of inner mental processes, you can imagine that there are even more things in our inner mental sea that we can be aware of, like motivations and longings and impulses.

These mental activities, the content of our mental life, can occur even without our being aware of them. But when we pay attention to these inner experiences, when we place them in awareness, something very important happens. When our mental lives become something we are aware of, we can develop the mindsight ability to sense this sea inside and to transform our inner life in a positive direction.

How can mindsight actually change our mental lives? To learn how this can happen and to learn how to make it happen for us, we need to ask a basic question about what the mind is. If this is a topic that is of special interest to you, please read an in-depth exploration of the mind in my *Pocket Guide to Interpersonal Neurobiology*, in which I discuss in great detail what we'll discuss in practical ways here. If you'd like to explore how these skills can be used to face various challenges across the life span, please see the range of examples illustrating this approach in my book *Mindsight*.

What is the mind? There is no single answer to this question. And many science fields actually have no answer to this simple but challenging query. Odd as that might seem, it's true. Here we'll explore the practical applications of what I think the mind is in ways that I hope will empower your life.

While the term "mind" is often used to mean our inner, subjective experience of life and the process of being aware or conscious, the mind also regulates the flow of energy and information. The mind regulates how energy moves both within us (embodied energy) and between us and others (relational energy). And since regulation entails both monitoring and modifying, the mind tracks and changes how that energy and information flow over time. A representation or map shows the pattern of energy regarding a specific image, memory, or thought in what is called information flow.

Recognizing the mind's role in regulating energy and information allows us to learn to direct their flow in a positive way. In order to move in a healthy direction, we must engage our minds in integration—linking different aspects of our inner and interpersonal worlds into a more harmonious and functional whole.

It is important to note that (1) the mind affects not just your internal processes, but your relationships with others as well, and (2) the mind is a regulatory process that is self-organizing in that it enables us to sense and then shape how energy flows within us and with others. This is how mental activities are formed.

What are mental activities, really? What do they all have in common?

Mental activities like feelings and thoughts can be described as patterns of energy and information that flow inside us. Energy comes in many forms, like light that enables us to see these words or the sound energy that we use to hear them. In the brain, ions flowing in and out of the membranes of its basic cells, the neurons, lead to the release of chemicals that allow these neurons to communicate with one another. That's electrochemical energy. At its most basic level, whatever its form, energy is the capacity to do stuff.

Certain energy patterns have information in them. When patterns of energy contain information, it indicates that the pattern means something beyond just the sensation of the energy itself. When I write "Golden Gate Bridge," that energy of the light of the letters or of the sound waves for hearing the words is not the bridge over the San Francisco Bay. Words are carried on energy patterns, yes, but they are patterns that contain information. Information is when energy flow represents something—it *re*-presents it to us. And this movement across time, this flow that we are saying is an aspect of the mind, is all about energy and information and how it changes across time.

Insight enables us to sense this flow of energy and information inside ourselves. How do we see this inner world? We begin with sensing energy and information flow by directing our attention inward. Attention, by the way, is defined as how we direct the flow of information. So consciously paying attention to our inner mental life means focusing the information of our minds into awareness. With awareness, we can learn to navigate our internal worlds, to see clearly and to move easily within the sea inside. This is how mindsight empowers us to develop more inner understanding and inner strength.

MINDSIGHT PRACTICE A: Insight and SIFTing the Mind

Right now, try closing your eyes and simply ask yourself, what am I *sensing* right now in my body? You may feel tension in your muscles or you may sense your heart beating, your lungs breathing, or simply a wash of sensations from the body as a whole.

What *images* come up in my mind's eye? Images may take many forms, including the familiar visual ones. But you can also have images of sounds and touch, an image of a time of your life or some hope for the future. Images may be hard to put into words, but don't worry about that—simply being aware of these inner mental experiences is what matters now.

And what *feelings* are inside me? Emotions can involve bodily sensations, yes, but they also link our bodies to our thoughts, to our memories, and to our perceptions. Becoming aware of your emotional feelings can fill you with a wash of energy that may be challenging to name, which is fine. Just becoming aware of your emotional state is a great starting place.

And now, what *thoughts* are streaming through my consciousness? It's funny, but no one really knows exactly what a thought or thinking really is! So don't worry if it's hard to define what you mean when you say you are thinking this or that. Some experience an inner voice that they can hear, others just a sense that has no words. It is fine however thoughts emerge; you just need to let yourself be aware of whatever comes up for you right now.

This is the basic way we can SIFT our sea inside to see what is going on. When we SIFT through our minds, we check inwardly on the *s*ensations, *i*mages, *f*eelings, and *t*houghts going on inside ourselves at any given moment. "Sift" is an apt term to describe the process, of course, because all of the many sensations, images, feelings, and thoughts that may come up in awareness are often connected to one another in a free-flowing process.

We don't need to worry about putting words to these inner experiences; simply becoming aware of our internal world is the essential component for this SIFTing practice. As we become more familiar with it, we can try journaling as a means for further exploration.

Physical Sight of the Material World Versus Mindsight of the Inner World

The way we interact in the world can be divided between two views of reality, one a view of the mind we call mindsight, another view into the physical nature of the world of objects.

Modern life often depends more on physical sight rather than on honoring the mental inner view. This lack of focus on the inner subjective world is a concern because not seeing the mind can lead to people treating others without respect or compassion. Since the experiences we have shape who we are, at home with family or friends, at school with teachers and peers, and in our interactions with the larger social world of culture and society, how we attend to those experiences can promote mindsight or discourage it. So if most of these experiences are externally focused, harnessing only our physical-object perceptual system, then we won't be developing our skills to see and shape the personal world of our inner and our interpersonal life.

When we close one eye, we can see the world in only two dimensions. Then, with both eyes open, we can see in binocular vision with the three dimensions that surround us. That shift in perception from 2-D to 3-D is a subtle analogy for how we move from object vision to mind vision. When we have mindsight, we see the mind within our human lives in its full dimensions. Without it, our perception is limited to the surface level of object-filled physical spaces that surround us, and we do not see the sea inside.

I once began working with someone who was in his early nineties, someone I'll call Stuart, who, sadly, lacked much mindsight ability. He lived mostly in a flat, physically defined reality. Stuart was not prepared to face some of the many challenges and changes in his life at that age, including his emerging illnesses and those of his wife of sixty-five years. As he has learned mindsight skills, his life has gotten fuller and freer and is now imbued with a deep sense of gratitude and joy.

How could Stuart learn a new skill? By focusing his attention, he could stimulate the activity of his brain in new ways.

And when the brain gets activated, it can change the connections among neurons in a helpful way. Focusing the mind can change the structure of the brain no matter our age.

As we move through life, the brain can be the driver in charge of which direction we take. For Stuart, that meant living in a flattened world he had grown accustomed to. His brain called the shots. Our brains can create automatic behaviors, automatic thinking, and automatic responding. The brain can run the show, for sure. But our minds can get our brains to fire and grow in new ways that we choose. That sounds pretty wild, but it is true. Science has clearly shown that how we focus our attention will grow our brains in specific ways. Amazingly, when we learn to see inside the sea inside with more depth, we can use the mind to change the brain toward a more integrated function and structure. Integration in the brain is what creates health and flexibility in our lives.

This is the key to mindsight's power. We can learn the skills that can place us in the driver's seat of our life's journey. We can do that by understanding the brain, as we'll see in Part II, and by learning how to use communication with others in a more effective way, as we'll see in Part III. And we can learn the skills of seeing the mind more clearly so that we might shape it in a way we choose that can change the brain's firing and even the physical connections that make up its wiring. That's what we'll be doing in all of these mindsight-building practice entries.

If we spend a lot of time learning a musical instrument, that encourages those activated parts of our brains to grow. If we spend a lot of time focusing our attention on a sport, the regions of the brain involved in that athletic activity will grow.

And likewise, the kinds of social media and video games we engage in on the Internet will shape our brains as well. The good news is that with balance, our brains can learn many skills, not just one. The key is to find things we love and develop those passions in our lives. Taking some time each day to see inside the sea inside will help us develop our mindsight circuits.

MINDSIGHT PRACTICE B: Mindsight Illuminated

Look around where you are now and locate an inanimate object, like a chair or a rock. If you are outside, see if you can notice something moving, like a cloud or a stream. Now try watching people walking down the street or in a television program or in a photograph, and imagine them only as objects moving through space, objects without an internal mental life. This is your physical sight that allows you to notice the surface features of objects. Now turn on your mindsight and look at those same people and imagine what they might be experiencing in their minds.

The energy we receive from those same images of the people can be processed inside us in two ways. We can see them as just images of objects—that's our physical perceptual system that makes a map of the physical world in time and in space. And we can turn on the mindsight perceptual system that enables us to map the mind of the other person. This is how we can "see" or sense the inner mental life of another person.

If you've never done much mindsight looking around, this may be new for you, so please be patient with yourself. If you've already learned a bit of this, there's always new skills you can develop as we go. And if you've spent a lot of time sensing the mind, then this will be a great review and strengthening of your skills.

Empathy

When we use our ability to make mindsight maps of ourselves, we call this insight. And when we use this same ability to sense and respect the inner mental life of someone else, to make a mindsight map of another person, that can be called compassionate understanding or simply empathy. The way we cultivate empathy can make the difference between a relationship that is rewarding for both people and one that is frustrating and unfulfilling.

But what exactly is a relationship?

When you speak with a friend, you are sending energy in the form of air molecules moving from you to your friend. Her eardrum picks up that energy and the nerve in her ear translates that energy of air molecules moving into electrochemical energy that streams now into the brain itself. The patterns of that energy flow contain within them information that stands for the sounds you are sending, the words that have meanings attached to them. Because you speak the same language, your friend gets the information in the energy patterns you've sent. That energy and information flow shared between people is really how we communicate with each other.

So a relationship can be defined as the *sharing* of energy and information flow.

When that sharing includes information about the mind itself, when you are interested in what is going on within the sea inside your friend, you are *attuning* to her inner life. That attunement is how you create a mindsight map of her inside you. And that is the essential aspect of empathy.

Instead of simply responding to the physical things someone does in their behavior, mindsight enables you to map out the inner mental life of your friend revealed by their physically sent signals, by their communication. Mindsight enables you to sense the mind that is creating the behavior.

You may have noticed that there are three elements to relational communication. One is sensing what is going on between you and another person. A second is being in touch with what is going on inside you, or insight. The other is what is going on inside another person, or empathy. For the "between" sense of your relationship, you can feel how communication is happening between you and another person. This means that signals being sent match what is being received. Does someone hear what you are really saying? Is he paying attention to you or is he distracted? Is he trying to make sense of what you say? And is this friend making an inner map of who you are and of your mind, not just what your behavior is. When we feel that another person feels our feelings, that can be called "feeling felt." This feeling is one of the most important aspects of a close and supportive relationship.

On the empathy side of relationships, we can map out those internal mental experiences we imagine are going on from what we are receiving as signals from other people. These signals include what they say with words and what non-verbal signals are being communicated. These non-verbal signals include eye contact, facial expressions, tone of voice, posture, gestures and touch, and timing and intensity of responses. Such nonverbal signals are often a direct clue as to what is happening in the mind before and beneath the world of words. Paying close attention to these signals can be a key to making mindsight maps of another's mind.

MINDSIGHT PRACTICE C: Empathy

Focusing on non-verbal signals can give us a feeling inside that may be difficult to describe with words, but it is an important way of turning on our mindsight circuits. A fun practice is to try turning off the sound on a television show or film and seeing if you can soak in the feelings being conveyed by the non-verbal signals on the screen. Try a foreign film in a language you don't understand, without subtitles, and leave the sound on so you can also take in the tone of voice of the characters in the story. Just let your mind SIFT the imagined world of the character, exploring in your own mindsight mapmaking view what the sensations, images, feelings, and thoughts might be of the characters in each scene. Don't worry about how accurate you are. Just inviting yourself to imagine the mind of another person activates those prefrontal regions in your brain that will become strengthened by such a perspective-taking practice as you try to see through the mental lens of another person.

Integration

Mindsight is not only the ability to sense the internal sea of others with empathy or of ourselves with insight; mindsight also cultivates integration, a skill that empowers us to coordinate and balance the internal world of others or of ourselves, and the relationships we have with one another.

What does integration really mean, and why does it culti-vate clarity from confusion, calm from chaos?

Integration is the linkage of different parts of something. When we integrate within a relationship, for example, we honor differences between ourselves and the other person. Then we promote linkage through compassionate understand-ing and communication. In the brain, integration happens when we honor the differences between our higher and lower regions and then link them, or between our left and right sides, and then link them.

When we are integrated, a system such as a relationship or a nervous system with its brain and whole body moves into a flexible and harmonious flow. Integration creates harmony. Integration is created as parts of a system are allowed to be unique and specialized, like you and me in a relationship or like members of a choir singing in harmony. The differentiated parts retain their unique aspects and they also become linked. The left and right sides of the brain work in a coordinated and balanced manner, and the communication between you and me honors differences and promotes compassionate connection so our relationship flourishes.

If either differentiation or linkage does not occur, then something very specific happens. When integration is blocked, a system moves toward one or both of two possible extremes: chaos on the one hand, and rigidity on the other.

I think of this like a river. The central flow is one of in-tegration and the harmony it creates. One bank outside this central harmonious flow is chaos; the other is the bank of ri-gidity. When things are chaotic, they are out of control, wild, overwhelming, completely unpredictable. And when things are rigid, they are stuck, unchanging, boring, and completely

The River of Integration

The river of integration represents the movement of a system across time. When the system is integrated, it is adaptive and harmonious in its functioning. When linkage of the differentiated elements (integration) does not occur, the system moves to rigidity or chaos, or some combination of both. From Daniel J. Siegel, M.D., *Mindsight: The New Science of Personal Transformation*, copyright © 2010 by Mind Your Brain, Inc. Adapted with permission.

predictable. Life has a natural movement toward, rather than getting stuck on, the banks of chaos and rigidity as we wind our way down the river of life, the river of integration.

You may be asking, "Where does this integration take place?" And you may be wondering what exactly is being integrated.

Great questions. Integration takes place inside you and between you and others. This is where the mind is—within us and between us. The mind is both embodied and it is relational. So what is being integrated? The core elements of the mind as we've been defining it: energy and information.

The process of mindsight has insight in which we look inward and honor our differentiated experiences and link them within awareness. Mindsight includes empathy with which we honor our differences with others and make maps of our minds within our own differentiated self. That's linking differentiated parts within an empathic relationship. And so we can see how insight and empathy naturally support the third fundamental power of mindsight to promote integration. Where? Within and between.

Now here's another amazing finding. People who use their minds to reflect on the inner nature of their mental lives grow circuits in the brain that link widely separated areas to one another. This linkage, called "neural integration," creates the coordination and balance of the nervous system. Another term that some researchers often use for this is "self-regulation." In the nervous system, regulation is created through neural integration. And not only can people who develop the skill of mindsight promote self-understanding and empathy, they create integration and regulation within themselves, within their relationships, and within others.

If we actively use our attention to explore the inner world, we can begin to see how mindsight can have positive effects that help make life, especially during adolescence, a more positive experience.

As we'll see in the next part, adolescent brain growth is all about increasing levels of neural integration. So with these practices that cultivate mindsight, we'll actually be creating more integration in our own brains and in those of others!

When we learn to use mindsight skills, we learn to focus our attention in a way that grows the important fibers in the brain that link widely differentiated areas to one another. You may see this repeating idea here: Mindsight is a way of focusing attention that integrates the brain! And that's why learning mindsight skills is such an empowering thing for us to do at any age.

MINDSIGHT PRACTICE D:
Sensing the Harmony of Integration

For this practice, you'll be learning to detect various states of integration. When a relationship you have with another person, or even with yourself on a given day, is working well, can you sense the feeling of connection you have? Try to observe how a state of harmony has the qualities of being flexible, adaptive, connected, energized, and stable. If you are considering your connection with another person, see if you can sense how your differences are being honored and compassionate communication is being cultivated between you. If you are focusing on your own inner life, then see if at this harmonious time you've enabled different aspects of yourself to be respected and then linked by how you've given time for the various needs you may have. For example, in my own life, I, like many people, have different states of mind, different "parts" of myself that have different needs. One part likes being social while another distinct part really loves and needs solitude. What can I do? It is literally impossible to satisfy my differentiated needs all at the same time. So the solution to create harmony in my life is to set out time during the day when each of the conflicting needs can be met separately. That coordination and balance of my various needs create a deep sense of being *f*lexible, *a*daptive, *c*onnected, *e*nergized, and *s*table inside me. If a part of you likes acronyms as much as I do, you might enjoy noticing that this collection of words can spell FACES. And it is this FACES flow that describes an integrated harmonious state.

When Integration Is Not Present: Chaos or Rigidity

Mindsight enables us to not only detect integration and harmony but also feel when integration is not occurring. We each can have moments of losing our temper; of saying things we shouldn't say, of reacting in a negative and sometimes hurtful way. We are all human. The key to living an integrated life is to embrace the human reality of these moments of impaired integration and make a repair, to take responsibility for what we've done, acknowledge those actions, and move toward a more integrated way of being back on a high road and repair the connection to others and to ourselves. When we realize, as do many people in workshops I teach, or patients I treat, or friends I know, that feeling disconnected feels bad and making a reconnection feels good, these feelings let us know the inner sense of harmony that emerges with integration. When your system—which is your body and its brain, *and* it is your relationships—honors differences and promotes linkages, when it creates integration within us and between us, that is the harmony of integration. And that feels good.

When the energy and information flow that is in chaos or rigidity in this non-integrated state are not brought into balance, our inner and interpersonal worlds are not very pleasant, to say the least. Inwardly we can feel like we've lost our minds. Interpersonally we can feel out of control and terrify not only others but ourselves as well. These abrupt emotional explosions are when we've "flipped our lids" or "gone down the low road." The actions that can happen down the low road are not necessarily "the real person revealed," as some people argue. They are the older areas of the brain, our primitive mammalian circuits and old reptilian brains, as we'll see in Part II, that are now acting without the oversight of the prefrontal region.

For some people, the time between a triggering event and the low road can be short. Those people need to work to identify the internal cues that reveal the low road process is starting. For others, the time between is longer, but the awareness that a process is unfolding, leading to the impairment of the prefrontal cortex and flipping our lids, is just not accessible. In retrospect, the trigger can be understood but not as it is happening.

MINDSIGHT PRACTICE E: Name It to Tame It

Repair of disintegrated low-road states starts with the self-reflection of mindsight. What was the trigger? What is the meaning of that hot button issue for you? What were the signs that let you know something was being triggered in you? Once down the low road, did you take a break and if possible leave the scene? Could you feel your way to lowering your nervous system's chaotic flooding or rigid shutting down? Drinking a glass of water, stretching, getting some fresh air, moving around the room are all ways of changing your present state of agitation or withdrawal.

Of course if you are the recipient of such low-road states,

in that moment there may be little you can do except to remove yourself from a situation. Out of the heat of the moment, it may be extremely useful to name this process "low road" or "flipping out." These are reactive states, far from the receptive state we need to truly connect with others. And so, even stating that "I am reactive now, I need a short break" is better than simply exploding.

In the brain, naming an emotion can help calm it. Here is where finding words to label an internal experience becomes really helpful. We can call this "Name it to tame it." And sometimes these low-road states can go beyond being unpleasant and confusing—they can even make life feel terrifying. If that is going on, talk about it. Sharing your experience with others can often make even terrifying moments understood and not traumatizing. Your inner sea and your interpersonal relationships will all benefit from naming what is going on and bringing more integration into your life.

MINDSIGHT PRACTICE F:
Detecting Chaos or Rigidity and Balancing the Mind

Try to recall a time when your life became filled with chaos or rigidity. This may have been within some interaction with another person in which you felt the chaos of being flooded with an emotion, like anger or sadness or fear. Or it may have been a time of rigidity, in which some repeating thought kept at you without changing, or you felt yourself withdrawing from interactions with others. If this memory is about a specific incident, can you detect any triggering event that may have been a part of a non-integrated experience? Was differentiation not occurring, such as someone was insisting on things being done their way and not respecting your viewpoint? Or was linkage absent, such as being ignored, misunderstood, or excluded? Notice how such blockages to integration put you in a period of chaos and rigidity.

If such a time was more extended, try to sense what might have been going on in your life then, when you may have been in a rigid, unchanging state of feeling bored or down in the dumps. Or chaos may have been your extended state, flooding you with emotions or thoughts or images or memories out of your control. Try to sense how some fundamental integration may have been missing at that time of your life and how you tried to pull yourself out of those uncomfortable states.

The key to this practice is to first detect chaos or rigidity. Next you can explore what aspect of your life may have been non-integrated in that it was not enabling differentiation or linkage to occur. One simple practice to try when you feel distressed by the memory of this chaotic or rigid time is to do the following physical positioning of your hands. When the memory of some chaotic or rigid time is in the front of your mind, try placing one hand on your chest—over your heart region— and one over your abdomen. Place a small amount of pressure from each hand and see how you feel. Now try moving the hand on your chest to the belly, and the other hand now up to your chest. Apply some gentle pressure and simply notice how you feel. Now place your hands in the positions that felt the best. What do you notice? Did you feel a calming sensation? Could you tell the difference between left on top or right on top?

I've offered this practice to many people in workshops with some fascinating results. For reasons we don't yet understand, this positioning of the hands on the body is calming for the majority of individuals who try it. And about three-quarters of people prefer the right hand over the chest, one-quarter the left hand. This preference seems to be independent of whether the person is right- or left-handed. I did a small study of one subject, showing that for me this movement (I'm a left-on-top person) created more integration, more coordination and balance, in my nervous system as assessed by some physiological monitoring of my heart. One possibility suggested by this single-person "study" is that the prefrontal region is activated to balance the brakes and accelerator of our bodies—the parasympathetic and sympathetic branches of the autonomic nervous system—and then soothes the heart and creates the state of calm in our minds, as we'll see more in Part II. Though we don't yet know exactly how or why this practice works, for so many it is helpful to bring calming within, and so I invite you to use this whenever your inner world becomes stuck on those banks of chaos or rigidity outside the flow of integrative harmony.

In Part II we'll dive into the brain's functions and how we can understand how to promote integration to achieve these balanced states. Then, in Part III, we'll explore how our attachment relationships may have shaped integration during our development so that we can become familiar with ways to make more harmony out of chaos and rigidity in our lives now.

Mindsight Strengthens the Mind, the Brain, and Our Relationships

As we move through these various practice entries, we'll be building the skills of mindsight to support the development of insight, empathy, and integration in our lives. Since the mind is both within us and between us and others—it is embodied and it is relational—then we can see how knowing about our body's brain and knowing about our relationships are both fundamental to strengthening our minds. In the pages that follow, we'll find important concepts that can help bring integration into our inner lives and our interpersonal lives. That's using mindsight to create a strong life for ourselves from the inside out.

PART II

■

Your Brain

A seventeen-year-old senior in high school, Katey looked terrified as her stomach was being pumped in the local hospital
emergency room after a night of heavy drinking. She was writhing
in pain from the emetic-induced vomiting, and still drunk from the
seven shots of tequila and four glasses of wine she had consumed at
an end-of-summer gathering that evening. At least that was her parents' version of what had occurred based on what Katey's friends had
told them. For her part, Katey couldn't remember much of what had
occurred that evening.

As it turns out, Katey brought the hard liquor to the party, shared
it with her classmates, and even coaxed the host of the event—the
daughter of the director of their school—into the drinking spree.

Katey was expelled from school the following week, which was the week she came in for her first therapy session. In speaking more with her about what happened, I learned that she had planned to "have fun" at the party even though it was at the home of the director of her school.

Katey knew how "off" it all sounded.

"What were you thinking before that party?" I asked her. She looked sheepish, glancing away with the beginnings of a smile appearing on her face. "What did you think might happen after the party when the school rules state that there is 'zero tolerance' for alcohol at school-related functions?" Katey looked at me, her eyes wide open and locked with mine, her half-smile widening, suggesting that perhaps her anxiety was increasing or that she was somewhat amused at the whole situation.

"Well . . ." she began, her smile now wide across her face. "I *did* think about it." She paused and looked around the room as if someone might be listening, and then she turned back to me. "I knew what might happen, I guess, but the *fun* of getting completely smashed at the director's own house just seemed like too much to turn down." Her eyes shone with a sparkle of delight.

The fact that Katey herself admitted that she had "planned" what would happen at the party even in the face of knowledge about the potential outcomes resonates in recent studies revealing that teenagers usually have awareness of the risks of potentially dangerous behaviors. As teens we are often not oblivious to the negative consequences of our actions. Instead, even though the negative consequences—the cons—are fully known, we place more emphasis on the potential positive aspects—the PROS—of an experience: the thrill, the shared experience, the fun, the excitement of breaking the rules. That emphasis on the positive, we now know, is a result of shifts in the brain's structure and function during the adolescent period.

Dopamine, Decisions, and the Drive for Reward

Katey's enhanced focus on the positive was in fact a natural consequence of the increased reward drive in the adolescent brain. The
brain is a collection of cells that communicate with one another using
chemicals called neurotransmitters. During adolescence there is an
increase in the activity of the neural circuits utilizing dopamine, a
neurotransmitter central in creating our drive for reward. Starting in
early adolescence and peaking midway through, this enhanced dopamine release causes adolescents to gravitate toward thrilling experiences and exhilarating sensations. Research even suggests that the
baseline level of dopamine is lower—but its release in response to
experience is higher—which can explain why teens may report a
feeling of being "bored" unless they are engaging in some stimulating and novel activities. This enhanced natural dopamine release can
give adolescents a powerful sense of being alive when they are engaged in life. It can also lead them to focus solely on the positive rewards they are sure are in store for them, while failing to notice or
give value to the potential risks and downsides.

The brain's increased drive for reward in adolescence manifests
in teens' lives in three important ways. One is simply increased
impulsiveness, where behaviors occur without thoughtful reflection.
In other words, impulse inspires action without any pause. Pausing
enables us to think about other options beyond the immediate
dopamine-driven impulse pounding on our minds. Telling that impulse to chill out takes time and energy, so it's easier just not to do it.
This said, with the drive for reward stronger and more pressing than
ever when we are teens, taking the time needed for processing—for
reflection and self-awareness—becomes very important. If any notion turns immediately into an action without reflection, we are

living our lives all gas pedal and no brakes. This can be very stressful for adolescents and the adults who care for them.

The good news is that such impulses can be put on hold if certain fibers in the higher part of the brain work to create a mental space between impulse and action. It is during the time of adolescence that these regulatory fibers begin to grow to counteract the revved-up "go" of the dopamine reward system. The result is a decrease in impulsivity. This is sometimes called "cognitive control" and is one important source of diminished danger and reduced risks as adolescents develop. As we'll see shortly, there are ways to enhance the growth of those regulatory fibers that create a pause, and they can be developed at any age.

A second way in which increased dopamine release affects us during adolescence is the documented increase in our susceptibility to addiction. All behaviors and substances that are addictive involve the release of dopamine. As teens not only are we more likely to experiment with new experiences, we are also more prone to respond with a robust dopamine release that for some can become part of an addictive cycle. A drug, alcohol for example, can lead to release of dopamine, and we may feel compelled to ingest beer or wine or hard liquor. When the alcohol wears off, our dopamine plummets. We then are driven to use more of the substance that spiked our dopamine circuits. Studies reveal that foods with a high glycemic index—those, like processed foods or even the simple carbohydrates of potatoes or bread, that lead to a rapid rise in blood sugar—can also lead to rapid rises in our dopamine levels and activity in the reward circuits of the brain. Sadly, in the United States such addiction to foods with high caloric but low nutritional value is thought to be responsible for the dangerous epidemic of obesity in adolescents, a medical crisis created and reinforced by our society's supplying us with just this type of addictive food. As with any addiction, we continue to engage in the behavior despite knowing its negative impacts on our health. That's the power of the dopamine reward centers.

A third type of behavior shaped by the increased reward drives of the adolescent brain is something called *hyperrationality*. This is how we think in literal, concrete terms. We examine just the facts of a situation and don't see the big picture; we miss the setting or context in which those facts occur. With such literal thinking, as adolescents we can place more weight on the calculated benefits of an action than on the potential risks of that action. Studies reveal that as teens we are often fully aware of risks, and even at times overestimate the chance of something bad happening; we simply put more weight on the exciting potential benefits of our actions.

What happens with hyperrational thinking is not a lack of thought or reflection as happens with impulsivity, and it's not a matter of merely being addicted to a particular behavior or something we are ingesting. Instead, this cognitive process comes from a brain calculation that places a lot of weight on the positive outcome and not much weight on possible negative results. By weight I mean that the evaluation centers of the brain downplay the significance of a negative outcome, while at the same time they amplify the significance given to a positive result. The scales that teens use to weigh out their options are biased in favor of the positive outcome. PROS far outweigh the cons, and quite simply, the risk seems worth it.

This positively biased scale can be activated especially when teens hang out with other teens or believe their friends will somehow observe their actions. The social and emotional context we experience as teens sets the stage for how our brains will process information. While that's true for any person whatever their age, the influence of peers is especially strong during adolescence.

In other words, in Katey's situation her brain focused on the rewarding images of the thrill, the core of sensation seeking, and she disregarded the potential negatives. The emotional meaning of her actions was woven together with her ability to plan and she hyperrationally calculated that this was a PRO thing to do. Katey's behavior was not impulsive—she planned her evening long ago in a hyperrational way.

As our teen years unfold, we move from the literal thinking of hyperrationality to the broader considerations called "gist thinking." With gist thinking, we consider the larger context of a decision and use intuition to aim for positive values we care about rather than focusing primarily on the immediate dopamine-driven reward.

So as you can see, it is not as simple as saying that teens are just impulsive. And it's also not as simple as saying, "Oh, raging hormones," as is sometimes stated. Research suggests that risky behaviors in adolescence have less to do with hormonal imbalances than with changes in our brain's dopamine reward system combined with the cortical architecture that supports hyperrational decision-making creating the positive bias that is dominant during the teen years.

When your dopamine circuitry is turned way up, it's like an amplifier with its gain turned up. Enhanced dopamine release drives us toward reward and satisfaction. The gain is turned up for how attention is drawn to the PROS, putting us at risk of deemphasizing the cons during these years.

Hyperrationality can be illustrated in the extreme example of Russian roulette, a game played with one bullet and six chambers of a pistol. You have five out of six chances to make the $6 million offered to you if you win. That means, overall, if hundreds of people play this game, then the average you are most likely to get, statistically winning five out of six times, is five-sixths of $6 million, which is $5 million overall. Let's go for it! The problem is, of course, if you are the one in six, you are dead. And for that one person in six, it is a hundred percent certain that life is over. You can see the challenge. It is true that "most likely" you'll get millions of dollars. If your brain circuits focus on that positive outcome, the PROS, and minimize the smaller chance of the risk, the cons, you'll take part in the activity. "Why not?" Yes, that seems like math gone mad. But to *not* jump into this probability assessment, the trap of "What is most likely to happen so I'll do it," requires a gut feeling, the intuition that is the basis of gist thinking, that lifts you out of hyperrational calculations. With development and the growth of the brain, a gut feeling rises and we get a feeling that the Russian roulette game makes no sense.

Paradoxically, intuition plays a very important role in making good decisions. This is because our intuitions, or gut feelings and heartfelt sensations, tend to focus on positive values, like the benefit of staying in school or driving at the speed limit or keeping fit. Many teens can be too rational, and need to incorporate the non-rational input of their intuitive gut feelings and heartfelt sensations, feelings that enable them to focus on positive values versus mythical rewards that, in reality, are often just out of reach. Learning to experience life from this standpoint is not about inhibiting impulses like driving fast or eating junk food, but rather about embracing positive goals that intuitively mean something to us. Katey's behavior was not impulsive and it was not intuitive or gist-like. It was dopamine-driven and hyperrational. She needed to work on being more aware of what her intuitive gut and heart feelings could tell her about the potential downsides to reckless behavior.

Family, Friends, and Fooling Around

Another important factor that contributed to Katey's decision making is that she was quite preoccupied with how her friends would react if she pulled this escapade off, literally, under the school director's nose, and with his daughter, no less! Here we see another aspect of the teenage brain. On top of the emotional spark and drive for the reward of novelty, intense social engagement with peers is also part of the essence of adolescence. Unfortunately, risk behaviors often significantly increase in the company of peers, as demonstrated in experiments that have measured how teens do when driving on a simulated automobile program when alone and when with their friends.

My son's friend Benji, now in his mid-twenties, tells the story of when he lived in southern Spain with his family as a thirteen-year-old. A half-dozen boys of the same age were running around the cliffs near the beautiful coastal town where he was staying. One of the locals decided to jump the fifty feet or so off the edge of the cliff and into the sea. Then, one by one, the group dynamics lured each of them to jump. When Benji jumped, he may have been just a few feet over from where the others entered the water, he told me, or perhaps it was because none of the local boys had remembered to tell him, as apparently they knew, that he ought to bend his legs right after entering the water. Straight in he went, hurtling toward the bottom and hitting a rock beneath the surface, severely fracturing his right leg. Struggling to the surface with the shock of such a crushing injury, he was losing consciousness when he was rescued by two of the boys and carried a mile back to the town to be hospitalized for much of his remaining time in Spain that summer. If those boys were not there in the water, Benji would not have been telling me the story.

I asked Benji if he thought he would have jumped if he was on his own. "Are you out of your mind?" he said. "No way."

The collective process of being with our friends, or even imagining the impact on our friends, as in Katey's planning stage of her escapade, increases the drive toward reward, the drive toward novelty, and the drive to take risks, and these reduce the focus on weighing the potential risks. So with peers we are much more likely as teenagers to engage in behaviors that may work out most of the time, but if they don't, they may have serious, sometimes irreversible, consequences. Benji's and Katey's behaviors were not impulsive. They both had plenty of time to see what was in the offing and change course. Their decisions were a combination of reward drive, peer process, and hyperrational, non-gist thinking. That's the nature of risky behaviors emerging from the teenage brain.

So the two broad ways that risky behavior emerges in adolescence are hyperrationality, the downplaying of the cons of an action, and impulsivity, or simply flying off the handle, as we'll discuss later. Katey did not, and generally does not, show a tendency to be impulsive. Neither does Benji. In Katey's case, this is what drove her parents mad when they picked her up. Katey is not impulsive, so why such a seemingly impulsive act?

Hyperrationality combined with an increase in her dopamine drive is the cause. And sometimes there are other things at play, such as the dopamine-dependent onset of addiction, that are not limited to being an adolescent but may also be influencing such behaviors, as we'll discuss for Katey and adolescents in general regarding drug use and abuse in Part IV.

The Purpose of Adolescence

In recent years, surprising discoveries from brain imaging studies have revealed changes in the structure and function of the brain during adolescence. As we've seen, interpretations of these studies lead to a very different story than the old raging-hormone view of the teenage brain. A commonly stated but not quite accurate view often presented by the media is that the brain's master control center, the prefrontal cortex, at the forward part of the frontal lobe, is simply not mature until the end of adolescence. This "immaturity" of the brain's prefrontal cortex "explains immature teenage behavior." And this notion also explains why rental car companies generally won't let someone younger than twenty-five take out a car. But this simple story, while easy to grasp, is not quite consistent with the research findings and misses an essential issue.

Instead of viewing the adolescent stage of brain development as merely a process of maturation, of leaving behind outmoded or non-useful ways of thinking and transitioning to adult maturity, it is actually more accurate and more useful to see it as a vital and necessary part of our individual and our collective lives. Adolescence is not a stage to simply get over, it is a stage of life to cultivate well. This new and important take-home message, inspired by the emerging sciences, suggests that the changes that occur in the adolescent brain are not merely about "maturity" versus "immaturity," but rather are vitally important developmental changes that enable certain new abilities to emerge. These new abilities, as we've discussed, are crucial for both the individual and our species.

Why should this matter to us, whether we are teens, in our twenties, or older? It matters because if we see the adolescent period as just a time to wade through, a time to endure, we'll miss out on taking very important steps to optimize the essence of adolescence. When we see our emotional spark, our social engagement, our novelty seeking, and our creative explorations as positive and necessary core aspects of who adolescents *are*—and who they might become as adults if they can cultivate these qualities well—this period becomes a time of great importance that should be not just survived but nurtured.

Yes, there are challenges in staying open to the "work" of adolescence. Important opportunities for expansion and development during this time can be associated with stress for teens and for the parents who love them. For example, the pushing away from family that adolescents tend to do can be seen as a necessary process enabling them to leave home. This courage to move out and away is created by the brain's reward circuits becoming increasingly active and inspiring teens to seek novelty even in the face of the unfamiliar as they move out into the world. After all, the familiar can be safe and predictable, while the unfamiliar can be unpredictable and filled with potential danger. One historical view for us as social mammals is that if older adolescents did not leave home and move away from local family members, our species would have too much chance of inbreeding and our genetics would suffer. And for our broader human story, adolescents' moving out and exploring the larger world allows our human family to be far more adaptive in the world as the generations unfold. Our individual and our collective lives depend on this adolescent push away.

Hard as it is for parents to worry about their teen's potentially risky behavior, the positive bias of hyperrational thinking helps adolescents take on risks that they'll *need* to embrace if they are to leave the nest and explore the world. As we've seen, the drive to have increased social connections can keep us safe as we associate with our adolescent peers who are also making the journey out into the unfamiliar world. Our increased sensitivity to our own heightened emotional states and to our peers' influence—our emotional spark and social engagement—are fundamental to this journey as well. Seeking out novelty and creating new ways of doing things also helps our species adapt to the ever-changing world. If the brain throughout the life span is indeed a "work in progress," as recent studies suggest, then the work that occurs during adolescence is so much more than simply a process of moving from immaturity to maturity. The essence of adolescence enriches our lifelong journey to embrace life fully.

What we are coming to see is that there is a crucial set of brain changes during our adolescence creating new powers, new possibilities, and new purposes fueling the adolescent mind and relationships that simply did not exist like this in childhood. These positive potentials are often hidden from view and yet they can be uncovered and used more effectively and more wisely when we know how to find them and how to cultivate them. We can learn to use cutting-edge science to make the most of the adolescent period of life. It's a pay-it-forward investment for everyone involved.

For the teen, the growth of the body itself, with alterations in physiology, hormones, sexual organs, and the architectural changes in the brain, also can contribute to our understanding of adolescence as an important period of transformation. Changing emotions revolutionize how we feel as teens inside, making more complex the ways of processing information and our ideas about the self and others, and even creating huge developmental shifts and transitions in the inner sense of who we are and who we can become. This is how a sense of identity shifts and evolves throughout adolescence.

From the inside, these changes can become overwhelming, and

we may even lose our way, and feel that life is just "too much" to navigate at times. From the outside, such changes may at times seem like we are lost and "out of control." Our adolescent years, a time of life filled with challenges that can strengthen who we are, can be challenging for sure. But the great news is that with increased self-awareness of our emotional and social lives, and with an increased understanding of the brain's structure and function, the powerful positive effects of the complex changes that occur during adolescence can be harnessed with the proper approach and understanding.

Making Decisions

Throughout adolescence, different areas of the brain link together, a process we've discussed called "integration." One outcome of integration is the growth of fibers of cognitive control that ultimately decrease impulsivity. As a result, adolescents are afforded more and more space in the mind to pause and consider other options of response than an initial impulse. Another outcome of this integrative growth is sharpened gist thinking, whereby the adolescent is able to rely more and more on intuition to see the larger picture of a situation and therefore make wiser decisions.

Let's see how a better focus on developing gist thinking in our earlier example of the car accident might have helped a teen make better decisions, decisions that could have saved a life. If the teen or his parents were able to acknowledge his longing for speed as a natural dopamine reward drive, then the urge could have been channeled in a constructive way. There are many options, including taking part in athletics where competition and speed and power are parts of the sport—racecar driving, running, bicycling, skiing—risky and adventurous activities that don't put innocent bystanders in harm's way. For example, when my son was in his early teens, we'd spend hours on the weekends racing long skateboards down closed multilevel parking garages at the university where I work. When we'd get to the bottom, we'd take the elevator back up and race down again. Having helmets on and wearing hard gloves to keep our skin from scraping on the concrete as we made those sharp turns helped minimize the damage to our bodies, most of which I seemed to get, not him. There's nothing wrong with the drive for thrills—the issue is how to harness those drives so as to minimize harm to oneself or others. The idea here is to respect the dopamine-driven need for speed or other risky activities, but then channel this drive in helpful ways. If we can instill awareness of the positive sides of these drives, and then find constructive approaches to addressing them, tragic outcomes like my teacher's death might be avoided. Not only might Bill still be alive, but the young man would not have the burden of living with the feeling of responsibility for that accident.

Sadly, instead of addressing a potentially dangerous problem with their son, his parents may have unintentionally rewarded his earlier risky behavior with a brand-new car. So why wouldn't he try something dangerous again? That's how risky behavior without a negative consequence can reinforce itself to happen again and again. Many of us know of other examples of reckless teen behavior that went unaddressed: driving a car without a license and losing the ability to drive later on, taking the chance of having unprotected sex and risking getting a disease or getting pregnant, trying combinations of street drugs without knowing their potentially lethal effects, or getting a tattoo from a disreputable source and risk getting hepatitis. There are even more minor risks, like not taking the time to sleep before an exam because you are talking with friends on the phone late into the night, or getting lost in social media and posting an insulting comment about someone's looks or a drunk party photo of yourself that a college admissions officer later sees. In all these situations the teen is seeing the PROS and de-emphasizing the risks. That's the positive bias of the adolescent mind.

Honoring the important and necessary changes in the adolescent mind and brain rather than disrespecting them is crucial for both teens and their parents. When we embrace these needed changes, when we offer teens the support and guidance they need instead of just throwing up our hands and thinking we're dealing with an "immature brain that simply needs to grow up," or "raging hormones in need of taming," we enable adolescents to develop vital new capacities that they can use to lead happier and healthier lives.

Gist thinking emerges with both experience and programmed brain development. In other words, the timing of the development of the brain is shaped by both experience-induced neural activation and by genetic information. Experience shapes the connections in the brain itself even if it cannot affect the general timing of such maturation. And studies suggest that gist thinking emerges from the growth of integration in our brains as teens. The timing may be in part genetically determined, but we can shape the degree of development of integration in our brains. Experience shapes our development during our adolescence and the rest of our lives. And experience can promote more integration in the brain, more connecting of its different parts so that they work in a coordinated manner. So how we set up our lives and the contexts we live in, what we do and whom we are with, can shape not only how the brain is activated but also how the brain will grow its integrative circuits. For these reasons, knowing the basics about the brain can be helpful in our lives because we can shape our brain's growth of integration in ways that are helpful for us now and for the future.

"Don't Do It" Doesn't Do It:
The Power of Promoting the Positive

Gist thinking draws on the gut feeling and heartfelt sense of a positive value, of aiming *for* something rather than inhibiting something.
So instead of trying to shut down an impulse by inhibiting it, adults
with adolescents in their lives and adolescents themselves should
focus on a positive factor to promote. Choosing not to get a tattoo at
an unknown place because you value your health is very different
from saying, "I won't do it because my mother told me not to." In
contrast, hyperrational thinking considers the impulse and senses the
reward drive to realize the positive thrill, the sensation-seeking
speed-driven adrenaline rush of getting a tattoo with some friends.
And it doesn't hurt that you are also breaking your parents' rules.

Public health advocates' efforts to reduce teen smoking are powerful examples of how appealing to the adolescent's emerging strength
in terms of gist thinking can help promote healthy behaviors. The
adolescent period is, as we've seen, a time of great vulnerability to
becoming addicted to various substances, including cigarettes. It's
not just that teens smoke more, but also that the changing teen brain
itself is open to becoming addicted in part because of its enhanced
dopamine response. If people are going to smoke cigarettes, they
most likely start during their teenage years. The same is true with
drug addiction. The most effective strategy to get adolescents to
avoid smoking was not offering teens medical information or trying to frighten them with images of graveyards, two strategies that
did nothing to reduce teens' taking up smoking or continuing to
smoke. The strategy that worked was to inform them about how the
adults who owned the cigarette companies were brainwashing them
to smoke so that they could get their money. Rather than getting

teens to say no to smoking because some adult was frightening them into it, this strategy focused on the positive value of being strong in the face of manipulative adults out to get rich. When this embracing of how the adolescent mind worked was taken up by public health advocates, the rate of teen smoking dropped. Simply saying "Don't do it" wasn't enough. Aiming for a positive value, like not letting someone—especially an adult—brainwash you, worked.

Knowing about these understandable and genetically based changes in the teenage brain can help adults support the adolescent's need for pushing back on the adult status quo and the exploration of new possibilities. Encouraging the reflection on values and on gut instinct, not simply the inhibition of impulses, is the difference between turning down a compelling impulse and embracing a thoughtful belief and value.

Integrating Your Brain

In many ways, how we decide to do things in life reveals who we are at that moment. When we understand how the brain changes during our adolescence, we can understand how the decision-making process changes, too. The brain changes during this period in two dimensions. One is how it *reduces* the number of the brain's basic cells, the neurons, and their connections, the synapses. This decreasing of neurons and synapses is called "pruning" and appears to be genetically controlled, shaped by experience and intensified with stress. How can we tolerate losing some neurons? During childhood there is an overproduction of neurons and their synaptic connections. The blossoming of our neuronal populations begins in utero and extends to our prepubertal period, to about eleven years of age in girls and twelve and a half in boys. Some pruning begins early as we learn and develop skills, but the removal of our overall number of neurons and their connections reaches its peak during the robust remodeling period of adolescence. In adolescence we prune those excess connections away, leaving the ones we've been using and discarding the ones we don't seem to need anymore.

Experience shapes which neural circuits—the neurons and their synaptic connections—will be pruned away. So if you want to have a musical skill, best to start it early, before the end of adolescence. And if you want to be a gold-medal Olympic athlete, best to start in your field before adolescence begins. Even if you're not aiming for athletic prowess, it's simply important to remember that your brain will respond to how you focus your attention in your activities. Attention streams energy and information through specific circuits and activates them. The more you use a circuit, the stronger it gets. The less you use a circuit, the more likely it may get pruned away during adolescence.

How you focus your attention throughout life, and especially during the adolescent period, plays an important role in shaping the growth of your brain. Attention maintains and strengthens existing connections, and as we'll see, it helps grow new connections and make those connections more effective. Our mindsight tools sections are all about learning to focus your mind's attention to integrate your brain's connections.

A second way the brain transforms during this period is that it lays down "myelin," a sheath covering the membranes among interlinked neurons. This myelin sheath enables the passage of the electrical flow, the "neuronal activations" among the remaining linked neurons, to allow faster and more synchronized information to flow. When that flow is fast and coordinated, it makes for a more effective and efficient process. As we learn specific skills and acquire knowledge, we grow new connections and even new neurons. Once we've established these new synaptic linkages, we can lay down myelin to make that circuit quicker, more coordinated, and more effective.

These two fundamental changes—pruning and myelination—help the adolescent brain become more integrated. Integration, the linking of different parts, creates more coordination in the brain itself.

We develop gist thinking as this pruning and myelination creates integration in the brain.

These more precise and efficient connections in the brain make for wiser judgment and discernments based not on the small details that are without a larger context but on the overall gist that sees the big picture. We use our intuition to guide our decisions as we aim for positive values, honoring what matters to us. That is gist thinking, one of the many things that the growth of integration in the brain during our adolescent years creates.

As we'll see, the very specific forms of change in the architecture of the brain enable us as adolescents to start to use judgment based on gist thinking, which is informed by experience and intuition rather than reliant on the reward drive and the literal calculations of our earlier years.

Think of it this way: With those neural connections from childhood that were so numerous, lots of details filled our minds. That's what we needed as children soaking up facts and figures from school. With adolescence, we have an increased reward drive and increased emotional reactions and increased sensitivity to social engagements. This combination means that we'll have lots of details still filling our minds before pruning, and intense emotions and heightened concern about our acceptance by peers will drive either impulsive behavior or reward-driven hyperrational decision-making that is based mainly on literal calculations. The upside of this period of functioning is the positive bias we need to take the necessary risks to get ready to explore the world as adolescents. From a decision-making perspective, the process looks like this: Details without perspective from experience win the day as probabilities are assessed and the Russian roulette gun is fired. Chances are most likely that all will be fine. But sometimes it is not. Just think of some of the things you may have tried in your younger years, or what you are trying out now. When you think about those risks you took, you may even shake your head in disbelief that you actually did those things. If your gist thinking and intuitive wisdom are at work, you may reflect on those times and wonder what in the world you were thinking. Now you know.

We can see why parents can be very concerned about the adolescent tendency to seek thrills. The tripling in accidental injuries and mortality during this otherwise very healthy period is not just in a parent's imagination; it is a statistical fact. It may be hard for you as an adolescent to have empathy for what your parents are facing, but in the big picture this understanding may be helpful not just for them but for you, too. When you communicate with your parents about these statistical matters, and then deal with your individual needs and plans, everyone can feel heard and more effective ways of coming to a decision can be created.

We need to increase our communication about these issues, honoring the healthy and necessary essential aspects of our adolescent years and learning to channel this power in more helpful ways. Knowing about the specific circuits in the brain that create this more integrated way of functioning can help us envision a more constructive approach to how we live and make our decisions as adolescents and as adults.

A Handy Model of the Brain

The reason to know some basic details about the brain is simple. When we know something about the parts of our brains, we can learn to direct our attention in new ways that help those parts work in a more coordinated and balanced way. What we know about the brain can help us grow our brains in integrative ways. That's it. And that's pretty useful.

We will look into the brain not only because it is what is chang-

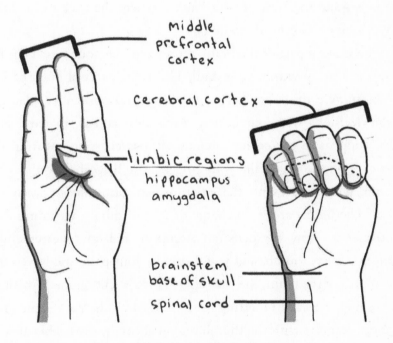

Handy Model of the Brain
The brain in the palm of the hand. This "handy model" depicts the major regions of the brain: cerebral cortex in the fingers, limbic area in the thumb, and brain stem in the palm. The spinal cord is represented in the wrist. From Daniel J. Siegel, M.D., *The Developing Mind: How Relationships and the Brain Interact to Shape Who We Are*, copyright © 2012 by Mind Your Brain, Inc. Adapted with permission.

ing in us as adolescents, but also because knowing about it can help us optimize the opportunities of adolescence. This understanding can help you think, feel, and behave in ways that help you get along better in your life, feel better, and be more the person you want to be. We won't need a plastic model or big poster of the brain for this exploration. We're about to get to know a very handy model of the brain, one you can take with you wherever you go.

If you fold your thumb into your palm, and then fold the fingers over your thumb, you'll have facing you a useful hand model of the brain. Give it a try right now and let's see how these parts fit together. In this model the area of your fingernails facing you is just behind the face—and the back of your hand is where the back of the brain at the back of your head would be.

The highest part of the brain, represented by your fingers, is just under your scalp within your skull. This is the *cortex* or outer bark of the brain. We think and reflect, perceive and remember, plan and make decisions with our cortex. Awareness comes, in part, from what happens in the cortex, and so self-awareness comes from this cortical region. If you lift your fingers, you'll see below them the thumb, which represents the emotion-generating *limbic area* of the brain. The limbic area is in charge of a lot of things, including what motivates us, how we focus our attention, and how we remember things. Lift the thumb, and you'll find in your palm the lowest and oldest area of the brain, the *brain stem*. This ancient region is involved in keeping us awake or letting us sleep. And it's the part of the brain that can interact with the thumb region above it, the limbic area, to create reactive states of being angry or scared. Since the brain stem and limbic areas are below the cortex, we call these the "subcortical regions." Lift your fingers and put them back over the thumb and palm and you'll see how the cortex literally sits on top of these two subcortical regions.

The brain itself sits atop the spinal cord, represented by your wrist. Input from this neural tube within the backbone, along with other neural inputs from the body and from the body's organs such as the heart and intestines, enables the processes of our organs, muscles, and bones to directly influence the neural firings in the skull itself, neural activity within the subcortical and cortical parts of the brain. Not represented here directly is the *cerebellum*, which would be just behind the limbic area and plays an important role in balancing the body's motions and also balancing the interaction of our thoughts and feelings. A band of neurons, called the *corpus callosum*, links the left and right sides of the brain to each other and coordinates and balances their activities.

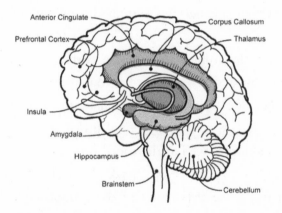

This is a leftward-facing model of the right side of the brain. The brain stem and the cerebellum are part of the "hindbrain" and regulate basic processes like heart rate and states of alertness. Connecting the two sides of the brain is a band of tissue called the corpus callosum. The amygdala and hippocampus, which are part of the old mammalian region called the limbic area, form the "midbrain" and help with functions such as emotional balance and memory processes. The cortex, also known as the "forebrain," makes representations or images of things. The front-most part of the cortex is the prefrontal cortex, which coordinates and balances the functions of many areas by linking input from the cortex, limbic area, brain stem, body, and social interactions. The insula is a circuit that connects bodily processes to the prefrontal area for self-awareness. From Daniel J. Siegel, M.D., *The Developing Mind,* 2nd edition, copyright © 2012 by Mind Your Brain Inc.

The cortex helps us be conscious in our lives, to think clearly about things, to assess a situation and reason through it, to remember other events, and to pause and reflect on what is going on. Those are a lot of important functions, and it's why the cortex, especially the front part, is called the executive region. It is the master control center that coordinates and balances the whole brain and the body itself.

The forward part of the cortex, the frontal lobe, develops a lot during infancy and toddlerhood, and it continues to grow during the remainder of childhood. When our adolescence begins, even more dramatic changes in this frontal region occur. The reason this area is so important is that it participates in the linkage of different neural regions to one another. In this way, the cortex has an integrative role as it coordinates and balances much of what happens throughout the brain, and even in the nervous system throughout the body as a whole.

As we'll see, the frontal areas of the cortex also link our own neural firing to the activity of other nervous systems, to other brains within other people. In this way, the frontal area is involved in both the shaping of our own internal mental processes such as thinking and decision making as well as the social processes such as empathy and moral behavior. So when we speak about changes in the adolescent brain, we'll see that many of these important changes involve increasing levels of integration, especially carried out in the cortex. This increased cortical integration enables such diverse abilities as cognitive control, emotional regulation, gist thinking, self-understanding and social functions to change and emerge throughout adolescence.

One of the central hubs that link the nodes of our larger cognitive, emotional, and social networks of circuits into a functional whole is in the frontal region of the cortex. A network contains many different parts, or nodes, and a hub is the aspect of the network that links those different nodes to one another. A node in the nervous system, for example, might be collections of neurons in the limbic area or in the cortex. One important nervous system hub that links the nodes together is just behind the forehead. Because it is at the front of the frontal areas, it is called the prefrontal cortex. Notice how in your hand model this integrative prefrontal region, located at the ends of your fingers, your prefrontal-fingernail region, connects the cortex to the subcortical limbic-thumb and brain stem–palm regions. In addition, this prefrontal region links input from the body itself and from other people. Energy and information from the cortex, limbic area, brain stem, body, and social world are coordinated and balanced by the prefrontal region. It is this integrative role, connecting and coordinating many differentiated inputs, that makes the growth of the prefrontal cortex so central to our understanding of how we change and become more integrated as adolescents.

Adolescence as the Gateway to Creative Exploration

In a nutshell: The overall movement of the brain's development is to become more *integrated*. What that means is that areas will become more specialized and then interconnected to one another in more effective ways. That's what the pruning down of connections and the myelination of remaining connections create—the differentiation of specialized regions and then their coordinated linkage. The result of such a process is to have more efficient and specialized processing of information. This is consistent with our discussions of the gist-based thinking that sees through all the details to find the wisest judgment about a situation. What are the basic ways such a transformation of thinking can occur? What are the basic units of the brain's structure that support such reconstructive and integrative changes in adolescence?

As we've seen, both our genes and our experiences contribute to how synaptic connections will form and interconnect the various parts of the network into circuits. What this means is that the changes in the brain will be due in part to genetic information we've inherited and in part to experiences we engage in. Experience streams energy flow through particular neurons and strengthens their connections with one another. It is important to know about our neuronal connections because they shape how we feel, think, reason, and make decisions.

Because this pruning and myelination restructures the brain's networks of connections, it is often called "remodeling." The remodeling changes in the integrative frontal areas of the cortex are responsible for the finding that as teens we begin to become aware of ourselves and to think about life in conceptual and abstract ways. Our emerging adolescent minds begin to consciously and creatively explore the deeper meanings of life, of friendships, of parents, of school, of everything. Even the ability to reflect on our own personalities emerges during the years of adolescence. While genes determine some of the timing of these changes, experience—what we think about, what we discuss with friends, how we spend our time—will help expand on this new way of thinking about the world. For example, some teens may not engage in such reflective thoughts or conversations with their friends or with their family. In this situation, their interpersonal experience of cultivating self-awareness may not be so well developed.

What we focus our attention on and what we spend time doing

directly stimulate the growth of those parts of the brain that carry out those functions.

Rather than the concrete way of thinking and the fact-based learning that dominates in children during the elementary school years, the learning curve for us as teens involves a focus on more complex concepts. Our literal experience of being aware of life ex-

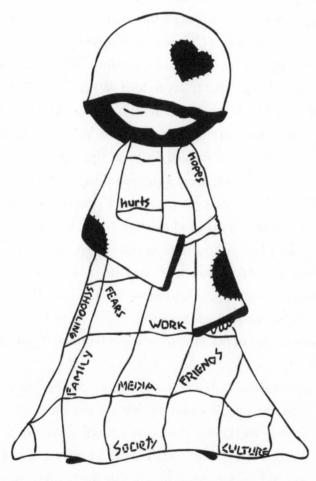

who's under there?

plodes with new visions of what is real, visions that in childhood may not have even crossed our minds. This is why adolescence is such an amazing time. The growth of the frontal lobes permits us to experience our human ability of knowing about knowing—of reflecting on how we think, how we feel, why we do what we do, and how we might do things differently. As Dorothy said in *The Wizard of Oz*, "We're not in Kansas anymore."

I remember that when I was a teen, this new awareness was overwhelming. I went from smiling a lot during my childhood to being more grumpy, more inward, more confused and pensive. When I first hit my teens, my father would ask me why I didn't smile anymore, and I just didn't know what to say to him. When I got older, I saw the film *Harold and Maude* with some friends and couldn't stop thinking of Cat Stevens's lyrics in the classic song "If You Want to Sing Out, Sing Out": "Well, if you want to sing out, sing out. And if you want to be free, be free." There were a million things I could be, the song said, and I could do whatever I wanted, I could make things come true. I used to sing it in my head, over and over; it played like an endless tape. When I listen to the song now as an adult, I can see that those lyrics capture the essence of our journey into those teen years. It's a coming-of-age song, of letting adults go into the background as we create a new world as adolescents.

This emergence of the adolescent mind is our birthright as human beings.

Our species name is *Homo sapiens sapiens*. *Sapiens* means "knowing." So with the double knowing we are the ones who not only know, but *know* we know. And this knowing we know emerges first in adolescence. Creative and conscious explorations of conceptual thinking and abstract reasoning enable the brain to approach old problems in new ways. A fifteen-year-old isn't simply a ten-year-old with five additional years of experience. Brain development means

that as adolescents we can think in conceptual and abstract ways a ten-year-old cannot even imagine. One aspect of this exploration can be divergent thinking, a way of approaching problems creatively to "think outside the box." We can approach problems in new ways, and we can approach our self-understanding in new ways never before possible. This creative exploration encompasses ways of perceiving and reasoning and problem solving with abstract capacities and thinking strategies and reflective capabilities that permit us to tackle life's challenges in more innovative ways.

The changes in how we think and expansions in our awareness are because of the brain's remodeling and are a healthy part of our adolescence. The reconstruction of the cortex enables conceptual thinking and creative explorations to emerge and blossom.

With this expanded capacity of consciousness, we are entering a potentially new way of approaching the world and how we fit into

it. Instead of the old pattern of just going along with earlier knowledge sponged up from adults when we were elementary school–aged
children, as adolescents our brains now permit this new form of
thinking that can challenge old ways of doing things. This new conceptual thinking even enables us to see that the old way of doing
things embedded in our brains is just one approach—and we can
now come up with another approach that may be just as good or
perhaps even better.

The power of the adolescent mind emerges from these brain
changes, which permit us to solve problems in new and innovative
ways. We might even say that this is also the primary work and purpose of the adolescent period—the essence of adolescence.

As we've seen, many revolutionary ways of interpreting and
shaping our world—in music and art and in the recent creation
of our digital age—emerge during the emotionally vibrant, socially
connected, novelty-seeking adolescent period. Adolescence is a
golden age for innovation because it is during this time of growth
and change that the brain's developmental shifts in the reward centers and in the cortex encourage creative thought and drive adolescents to explore the world in new ways.

So abstract and conceptual thinking, increased reward drive, and
enhanced novelty seeking are three sources of the potential and
passion for creative thought. These capacities need to be blended
with disciplined study, naturally, to allow knowledge to inform
innovation.

Yes, these years can be challenging to navigate because in addition to innovation, they also involve risk and rebellion, as we've seen.
Impulsivity and hyperrational thinking enable us to drive too fast,
take on unnecessary risks, and endanger ourselves and others. We
jump off cliffs into the sea and get hurt. But there is a middle ground,

a place to honor the drive for novelty and the creation of new explorations. If we as adults push back severely against these natural changes, rejecting adolescents as they reject us, the result can be a shutting down of all communication between the generations.

The call is to increase empathetic understanding and respectful communicating, creating integration across the generations.

Just as when adolescent elephants are deprived of their male elders in a herd and then run wild and become destructive without the adults' presence, total isolation of adolescent humans from the adult community can be an unhelpful standoff. Technology's products—cars, synthesized drugs, weapons, the worldwide web—make the stakes higher. So an important lesson for adults and adolescents is this: Adolescents' pushing away is not the same as shutting completely out. If both sides of the generational divide understood each other more fully, perhaps these important years of innovation and transition could be navigated better, helping adolescents grow into the people they have the power and potential to become.

Our challenge, simply put, is to see the power and potential of the teenage brain and the emerging adolescent mind as assets rather than liabilities.

Creating Collaboration Across the Generations

In middle school, my son and his fourteen-year-old band mates once stacked up all the amplifiers in their music practice room to see how huge a "wall of sound" they could make with all the instruments being played at the same time through the same system. On the floor above the practice room were the school's administrative offices. Needless to say, the nearly shattered windows in the building were an incentive for the head of the school to come down on my son and his friends with severe consequences. One of those consequences was to bar them from using the practice room for three months. The result was that those adolescents, not being able to have their creative outlet of music at school, started doing even more egregious things. The cycle of pushing back by the teens and then pushing back by the adults began. At a meeting, I suggested that the administrators, as the adults in the cycle, try to see through the vicious feedback loop and consider the drive for novelty and exploration that the amplifier-stacking experiment was really meant to be.

Fortunately, one of the administrators remembered her own brother's experience of a similar cascade of events. She suggested they try a different approach. The school administrators brought the band mates in, told them the negative effects of their actions, gave them back their privilege of using the practice room, and said they could keep that privilege if they didn't violate the basic rules of the school. All of their "conduct problem" behavior disappeared for the next five years.

The key to this creative solution was honoring the natural adolescent drive for innovation and the creation of new ways of doing things. Honoring does not mean setting no limits. It means acknowledging the intention behind the actions. Adolescence is all about experimentation. If adults shut that down, the passion for novelty will be thwarted, the teens will become disillusioned and disconnected, and no one will benefit. I felt grateful that those administrators could think in creative and collaborative ways, as they drew on the essence of their "inner teenager," to come up with a developmentally appropriate, behaviorally and psychologically effective plan. They understood that the waterfall was going to flow, so they used their adult skills to channel its path. It was a win-win situation for everyone. And the band went on to create and perform some really fine music.

Sometimes as adults we see the adolescent drive toward experimentation to create novelty as only a negative change, as only a problem, as a sign of teens being "crazy." As an adult and as a parent, I understand the idea behind this sentiment. But perpetuating the notion that these natural and healthy pushes toward novelty mean teens are only "out of their minds" is not a helpful message for anyone. We are moving out of our old minds and into new ones as adolescents, and our adolescent mind is full of positive power and the potential for creativity. And this power is something we all need to honor. The key as an adolescent or as an adult is to tap into that potential and help cultivate that power.

Vulnerability and Opportunity

Adolescence can be seen as a transformative period in which individuals go from being open to everything (in childhood) to becoming expert at a few things (in adulthood). We've seen that one aspect of this remodeling is pruning, or letting go of the connections in the brain that are not needed. Pruning in general can lead to important changes in how we function as teens—and sometimes it can unmask potential problems. This is why a number of mental health challenges, like mood difficulties such as depression and bipolar disorder, or thinking difficulties such as schizophrenia, may emerge more in adolescence than in childhood. Pruning, along with hormonal changes and alterations in how genes are expressed, shapes our neural activity and synaptic growth and makes the brain's functioning change dramatically during the teenage years.

If there is any vulnerability in the brain's makeup during childhood, adolescence can reveal those brain differences because of the paring down of the existing but insufficient number of neurons and their connections. Such vulnerability may have a wide array of causes, from genetics to toxic exposures to adverse childhood experiences such as abuse or neglect. This developmental view proposes that the vulnerability of the adolescent period happens because the pruning of childhood circuits that may have been "at risk" leads to the unmasking of those deficiencies. The new activation of genes during adolescence, which shape how neurons grow and how they interact with other neurons, may also influence the vulnerability of a teenager's brain. Even if average pruning occurs, what remains may be insufficient to enable mood to be kept in balance or for thought to be coordinated with reality. If stress is high, this pruning process may be even more intense, and more of the at-risk circuits may be diminished in number and effectiveness. The result is the unmasking of underlying vulnerability during the pruning of adolescence. The brain's integrative growth will not occur optimally, and depending on which circuits are affected, impaired coordination and balance in the brain can happen.

During high school and the college years, major psychiatric disorders, such as depression, bipolar disorder, or schizophrenia, can express themselves for the first time, even in otherwise well-functioning individuals. When mood or thought becomes dysfunctional, filled with rigidity or chaos that disrupts adaptive functioning for long periods of time, it is possible that a teen is experiencing not simply the unavoidable intense emotions of adolescence but something more. Perhaps there is simply a period of impaired integration during remodeling in the brain that temporarily leads to such chaos and rigidity and further development may correct that impairment. But sometimes that onset of severe behavioral issues is the sign of a disorder that may be appearing and that needs evaluation and treatment, as with a mood disorder, a thought disorder, or an anxiety disorder with obsessive-compulsive or panic behavior. Since some of these serious psychiatric conditions go along with suicidal thoughts and impulses, seeking help to figure out the significance of such changes in yourself, in your friend, or in your teen, can be extremely important. I myself have a friend whose daughter developed such a mood condition in college, and no one in the dorm helped her find support. She was just called "nuts" and became isolated, and no one reached out to help her until it was too late.

Naturally, with impaired integration in the brain, the mind will not be as flexible or as resilient. Sometimes that lack of integration can respond to therapy with a psychotherapist, sometimes it may also require a medication, but always it should begin with an open mind and a good evaluation. When your own mind stops working well, it can be very distressing for yourself and for others. And the stress of having a tumultuous mind can itself create more stress. Here, remodeling has uncovered an underlying vulnerability, and the dysfunction that ensues from the impaired integration may create its own intensification of the pruning process. This is why getting help can be very important to reduce stress and reduce excessive pruning. The key that is being explored now in research is how this pruning process, intensified by stress, may create inadequate ways in which the connections in the brain can function.

Clearly, early interventions to create a stable life experience for the individual and reduce stress are essential to support the healthy growth of the brain during this period of change and development. This is not an "all-or-none" proposition in which a genetic vulnerability always becomes a psychiatric disorder. The reality is far more complex. Even identical twins who share the same genetic makeup do not have one hundred percent probability that both of them will develop a disorder. Experience plays a big role in how the brain develops, even in the face of same or other risk factors. We can look at genes and other important variables as some of the many factors that contribute to a larger picture of brain growth. Genes may influence some aspects of neural growth, but there is a much fuller set of factors that contribute to our well-being than genetics alone. How the mind unfolds, how relationships are supportive, how people feel a sense of belonging to a larger group all influence how the brain achieves and maintains integrative development at the root of our pathway toward health.

During adolescence, the pruning and myelination and the remodeling that they create happen primarily in the cortical regions. While one of those areas is the prefrontal cortex, it is important to keep in mind that this most forward part of the frontal cortex is not super-special by itself; it is more accurate to say that the prefrontal region and related areas are important because they coordinate and balance other regions of the brain. In this way, we can say that the prefrontal cortex is integrative as it links differentiated areas to one another. This integration enables the "whole to be greater than the sum of its parts." With this integration we achieve more complex and useful functions. As we've seen, examples of these include self-awareness, empathy, emotional balance, and flexibility.

As the prefrontal region serves as a master integrative hub, what some might call a master control center or an executive region, its rewiring during the adolescent period permits a more extensive form of integration to be achieved in the transition from childhood to adulthood. As we've noted earlier, this hub is both for the networks within the brain and body as a whole, and for the networks of interconnecting brains we call relationships. Here we see how the integration of our inner networks and our interpersonal networks shapes our experience of mind. The mind is embodied within us and it is embedded between us. Our mind is within us and between us.

The Remodeling Brain and Flipping Our Lids

Under the active influence of various drugs including alcohol, our minds can stop functioning well because our prefrontal region is no longer able to carry out its coordination and balance of the streams of information from within our bodies and from the outside world. While various drugs can shut off our brain's integrative functioning in the short run and chronic drug usage can distort that coordination and balance in our lives in the long run, we can also be prone to losing integration in other ways that don't involve drug use. Sometimes we can simply "flip our lids" and have the prefrontal integrative fibers of our brains stop coordinating our whole system. Since the prefrontal area is in a state of reconstruction during adolescence, it may be especially prone at certain times to temporarily lose its integrative functioning in linking separate areas to one another.

Even when we are developing well, sometimes during this remodeling period the prefrontal region's ability to carry out the coordination and balance of its integrative role may not function optimally. Remodeling in the brain is a necessary part of its development and builds integration through the adolescent years. This remodeling involves different phases, with females and males undergoing pruning and myelination in different regions at different times. And remodeling is energy consuming. But while trajectories do differ between the genders, where this remodeling process ultimately ends up is actually quite similar across the genders.

The brain functions in a state-dependent way, meaning that while it is in a calm state, certain integrative functions may work well and efficiently. But in other situations, those same functions may not work so well. For many of us, by the middle of adolescence, when we are away from our peers and our emotions are in balance we can be as efficient as adults. But under settings with increased emotion or in the presence of peers, reasoning can become skewed. The context we are in and the internal emotional state of our minds directly shape how sensitive we are to losing certain functions. This can be interpreted as being "too emotional" or "too swayed by peers," but another view is that our emotional sensitivity and interest in peers is adaptive. This is not immaturity but a necessary step in human development. We need to listen to our peers in order to become a part of that vital survival group as we leave our family home.

From a family point of view, this increased emotionality and social influence can become disruptive to life at home. An extreme form of this is when we get really agitated and "flip our lids" or "fly off the handle." Such a state of non-integration can happen abruptly in anyone, but in our early adolescence we may be especially prone to being this way under certain conditions, as when our parents interrupt us when they know we are busy, or when a friend does not call even though she said she would.

If you put your hand model together and then suddenly lift up your fingers, you'll see the anatomic way we can symbolize how we lose the integrative role of the prefrontal cortex. Without the calming influence of that cortical region, sudden outbursts of limbic lava and bursts of reactivity—the ancient reactions of fight, flight, freeze, or faint—can emerge suddenly, sometimes without warning to anyone. These are our early, primitive, subcortical reactions to threat. Since the cortex is a center for awareness, these lower brain areas can become active without our conscious mind's knowing what is stirring deep inside the brain. Then *wham!* Out comes a set of reactions we didn't even know were cooking inside us. Sound familiar? It happened to me a lot when I was a young teen. And it can certainly happen to us as adults, too. It is at these moments when a vulnerable prefrontal cortex is not at the top of its game monitoring and managing the subcortical world that such "low road" reactions can erupt. If we haven't slept well, haven't eaten, are under pressure, or feel some underlying emotional agitation, the prefrontal cortex's calming influences may not work so well and we can flip our lids. Adolescent or adult, this is a part of being human.

The Low Road

Now, when it comes to teenagers, this flipping one's lid is often seen as being a "crazy teenager." But let's make an agreement not to call this crazy; let's call it what it is—remodeling and shifts in integration. In a construction site, sometimes the previously working plumbing and electricity are temporarily disabled. We don't have to call that a faulty building—it's just a reconstruction project. Remodeling has its inevitable downsides, for sure. For a short time, or for bursts of time, those utilities on the construction site are off-line. No effective electricity, no plumbing, no workable staircase. These are all temporary shifts in what works well. The good news is that remodeling is a process that will create new and improved ways of functioning. Remodeling is necessary to adapt the structure of our neural foundation to adjust to new needs, and remodeling in adolescence is necessary to adapt our human family to the new needs of a changing world. New levels of integration are being created and new capacities are being established and strengthened. Remodeling constructs new integration.

That said, sometimes the remodeling comes with challenging ways of thinking and feeling and interacting that are par for the course in neural remodeling.

The reconstruction zone of the prefrontal cortex in particular means that many of the functions that this frontal area of the brain enables through its integrative role—balancing emotions, planning for the future, having insight and empathy—are more easily thrown off-line with intense emotions and peer influence. They may be more fragile, more easily disrupted, than they will be in the years ahead. In fact, one of my friends, whose son is a few years younger than my son, once said that it felt like night and day when his son went from nineteen to twenty years of age. After his son completed his first year of college, my friend told me that he "seemed to have returned to the world of normal human interactions." Now what did he mean by that? His son's balancing of emotions had been turned off, planning for the future was not happening, insight into himself—or empathy for others—seemed not to have been displayed, at least to this young man's dad. How can we make sense of this common experience?

When you understand that the prefrontal region is necessary for each of these important functions to occur, then you can understand why the change toward a settling in after some intense periods of remodeling feels so different—likely because the remodeling period is stabilizing and the prefrontal region can do its thing.

What is that thing exactly? This region coordinates and balances the whole brain with the whole body, and even our inner networks with the social world. Yes, this region behind the forehead connects all the parts of the brain in the skull to one another, and links those functions to what is going on in the body (signals from the heart, intestines, muscles). Then those connected signals are woven together with the input from other people. That's a lot of integration, the linkage of different parts. So as adolescents we need to cut ourselves some slack, and as adults we need to give respect to the remodeling adolescents are going through. That doesn't mean the shop is closed, it means we make adjustments for the fact that the adolescent mind is shaped, at times, by a construction zone.

Adolescence Builds Integration in the Brain

Take a look at your hand model of the brain. Put your limbic-thumb area over your brain stem–palm area. Those are the lower parts of the brain, the ones that generate emotion and reactivity and reward drive, among other things. Now put your fingers over your thumb, and take a look at the middle two fingernails. This is the prefrontal region. Notice how when you lift up your fingers-cortex and put them back down, you can see how this prefrontal-fingernail area is connected to the cortex; it sits on top of the limbic-thumb, and also connects directly to the brain stem–palm. In addition, signals from the body itself—from muscles and bones, from the intestines and heart—all come up to this prefrontal region, too. And if that was not enough, this prefrontal region also makes maps of what is going on inside other people's nervous systems. That's right! The prefrontal region maps the social world. It is this prefrontal area that creates our mindsight maps of you for empathy and of us for morality, as well as a mindsight map of me for insight.

So let's review this now with your hand model in mind. Five separate areas of information flow are coordinated and balanced by the prefrontal region. Here they are. The cortex. The limbic area. The brain stem. The body proper. And the social world. When these separate sources of information flow are linked together, we call that "integration." And integration is what creates the master functions of self-awareness, reflection, planning, decision making, empathy, and even morality—thinking about the larger social good.

When the prefrontal region achieves a new state of being remodeled, those important functions become more dependable and stronger. Integration can now happen more consistently and reliably. Brain, body, and social world are woven together into one whole by the prefrontal cortex. Knowing about how this prefrontal remodeling happens can help us as adolescents and as adults not only to understand better what is going on inside the brain but to do something about it that is constructive, as we'll soon see. In fact, the mindsight practices we'll explore throughout the book can promote the growth of these integrative regions of the brain. Yes, it turns out that we can cultivate the growth of the integrative fibers of the prefrontal cortex. Positive interactions with others and self-reflection are two ways to increase prefrontal integration. That's right: You can grow those fibers if you choose to learn how to do that!

The Emotional Lower Brain

Did you know that along with these prefrontal changes, the lower brain areas below the cortex (your limbic-thumb and brain stem–palm in the hand model) are more active in adolescents than they are in children or in adults? What this means is that emotions can arise rapidly and intensely without the calming influences of the prefrontal cortex. The prefrontal region can send soothing circuits, called "inhibitory fibers," down to these lower areas and keep their firing calmed.

Brain scans reveal that when teens are shown a neutral face in a photograph, a major area of the limbic region, the amygdala, becomes activated, whereas in adults the same photograph merely activates the reasoning prefrontal cortex. The result for teens can be an inner sense of conviction that even another person's neutral response is filled with hostility and he cannot be trusted. A blank expression or a bump in the hallway can be interpreted as intentional, and a teen responds with an irritated remark even when the look or bump may have been completely innocent. Knowing this scientific finding has helped me as a parent to understand the often intense reactions of my own adolescents to statements I made that, in my view, were pretty neutral, but they experienced as aggressive.

There are two routes that send information to the amygdala. One is a slow route, in which the higher cortex sifts through information, reasons, reflects, and then informs the amygdala in a calm and rational way. There's a second route, one that bypasses the cortex and simply sends incoming streams of perception directly to the amygdala. This is the fast route. Studies of adolescents reveal that even under calm conditions, the fast route to amygdala activation often occurs more readily in teens than in adults; the slow route is used more in adults. What this means is that the intense emotions of a pure amygdala response may rise up even when nothing is shutting off the cortex, as when we've flipped our lids in an agitated, chaotic state or in a shutdown, rigid state. As teens we may simply have a more immediate emotional response that is not filtered by cortical reasoning. That's the fast route in action. This is what we mean, in part, when we say that adolescence is a period of more emotional intensity, more emotional spark. The fast route to the amygdala is more readily activated during this period than it ever was, or ever will be.

For all of us, as teenagers or adults, when intense emotions erupt in our minds, we need to learn to feel them and deal with them. As Fred Rogers used to say on television, if feelings are mentionable, they can become manageable. As we have seen in the Mindsight Tools #1, we can use the notion of "Name it to tame it." Learning to deal with emotions means being aware of them and modifying them inside us so that we can think clearly. Sometimes we can name it to tame it and help balance our brain's emotional intensity by putting words to what we feel. If we say the name of an emotion inside our own minds, it can help. There are even some brain studies that show how this naming process can activate the prefrontal cortex and calm the limbic amygdala! Learning to manage our emotions in adolescence is an important part of becoming independent of our parents and becoming strong in life. In the mindsight tools sections, we'll explore the many helpful emotion-balancing strategies that can support our growth in this way during adolescence and beyond.

Hardwired for Adventure and Connection

When we compare our own adolescent period with the similar transition of other animals, we find some amazing parallels. In *Zoobiquity*, a book on the subject of how we have a lot in common with our animal cousins, Barbara Natterson-Horowitz and Kathryn Bowers write: "A similarly lowered risk threshold—indeed, a new *pleasure* in risk taking—likely propels nearly grown birds out of nests, hyenas out of communal dens, dolphins, elephants, horses, and otters into peer groups, and human teens into malls and college dorms. As we've seen, having a brain that makes you feel less afraid enables, perhaps encourages, encounters with threats and competitors that are crucial to your safety and success. The biology of decreased fear, greater interest in novelty, and impulsivity serve a purpose across species. In fact, it could be that the only thing more dangerous than taking risks in adolescence is *not* taking them."

Indeed, the natural process of moving away from the nest is filled with risk. The risk of not taking risks that Natterson-Horowitz and Bowers are referring to is that the individual will not be able to take the chances needed to leave the nest, and with such stagnation our species will not survive. Risk breathes new life into rigid ways of doing things. We can see that deep in our brain's structure, we may have the urge to take on risky behaviors that can feel as if they are matters of life or death. For the health of our family across the generations, they are essential. And for our species as a whole, they in fact *are* a matter of our survival. The adolescent brain sets up a positive bias, emphasizing the PROS and majorly de-emphasizing the cons in order to preserve our human family.

We might be driven as well to connect with our peers, who are also moving out into the world, because in groups we can find the safety of belonging. More eyes to watch for predators, more compatriots to join in our shared journey away from home, more companions to connect to as we create a new world that is necessary for the survival of our species.

I once had a patient come into my office with his pants' waistline beneath his rear end. It was quite the fashion a few years back (it may still be), and it puzzled me. I couldn't stop myself from asking about it. So with curiosity, but also I believe quite respectfully, I asked, "Why do you wear your pants below your butt like that?" I'll never forget his frank response: "I need to wear these pants like this so I can be like everyone else who is trying to be different. I am trying to be like everybody else who is trying not to be like everyone else." Exactly.

So that helps us understand the situation. Teens often feel that they need one another much more than they need adults. Adolescents are our future, and it is through their courage and their sometimes outrageous but creative efforts "not to be like everyone else" that our species has been adaptive. If we are to survive on this fragile and magnificent planet, we are going to need all the ingenuity of the rebellious adolescent mind to find solutions to the grave problems that our and previous adult generations have created in this world.

As a parent, I have tried to take to heart these lessons from science about adolescence. I take a deep breath and try to remind myself the best I can that their push-back behavior is embedded not just in *their* brains but in all *our* DNA. Their push back now was our push back then, when we were adolescents. With this universal human quality in mind, the challenge at a minimum is to find a way to help adolescents navigate these years without seriously harming themselves or others. That can be a foundational goal: *At least do no harm.* After that, everything is icing on the cake. But naturally we can start there and have much greater expectations. Another central goal is to keep the lines of communication as open as they can be. This view sets a framework that can help the most challenging situations become a bit more manageable and make this period a time of collaboration as best we can across the generations.

MINDSIGHT TOOLS #2

■

Time-In

Want to create integration in your brain? Taking time to reflect inwardly is the science-proven way to do that. I call this taking "time-in."

We've been discussing how an integrated brain gives you a strong mind and enables you to have healthy relationships with others. If you are interested in developing integration in your own brain, taking time-in to focus your attention on your internal world has been shown in research to grow those important prefrontal fibers that integrate your life. This mindsight tool will teach you how to grow the integrative fibers of your brain by learning how to focus your attention in very practical ways.

Time-In, Mindsight, and Mindful Awareness

"Time-in" is a term I use to describe the time we can take—be it a minute a day, ten minutes a day, or throughout the day—to intentionally focus our attention on the inner world of our mental, subjective experience. Much of what happens in families and in schools, and even on the Internet with social media, pulls our focus of attention to the outer world. Think of how much time many of us spend on smartphones, iPads, and other devices absorbing an endless stream of information. For many adolescents who've grown up with the Internet, e-mailing, chatting via text, and surfing the Net are just a regular part of life. And while there are a lot of great connections we can make through social media that enhance friendships and social connections in general, the danger is that we fail to pay attention to other aspects of our lives. Hours and days can go by without our taking time-in to just be with our inner life, the life of our own mind.

Why is that an issue? you may ask. Because without at least some time spent exercising our mindsight circuits focusing on the inner world—of ourselves or others—those circuits won't remain healthy and strong. To move our lives toward integration, we can't focus solely on the outside world of physical objects. We need mindsight to develop the integration in our inner lives that cultivates our insight and empathy.

Taking time-in on a regular basis is helpful because it exercises the mindsight circuits that can integrate our brains and empower our lives. One way of taking time-in is to develop mindful awareness, ways of training the mind that help us develop the ability to be present with what is happening in the moment and to let go of judgments and focus instead on accepting life as it is rather than on how we expect it to be. The way we focus attention to train the mind in general is called "meditation," and studies of mindfulness meditation show how it supports healthier functioning in the body, in the mind, and in relationships. For example, research has shown that the more present we are in life, the higher the level of the enzyme telomerase in our bodies, which maintains and repairs the life-preserving ends of our chromosomes, called telomere caps. With the day-to-day stresses of life and the natural progression of the aging process, these chromosome caps are slowly whittled down. Building up more telomerase can help us be healthier and live longer. Some people have come by presence naturally; others may learn it through mindfulness training. For those who were taught to train their mind to be mindful, their ability to be present was increased, their immune system functioned better, and their level of telomerase increased. Amazing, but true: How you focus your mind's attention inwardly can change molecules in your body that make you healthier and make your cells live longer.

With presence, too, our ability to be aware of our emotions and make them work for us instead of against us will be improved. And our ability to focus attention so we can learn what we want to learn will be strengthened. As if that were not enough, other studies of mindfulness meditation show that we will be able to approach, rather than withdraw from, challenging situations and actually feel more meaning and fulfillment in life. Some people call that happiness. It is a way of living a life of meaning, compassion, and purpose. Simply put, time-in helps us to be at our wisest.

For our relationships, time-in and the mindful awareness it creates will help us become more empathic with others. Not only is the compassion that arises from such a skill set directed at being aware of others' feelings and helping them feel better, it also helps us feel more compassionate toward ourselves.

So, yes, time-in is a fundamental part of having mindsight. And time-in is a win-win-win situation, helping our bodies and brains, our minds and inner lives, and our relationships with others. It even helps how we relate to ourselves in a kinder and more supportive way.

Why, then, isn't every school teaching time-in practices? Teachers could expand their focus beyond the traditional three R's of reading, 'riting, and 'rithmetic to teach reflection, relationships, and resilience. I think this is generally not being done because people are simply not aware of these scientifically proven outcomes of such inner practices. And teaching such internal education in schools would mean taking a step back from routines and busy schedules and creating a new approach to education overall. Yet there is a lot of research to suggest that taking time-in and developing the mindsight foundations of social and emotional intelligence enhance academic achievement. Schools can embrace these findings and support adolescents in developing this prefrontal program that supports a healthy mind. A number of innovative programs are being adopted in some schools to bring this new approach of internal education into the classroom. Since presence has been proven to promote happiness, the presence that such a time-in curriculum fosters may even make a happier set of students, and probably teachers, too.

And as families, we can make time-in a part of our daily lives. In many ways, parents are their children's first teachers. So why not have this internal education begin at home for everyone in the family?

There is no better place to begin than with ourselves. Mahatma Gandhi had a great saying: "We must be the change we wish to see in the world." And with this idea in mind, I invite you to join me in developing these basic time-in practices so you can become a mindsight maven and develop more presence in your life. Whether you are beginning your adolescence or are in the middle of it, whether you are at the end of adolescence or deep into adulthood, these time-in practices can work to bring presence into your life, catalyze integration in your brain, and strengthen your mind.

Getting Started

First, I'd like you to think of time-in as a regular daily practice you are doing to activate the mindsight circuits of your brain. A bit like brushing your teeth for oral hygiene, time-in should be a daily habit that you just do because it is a needed part of a healthy life. When we exercise a muscle, the repeated tightening then relaxing, tightening then relaxing of the muscle ultimately strengthens it. There is no muscle in the brain, but the practice of activating and strengthening a part of your body is the same idea for strengthening the brain. Here the practice is not moving a muscle but focusing your attention.

How you focus your attention drives energy and information flow through your nervous system. Where attention goes, neural firing in the brain occurs. Where neural firing happens, neural connections are strengthened. Attention is the way we activate specific circuits in the brain and strengthen them. And when you strengthen neural connections that are linking differentiated areas of the brain to one another, you are creating integration in the brain.

Put simply: Focusing your attention in regular time-in practice can integrate your brain.

Time-in and the mindful awareness and presence it creates will enable your brain to literally grow more integrative fibers that create your ability to regulate emotions, attention, thinking, and behavior, and your sense of well-being and connections to others will be optimized. If carefully conducted scientific studies did not reveal this, I myself would look at this list and say, "That is too good to be true!"

But these positive outcomes have all been shown to be true.

So the simple question is this: Are you ready to get started? And if you are, please take your time, but let's get ready now to dive into time-in.

Being Present for What Is Happening
as It Is Happening

Taking time-in can happen at any moment of the day. If I am washing the dishes, I can simply create the internal stance, called an "intention," to let this be a time to mindfully wash the dishes. What this means is that I will let the internal sensations of the experience fill my awareness. When my mind wanders and I begin to think about what I did last week, or what I'll be doing next month, then I am no longer being aware of the present-moment experience, no longer taking in the sensations of the water or the dish soap or the dish in my hands at that very moment, no longer allowing my mind to be filled only with awareness of the sensations of that moment. Taking time-in and being mindful mean being present for what is happening as it is happening.

You might be wondering: Couldn't awareness of one's thoughts about the past or the future be what is happening at that present moment? If so, isn't this taking time-in because your thinking about the past and future is *inside* you right now? And because it is what is "happening as it is happening," doesn't this also mean that you are being mindful of your thoughts at that very moment? These questions have yes answers if we are *intending* to let our minds wander on purpose and are then open to whatever arises in our thought processes. But if our intention is to focus on the sensations of the experience of washing the dishes and our minds *unintentionally* get distracted as our attention wanders and our awareness becomes filled with the uninvited focus on the past or the future, then no, this is not being mindful, and no, this is not what we mean by time-in practice.

When we take time-in, we intentionally focus on some aspect of our inner world. We are SIFTing our minds as we focus at least on some aspect of our sensations, images, feelings, and thoughts. This is how we strengthen our ability to be present, to be aware of what is happening as it is happening. Learning to be present in life, at any age, will help us become more resilient. Resilience means being flexible and strong in the face of stress, and it is what we need to approach any of the challenges of life and rise above adversity, learn from the experience, and move on with vitality and passion. These are some of the likely reasons that, research has shown, presence creates happiness and well-being in our lives.

Before we can take the steps to be present with strength and reliability, we need to learn the first step of presence, which is to use awareness to stabilize our attention. This is how we strengthen the monitoring ability of the mind.

MINDSIGHT PRACTICE A: Breath Awareness

Here are the basic instructions for this time-in practice with breathing. The task is to focus on the sensation of the breath. When the mind gets distracted, take note of that and redirect attention to the sensation of the breath.

That's it.

This universal mindfulness of the breath approach can be done sitting down or standing up. It can be done in two minutes or twenty minutes. You can do this once a day or many brief times a day. Many people like to have a regular time to carry out this breath practice and find the mornings are a great time to do this. Some researchers suggest that the key to long-term benefits is regular, daily practice. Some have said that for adults a minimum of twelve minutes seems to be important each day. But it's better to do a couple of minutes each day if those daily dozen are not possible. Just as with aerobic exercise, while thirty to forty-five minutes a day is ideal on a regular basis, if you don't have that time, it is better to do something each day rather than nothing.

Great. So now what do you do with your body while you're focusing your mind? Some people like to sit comfortably in a chair, feet flat on the floor, legs uncrossed, back straight but comfortable. Some like to sit on the floor, legs crossed. And if you can keep from falling asleep, some with back troubles like to lie flat on the floor, legs elevated either on the seat of a chair or on a cushion to ease the tension on the lower back and knees. Whatever works for you is fine.

And what do you do with your eyes? Some like to keep their eyes open, some partially closed, and others fully closed. Do whatever works well for you to focus on the breath's sensations. Since the focus is on time-in, turn off any digital objects and try to have some time when you won't be easily distracted or interrupted. You can do this alone, or you can do this with others. Whatever works is fine!

When it is new to you to focus on the sea inside, it can be challenging. So while I am saying this is simple, it doesn't mean it is easy. One challenging aspect of this experience is that we are so used to focusing on the outside world of stimulating sounds and sights that focusing on the internal world of sensations can be less captivating. In short, you may get bored!

Part of the practice is to monitor if you are falling asleep from boredom. Please don't become discouraged, but if you do feel discouraged, or anything else for that matter, just be open to whatever feelings arise. That's what being present is all about. If any particular feeling gets in the way of your focus on the breath, name it to tame it by simply saying something like "feeling discouraged" or "feeling anxious" or simply "feeling, feeling" and then let the feeling cease to be the focus of your attention by returning to the breath. The key is not to try to get rid of something, like a feeling of discouragement, but rather to be open to it, sense it as simply an object of attention, and then let your mind redirect attention to the sensation of the breath.

Being mindful has a sense of kindness, a positive regard toward yourself and others. Some people call this self-compassion, meaning you are patient with yourself and realize that you are just human. The mind has a mind of its own, and getting distracted is just what it means to be a person. Welcome to the human family! So instead of beating yourself up for being "bad" at taking time-in, you should simply acknowledge that your attention wandered to the conversation in the hallway, and then lovingly and gently redirect the attention toward your breath. Again and again, one breath at a time.

Mindful practice has the elements of COAL—that is, being *c*urious about what's happening, being *o*pen to what is going on, *a*ccepting that this is the present moment and letting go of judgments about it, and having a *l*oving stance toward the experience, and yourself. This is the COAL that warms the experience of time-in.

Let's Begin

(You may want to either have someone read this to you as you try the practice, or simply record it yourself and listen to your own voice. If you want to listen to me speaking a version of the Time-In with the Breath Awareness practice, go to my website, DrDanSiegel.com, and click on the Resources tab and the everyday mindsight tools and you'll find the breath awareness practice.)

The first time you do this, get started with a focus on the visible outside world. With your eyes open, let your attention focus on the middle of the room. Now send your attention to the far wall or ceiling. Now direct your visual attention to the middle of the room again. And now bring your attention to about book reading distance, as if you have a book or magazine in your hands. Notice how you can direct the focus of attention.

For this practice, let the sensation of the breath be the object of attention. Let's begin at the level of the nostrils with the subtle sensation of the air coming in and going out. Ride the wave of the breath, in and out, and just sense that sensation. Now notice how you can direct attention from the nostrils to the chest. Let the sensation of the chest rising and falling fill awareness. Up and down, simply ride the wave of the breath in and out. Now redirect attention to the abdomen. If you are new to this abdominal breathing, you can place a hand on the belly and simply notice how the abdomen moves out when air fills the lungs, and the abdomen moves in when air escapes the lungs. Simply ride the wave of the breath by focusing attention on the sensation of the abdomen moving out and moving in.

For this breath awareness practice, just let awareness become filled with the sensation of the breath wherever it feels most natural. It may be the abdomen moving in and out, the chest rising and falling, or the air at the nostrils. Or it may simply be the whole body breathing. Just let the sensation of the breath fill awareness wherever you feel it most readily.

As you ride the wave of the breath, in and out, let's take a few moments to focus on an ancient story that's been passed down through the generations. The story goes like this. The mind is like the ocean. And deep beneath the surface of the ocean, it is calm and clear. From this place of clarity beneath the surface, it is possible to just look up and notice whatever conditions are at the surface. It may be flat, or choppy with waves, or there may even be a full storm, but no matter the conditions, deep beneath the surface it remains calm and clear.

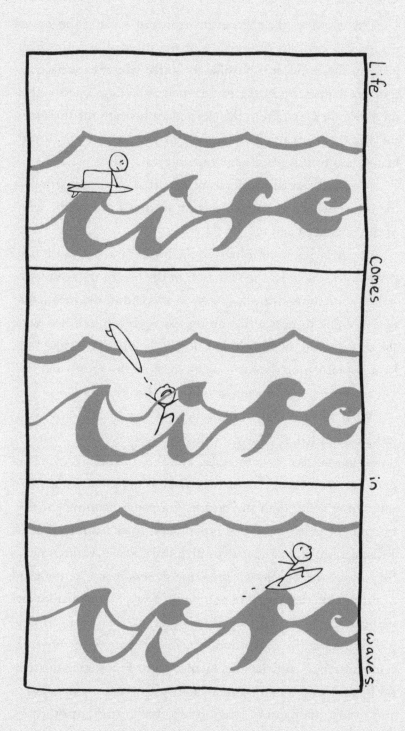

The mind is like the ocean. And just sensing the breath brings you beneath the surface of the mind. From this deep place in the mind, it is possible to notice whatever surface activity is happening in the mind, such as feelings or thoughts, memories or ideas. From this deep place beneath the surface of the mind, it is calm and clear. And just sensing the breath brings you to this place of clarity and tranquility.

Now let's return to a focus of attention on the sensation of the breath wherever you feel it most readily. Just ride the wave of the breath, in and out.

For this basic mindfulness of the breath practice, we'll take time-in to simply let the sensation of the breath fill awareness. When something distracts attention away from the breath and you've come to notice that awareness is no longer filled with the sensation of the breath, just notice the distraction and then let it go, returning the focus of attention to the breath and filling awareness with the sensation of the breath.

We'll practice this mindfulness of the breath now for a few minutes. (If you have a timer, you can set it to whatever duration you like, five minutes, a dozen, twenty.) As you experience the practice, you may find your attention goes to something other than the breath. For some, naming the distraction helps to let it go. For others, such naming is itself a distraction. If you choose to give this a try, it is often helpful to give the distraction the same general name as the kind of distraction that took your attention away. So if a memory of being at the beach distracts your attention, then you can simply say quietly in your mind, "Remembering, remembering, remembering," and let the memory go. For some, this can be helpful to strengthen their ability to release a distraction and return the focus of attention to the breath. For others, it is not helpful and may even be distracting. Find what works for you.

Remember, in addition to the task of simply focusing on the breath, it is recommended that you consider regarding yourself with kindness as you go through this practice. Everyone's mind wanders at times, and that is just what it means to be human. In fact, part of the strengthening aspect of this practice comes from the redirecting of attention, which is like contracting a muscle. The unintentional distractions are like relaxing a muscle, the refocusing on the breath is the tightening of the muscle. Focus, distraction, refocus, distraction, refocus again. That's how we work out our minds with this time-in practice. This time-in can be new to many, focusing on the internal sensations of our mental lives. If you find yourself getting sleepy, you can always open your eyes a bit if they are closed. And if that doesn't help to energize the mind, you can try this exercise standing up. Same practice, only now you are vertical.

Let's give this a try.

After a designated period of time, when you are ready, you can take a more intentional and perhaps deeper breath and let your eyes come open, if they are shut, and we'll bring this time-in breath awareness practice to a close.

How was that for you? If you are new to this, welcome! As we said, this may be simple, but it is not easy for most of us. The mind does get distracted easily, and that is just part of the reality of having a human mind. To carry out this practice, we train our minds to be present. With repeated practice, this mind-training exercise has been shown to grow important parts of the brain that are connected not only with attention but with emotion and empathy as well. These are integrative circuits, and so this basic mindfulness of the breath practice helps integrate the brain. It is a form of brain health, a way of creating mental resilience and well-being.

Building Mindsight's Lens

We can think of taking time-in as a way of building the lens that enables us to see the sea inside with more stability so that what we see is in better focus and gives us more detail and depth. Think of mindsight as having a metaphoric lens, one that is stabilized with a tripod. Each of its three legs represents an aspect of what time-in creates for us. Having a sense of these three factors of a stabilized attention can help us as we practice time-in and strengthen our mindsight skills.

The first tripod leg is *openness*. This is the openness in our COAL work, how we are simply open to whatever arises as it arises. This is an invitation to let happen whatever will happen, a deep presence to the moment that embraces whatever may stream into our awareness from attention.

The second leg is *objectivity*. This is akin to the acceptance of our COAL acronym in which we just accept the object of attention into our awareness. We don't try to distort what we think is happening; we simply let into our awareness whatever is happening at the moment and then see it as an object of our attention, as a known in the larger knowing of conscious experience. When we do our next mindsight practice, this distinction between knowing and known will become the focus of our experience.

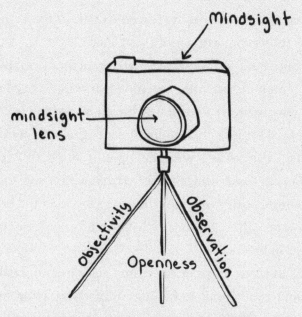

From Daniel J. Siegel, M.D., *Mindsight: The New Science of Personal Transformation*, copyright © 2010 by Mind Your Brain, Inc. Adapted with permission.

The third leg of the tripod that stabilizes mindsight's lens is *observation*. When we are tracking our designated goal for a practice and paying attention to our intention, we are observing our experience.

Interestingly, two distinct circuits have been identified in the brain. One is a sensing circuit that streams sensations directly into awareness. Another circuit is an observing circuit that enables us to bear witness to an event and to then be able to narrate that moment of time in our lives if we choose. This observing capacity gives us a bit of distance from direct sensation so that we may be more flexible in how we respond. As one of my students pointed out, this is how we "own" an experience—observe, witness, and narrate.

It is this observing capacity that lets us do something like this during a time-in practice of the breath: Ummm. Interesting conversation in the hallway. I need to talk to Steve. . . . Oh, whoops [observing distraction] . . . That's right . . . I want to talk to him, but this is a time-in practice on the breath [witnessing] . . . listening, listening, listening [narrating] . . . [observing circuit now redirects attention to breath on purpose] . . . Now: Sensation of breath fills awareness as it engages the sensing circuits that fill awareness with the input of simply the sensations of the breath. Observer feels satisfied that we are now following the intention of this time-in practice to focus on the breath by being aware of the sensations of the breath. Now we've "owned" the time-in practice!

This distinction between sensing and observing may seem subtle, but it turns out to be quite important. Time-in builds both circuits, empowering us to simply be in the flow of sensations, and also to observe our inner workings, such as our focus of attention, so that we can modify them as needed depending on our intention. Being mindful embraces at least these two streams of awareness, sensing and observing. To build the capacity for both abilities, we'll turn now to the next practice and explore more about how to build our mindsight skills.

Integrating Consciousness with the Wheel of Awareness

A time-in practice that is specifically designed to integrate consciousness is called the Wheel of Awareness. In our daily lives there are many aspects of our conscious experience, of what we are aware of and the nature of our awareness itself. When we allow these different aspects of consciousness, of being aware, to be seen for their unique qualities—like distinguishing vision from hearing, sensing the body from thinking—and then we connect them through systematically focusing attention on each within awareness, we develop a more coherent sense of ourselves. This is what I mean when I say integrate consciousness. It's the linking of the different elements of being aware into a harmonious whole. It is quite simple but quite empowering as it integrates our minds. The wheel practice is more elaborate than the breath practice offered in the prior practice entry, but taken together, they make a good pair of mind-strengthening time-in exercises. My suggestion to you is that if you have not worked on the time-in with the breath awareness

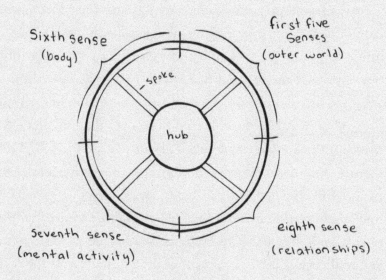

Wheel of Awareness
The hub represents the experience of knowing within awareness; the spokes are focused attention; the rim is the known, including sensations and other mental processes. The sectors of the rim are as follows: first through fifth (outer world), sixth (body), seventh (mental activity), and eighth (relationships) senses. From Daniel J. Siegel, M.D., *The Mindful Brain*, copyright © 2007 by Mind Your Brain, Inc. Adapted with permission.

practice for a week or so, you may want to do that before trying out the wheel practice. Some just dive in and it goes well, but this practice is both a bit longer—it can take about twenty minutes or so in its full form—and a bit more elaborate.

In my office at work there's a table with a glass center and an outer wood rim. When you look through the glass, the legs of the table appear like spokes connecting this center hub to the outer rim. One day that table seemed to be a good metaphor for consciousness. As an image, the hub could represent the sense of knowing in consciousness, the rim could stand for the known (like a feeling or thought or memory), and the spokes could be the process of attention that streams the known into the knowing.

As integration is the differentiation and then linkage of parts of a system, how can we integrate consciousness? At a minimum, consciousness or being aware has two components: our sense of knowing and that which is known. We can use attention to link these differentiated aspects of consciousness to each other. It is also possible to differentiate the different elements of the known, represented in our metaphoric wheel on the rim, into four segments. This process of creating a linkage of the differentiated parts of being aware creates a powerful state of integration in our minds and can soothe anxiety, create clarity, and open us up to being present in life with strength and resilience. The first segment of the rim represents the first five senses, sight, hearing, smell, taste, and touch. The second segment of the rim contains the interior of the body—what is called the "sixth sense"—that includes the inner sensations of our muscles and bones, and of the internal organs such as intestines, lungs, and heart. A third segment represents our mental processes of feelings, thoughts and memories, intentions, beliefs, and attitudes—our "seventh sense." And a fourth segment can also be differentiated and represent a kind of relational sense, our "eighth sense," where we perceive the connections we have with other people and with our natural environment, our planet.

How could these various knowns of the rim actually be connected to the knowing of the hub? That would be the distinct but related process of attention. Attention is the process that directs the flow of energy and information. We focus attention from the hub of knowing in awareness toward the rim of the known. And when we do this in a systematic way, a "rim review," we then link the differentiated elements of consciousness. That is how the Wheel of Awareness practice integrates consciousness.

So I offer this wheel practice to you as an invitation to explore your own inner life—and to integrate consciousness. The wheel has been vetted by my mindfulness colleagues as a mindfulness practice, but it was not designed to be that. Preliminary research suggests it also has powerful positive effects on how we regulate our emotions and helps develop a clear mind—two outcomes of integration. The Wheel of Awareness was created to integrate consciousness and offer a systematic way of exploring the sea inside.

MINDSIGHT PRACTICE B: The Wheel of Awareness

You can record this practice yourself and listen to it, or you can simply go to DrDanSiegel.com and download it. This practice takes about twenty minutes, so it certainly offers you one variation on doing your daily dozen. If you don't have the twenty minutes, you can also do one segment of the rim review only, tailoring it to your needs as you go. And there is even a way to move more quickly through the rim if needed, covering it all but making the practice more like a dozen minutes, by letting alternate breaths be your guide for timing the movement of your spoke in reviewing the sensations of the outside world and body. I suggest starting with the full timing to get familiar with the wheel and then modifying your practice to fit your needs. You choose what works best for you.

■

We'll begin the practice here.

In the illustration of the Wheel of Awareness (p. 129), you'll find a drawing of the table in my office that serves as the wheel for our practice. Take a look at the wheel, and let's review its parts. The hub represents the experience of knowing within awareness. The rim represents anything you can be aware of, such as sights or sounds, thoughts or feelings. And the spokes represent attention, the way you can stream energy and information from the rim into the hub.

Let's focus on the breath for a few waves of the in breath and the out breath. If you've been practicing time-in with the breath, you'll be ready to sense the breath wherever you feel it most naturally. Now that deep place beneath the surface of the mind, the place where sensing the breath can take you to notice whatever arises on the surface, is like the hub of the wheel. And just sensing the breath brings you to the hub of the mind. Now let the breath go, and simply visualize or imagine the idea of the Wheel of Awareness, with its central hub of clarity, the spokes of attention, and the rim. We'll now begin our rim review to explore each of the segments of the rim.

Imagine sending a spoke of attention to the first segment of the rim, that part that has sight, hearing, smell, taste, and touch. Let's begin with hearing, letting any sounds in the room fill awareness . . .

Now move the imaginary spoke over a bit in this first segment and let the light coming in through your eyelids, or slightly opened eyes, fill awareness . . .

Now move the spoke again and let any odors fill awareness . . .

And now move the spoke to the sense of taste, letting any tastes fill awareness . . .

Now let anywhere where skin is touching something, touching clothes, touching a chair, touching skin, let the sense of touch fill awareness . . .

Now taking a bit of a deeper breath, we'll let this first segment of the rim go and move the spoke over to the second segment of the rim. Let's begin by focusing attention on the facial area. Let the sensations of the muscles and bones of the face fill awareness. Now move attention to the scalp, and let the sensations from the top of the head fill awareness. And now focus attention on the back of the head and sides, filling awareness with those sensations. Now moving attention to the muscles and bones of the neck and throat, fill awareness with their sensations.

Let attention now go to the shoulder area, letting the muscles' and bones' sensations fill awareness. And now stream attention down both arms, to the elbows . . . wrists . . . and the ends of the fingers . . . Now bring attention to the muscles and bones of the upper back and the chest . . . And now to the lower back and the abdomen . . . Now send attention to the hips, and down both legs to the knees and the ankles and the ends of the toes . . .

Now bring attention to the pelvic area, filling awareness with the sensation from the genitals . . . and now move attention inward, to the intestines, letting these gut sensations fill awareness . . . Now let attention go to the stomach . . . and now up to the interior of the throat. . . And now let attention move to the interior of the lungs . . . And now center attention in the heart region, and just let those heartfelt sensations fill awareness . . .

And now let awareness become filled with the interior of the whole body, from head to toes . . .

Knowing that the body's signals are a deep source of wisdom always available to you, we'll let this segment of the rim go as you take a deeper breath and move the spoke of attention over to the third segment of the rim. This is the segment that represents your mental life of feelings and thoughts, memories and intentions. Whatever the mind can create is represented here. For this aspect of the rim review, we'll have two parts.

In the first part, you'll send the spoke from the hub to the third segment of the rim. Then you'll simply invite into awareness in the hub whatever may arise, whatever comes up to enter awareness. In many ways, this is the opposite of the breath-awareness practice where you intentionally focus on the breath, and when a mental process—like a thought or memory—distracts attention, you let it go and return the focus of attention to the breath. Here you are simply being open to whatever mental life may or may not come into awareness. It's like an internal open stance of "Bring it on." Just sense whatever may arise in awareness. Let's do that for a few minutes . . .

For the second part of this aspect of the rim review, we'll again invite anything into awareness from this third segment of the rim. Now, though, I'll invite you to also study the ways in which a mental activity is experienced in awareness. How does it first come into awareness? Does it come suddenly or gradually? From one side or another? And once it is in awareness, how does it stay there? Is it constant or vibrating, is it steady or intermittent? And then how does it leave awareness? Suddenly, or gradually, or is it just replaced by another mental activity, another thought or memory or feeling or image? If it is not replaced by another mental activity, what does the space feel like between two mental activities in awareness?

So for this part of the rim review, I'm inviting you to become a student of the architecture of your own mental life. Let's begin that practice now for a few minutes . . .

Now I invite you to find the breath, in and out, and take a deeper breath as we let this segment of the rim go for now and move the spoke over, one more time, to the fourth segment of the rim. This is the part of the rim that represents our sense of connection to others and to our environment. First, if there are people in the room near you, let the sense of closeness to them fill awareness. Now let that sense of connection expand to your relationships with friends and family . . . Now let that sense of connection move out to your classmates if you are in school, or to your work colleagues . . . And now let that sense of connection open to all those who live in your community . . . in your city . . . in your state or province . . . in your country . . . on your continent . . .

Now let that sense of connection open up to all people

who share this home we call planet Earth . . . And now see if you can expand that sense of connection to all living beings, animals and plants, who share our common home, this planet, together . . .

Knowing that scientific research has validated what wisdom traditions throughout the world have taught for centuries, that positive intentions and wishes for the well-being of others lead not only to positive changes in the world but also to health benefits to yourself, I invite you to imagine sending wishes of kindness for health and happiness, safety and well-being to all living beings on Earth . . . And now, taking a bit of a deeper breath, sending kindness and compassionate wishes of health and happiness, safety and well-being to your own inner self . . . Now let's find the breath and ride the wave of the breath, in and out . . . And taking now a more intentional and perhaps deeper breath, we'll bring this Wheel of Awareness practice to a close for today.

Reflecting on the Wheel

One amazing thing about the Wheel of Awareness practice is that each time you do it, it is different. People from all walks of life from all over the planet have shared the challenges and the benefits of the practice. You can see for yourself what doing this practice is like, and only you can say if it is useful to you in some way.

When adolescents have reported on their experience with the wheel, they've told me that the sense of the hub has given them a kind of freedom from whatever might be coming up on the rim. One twenty-one-year-old said that her anxiety about being with other people was greatly reduced because her "nervousness and worries just became points on the rim that I could sense from that calmer place on the hub." And she is not alone. Many people, adolescents and adults alike, have reported all sorts of relief from painful emotions and even painful bodily sensations when they've strengthened the hub of their mind.

There is a more advanced practice, Wheel of Awareness III (with the hub-on-hub practice included), in which you are invited to experience sending the spoke out from the hub, only this time it is bent back to return to the hub itself. This is how you are focusing attention on awareness, and experience what awareness of awareness feels like.

For people new to time-in practices of reflection inwardly, such an advanced awareness of the awareness part of the wheel may be too much at first. Rather than frustrating someone new to this important reflective work, I just leave out that more advanced step for the initial experience. But if you've been practicing the breath awareness for a while and feel that it works well for you, and if you've tried out the wheel for a while and feel ready for a more challenging aspect of that process, you may be ready to try out Wheel III.

I suggest that if you feel ready, go ahead to the website and give it a try. That bending of the spoke to come back to the hub is generally done after the fourth segment of the rim is reviewed, just before the end of the whole practice. It's best to do the whole wheel first, and then add this hub-on-hub part at the end so that your mind is prepared. Just let yourself sense whatever focusing attention on awareness itself feels like. After a couple of minutes, let yourself find the breath again, in and out, and then, when you are ready, take a more intentional and perhaps deeper breath and let your eyes come open if they're shut, and let the wheel practice come to a close.

■

There are many other forms of taking time-in on a regular basis, including focusing on being more compassionate with yourself and others in a systematic way. Even when you are in motion there are ways to take time-in. You can mindfully walk by focusing on the internal sensations from the bottoms of your feet with each step. And you can do other mindful movement practices that encourage you to focus on your intentions, awareness, and sensations. Focusing attention on your intention, being aware of your awareness, and staying present with a stance of kindness and compassion are the essential elements of time-in practices. Each of these practices offers a research-proven way to empower your life. Many studies suggest that taking time daily, even just three minutes several times each day, to focus mindfully on your breath can greatly support your well-being. Time-in integrates your brain, improves your relationships, and strengthens your mind. In so many ways, taking time-in on a daily basis is the powerful starting place to create more integration in your life.

PART III

■

Your Attachments

Close relationships shape us across the life span. Learning about the fundamental ways our connections to others can enrich our lives as they support a healthy mind and likely promote integration in our brains can guide us in creating the relationships that are best for us no matter our age. Our experiences in the first dozen or so years of our lives have a powerful impact on the people we become. Friendships, experiences in school, activities we participate in, and relationships with family members all influence how our brains develop during the years leading up to adolescence. But even after these early years, relationships continue to play a crucial role in our growth and development. In this part we'll explore how the ways we relate to our caregivers shape how our minds develop to reveal some basic

guiding principles of relationships. The great news is that by understanding what happened to you and how you responded to those
experiences in the past, you can open your life now to more productive and healthy ways of relating to others, and even to yourself.

Especially influential in terms of how the brain develops—and,
in turn, how we learn to calm our emotions, how we understand
ourselves, and how we relate to others and the larger world—are our
experiences during infancy. The relationships we have with our parents and other people who care for us when we are very young most
directly shape who we become. But it is crucial to keep in mind that
our minds are continually emerging, our brains continually growing
in response to experience, and whether you are an adolescent or an
adult now, how you make sense of your life and understand these
patterns of connecting with others can empower you to optimize
how you live.

If you are an adolescent still living with a parent, you may feel
intense and complex emotions as you explore these ideas about family life still going on in the present. I also know, from personal experience as a parent, that reflecting on ways we parent our children and
adolescents can be challenging as we face some at times non-ideal
patterns of communicating that have been present in our parenting
approach. Naturally, we want to do well with our kids. But doing
well may sometimes elude us if we've had challenging experiences in
our own past. So much of what I've tried to explore in earlier books
is how important it is for us to be honest with ourselves and open to
the important continuing growth we can model for our offspring.
There is no such thing as perfect parenting. But there is a way to
make sense of our lives so that we move toward authentic ways of
relating that are supportive of our kids and ourselves. So please keep
this in mind: It is never too late to course correct, to come to a
deeper understanding and enhance the way we connect in our fami-

lies with the people we love and care so deeply about. If change were not possible, there wouldn't be much reason to dive into this material. But science and experience reveal that with self-reflection and understanding, non-ideal patterns we've adopted from our own pasts can be transformed. Be patient with yourself and with your family members. With kindness and understanding, to yourself and to others, change can be nurtured and good things can emerge.

Connections with others, our relationships, come in many forms. These important connections with our parents or other caregivers are called "attachment relationships." We carry these selective few attachment relationships forward inside us in what are called "models of attachment." The term "model" broadly means the mental way, shaped by brain-firing patterns, that we summarize across experiences and generate a schema that lets us anticipate what is happening next, how we should behave, what emotions we will have, and how we filter our perceptions. Models are really useful in learning and knowing how to behave, and they often influence our ways of seeing and being in the world without our awareness.

An attachment model is in effect the way in which our brains remember the attachment relationship(s) we have had, or still have, and how we have adapted to these formative attachment experiences. The models we carry with us in our minds are very influential in terms of how we feel, how we think, how we behave, and how we connect with friends, teachers, and later on, our romantic partners as we move through our lives. And since we can have more than one model if we've had more than one attachment figure, then each of these brain states, these models, can influence how we behave and react in different situations.

Our attachment models get activated in specific situations that may resemble the particular kind of attachment relationship we had in the past, and then they shape how we interact in that present moment. If we are with an assertive older female friend, for example, we may begin acting as we did with our mother, who, too, may have been an assertive personality. In contrast, if we adapted to a mild-mannered father with our own withdrawal, with a quiet male friend we might find ourselves becoming withdrawn and not even know the reason why. Models become engaged automatically, without our awareness or intention. For all of us, adolescents and parents, understanding what kinds of attachment models we constructed in our early childhood can greatly help us understand how our lives are unfolding now, and how we might create a new way of living that frees us from any kind of limitations such models may be making in our lives.

There are two broad types of models, one secure and the other non-secure. Secure models support our living with flexibility, self-understanding, and ease of connection with others. Non-secure models come in several forms we'll explore here, and each of these in some ways challenges our ability to be flexible, understand ourselves, and connect with others. Because we can have many models and their activation is dependent on the situation we find ourselves in, we can seem quite different in different settings with different people.

In many ways, developing secure attachment models is an important way to support the ESSENCE of adolescence. With security our emotional spark can be freed to enrich our lives with passion rather than pushing us toward states of being chaotically overwhelmed or rigidly shut down. With secure models, too, we can have social engagements that are mutually rewarding and enable us to feel both differentiated and linked within the integrative social connections that help us thrive as adolescents. We will see that secure attachment is as much about offering a safe harbor of support, to turn to when we are distressed or tired, as it is about supporting how we go out and explore the world. With such a secure launching pad, we can

I support you.

take on our drive to seek novelty with more gusto and strength. Security supports the development of a resilient mind. And as our minds find new ways of experiencing how we think and reflect on life during adolescence, having secure attachment models can support our creative explorations during this new period of our growth.

In this part we'll explore what your experiences with attachment figures in your life have been and what attachment models you may have now. We'll then see how we can use this understanding and specific strategies to develop secure attachment models that set the foundations of resilience and support the ESSENCE of adolescence to help you create a life that's best for you, whatever your age.

Safe Harbor and Launching Pad

I have an aquarium in my office and I love to sit and stare at the fish as they swim about. Interestingly, while some fish do care for their young, my fish are typical of most fish (and reptiles and amphibians, for that matter) that fertilize their eggs, deposit them in the sand, and leave them to fend for themselves after they hatch. We mammals are very different. A key feature of our mammalian heritage is that our young require the close care of an adult figure, often the mother, who provides safety and nurturance. That's attachment.

One important feature of human child rearing is that we don't just have one attachment figure as most mammals do. We humans practice what is called alloparenting, which means "other parenting," sharing child rearing with other trusted adults or older children. This ability is crucial for us as a social species and may have shaped how we evolved as a species in general in terms of our unique abilities for communicating and building collaborative relationships. Alloparenting also means that we can have attachments to more than just our mother; we can form attachments to a selective few older, stronger, and hopefully wiser individuals to whom we turn for protection and comfort.

As complex social creatures, we have a very extended period of dependency on our attachment figures. The human brain needs the relationships with our attachment figures and other adults to shape how it grows. Our childhood period of dependency goes on for a good 15 percent of our lifetime—a really long time in mammalian terms. And if we include the period of adolescence, now extended into the twenties, that percentage before we reach adult status in our society is higher still, approaching a third of our lives.

Human attachment can be understood as involving four S's. We need to be *seen*, *safe*, and *soothed*, in order to feel *secure*. Being seen means that our inner mental life is sensed beneath our behavior. Our caregiver hears our cry, figures out what our inner need is, and then offers us something that meets that need. Being safe means we are both protected from harm and not terrified by our caregiver. To be soothed means that when we are distressed, our caregiver's response makes us feel better. When we need comfort, we get a hug. And all of this—being seen, safe, and soothed in a reliable way—gives us an overall sense of security in the relationship.

These ways our attachment figures treat us give us a sense of a safe harbor in which we can feel secure. But attachment relationships also serve as a launching pad from which we can take off and explore the world. When we have a secure attachment model, we have the security to venture out into all that lies ahead in the world beyond our home. And when we are tired, or distressed, or just need to touch base, we return to the safe harbor of our attachment home, our relationships with our attachment figures.

As we grow from infancy into toddlerhood, this sense of security in our relationship is internalized in our brains in a "state of mind"

that is secure. We feel good about ourselves, good about connecting with others, and feel that our needs will be met. Even more, in a humble and solid versus demanding and entitled way, we feel we'll be able to have connections with others who will see our minds, feel our feelings, and meet our needs. This is the solid sense of self that emerges for those with secure attachment models.

When we hit adolescence, having a secure attachment model can be a real blessing as we go out into the world and experience all the many changes that becoming an adolescent means and what the journey toward adulthood may entail. If we've had secure attachment in our earlier childhood, then we enter these early adolescent stages with a more secure model, a state of mind that is filled with many of the prefrontal functions that emerge with integration strong and well-developed. Science has shown that secure attachment is associated with the integrative prefrontal functions that include regulating the body, attuning to others and ourselves, balancing our emotions, being flexible, soothing our fears, having insight into ourselves and empathy for others, and having a good grounding in a sense of morality.

To put this proposal in a nutshell, when we've had secure attachments, our relational experiences have supported the development of integration in the brain and resilience of our mind. When we have had insecure attachments, the development of our non-secure models reflects states of non-integrated brain functioning. You can see the basic idea here: If you've had a history of insecure attachment, to grow toward security happens by moving from non-integrated brain functioning to the development of integration in your brain. And that development can potentially happen at any age.

Secure attachment confers resilience as it likely stimulates the growth of integrative connections of the prefrontal cortex. Recall that the prefrontal region links cortex, limbic area, brain stem, body, and even the social world into one coordinated and balanced whole. This is the power of attachment relationships to create healthy and adaptive functions in our lives, functions that emerge from integration in our brains.

While entering adolescence with a secure model of attachment makes it more likely that the adolescent period will be smoother, it does not guarantee it. Resilience is important, but it does not confer absolute immunity to the many curve balls life sends our way. As we're seen, the remodeling period of development that occurs in adolescence can play a role in the emergence of many challenges to well-being, including the onset of various psychiatric conditions such as mood, anxiety, and thought disorders, as well as drug abuse and addiction. These conditions are not caused by attachment and their onsets are not necessarily prevented by secure attachment. Any of these can emerge even with a history of secure attachment, as many other factors in life influence our development besides attachment, such as our temperament, our extended social relationships, our socioeconomic status, our genetics, and our use of dopamine-activating substances. Studies suggest, for example, that certain variations in our genetic makeup that influence ways we process dopamine, serotonin, or oxytocin may have a direct effect on how we respond to certain challenging experiences in life. Attachment is one important element of our lives, but not the whole story. Still, since attachment influences so much, and because we can actively empower our lives as we shape our attachment models in a positive way, knowing about attachment is vital for any of us. You may not be able to alter your genes, but you can alter your mind and your behavior to change your brain. In other words, your attachment models are changeable, and knowing about your attachment models is crucial so that you can move them toward security whatever your age.

For about one-half to two-thirds of the general population, secure attachment is where we start out in life. If that is mostly where you've come from, you've got a great starting place to enter adolescence, a boost in your ability to be resilient when life throws challenges your way. But for about one-third to one-half of us, which means about 150 million people in the United States alone, we have had attachment relationships that were not secure. These insecure attachments don't necessarily mean that we are insecure on the whole as people, it simply means that we didn't consistently receive those S's of being seen, safe, and soothed, and so did not feel secure in our primary attachment relationships. Our non-secure models of attachment reflect how we had to adapt to this insecure relationship when we were younger. And these models of attachment persist throughout our lives. They are changeable, yes, but only if we come to understand them.

With a history of insecure attachment, our brains may not enter the adolescent period with the same baseline integrative growth that a securely attached person has been able to develop in childhood.

The great news is that it is never too late to develop integration in our brains! We can move from non-secure models of attachment, those states of non-integrated brain functioning, to secure, integrated models by developing integration in our brains. One way we can do this is to make sense of what has happened in our lives. Making sense moves us from a non-secure, non-integrated model of attachment to a place of security and an integrated model of attachment.

In this part, we'll explore your life history and try to make sense of the different kinds of attachment that you may have experienced in your childhood and the attachment models that may now be a part of your internal world. Whether you are an adolescent still living with your attachment figures, your parents or others, or you are an older adolescent or adult living away from your attachment figures, making sense of your life is a science-proven way to move from non-secure to secure models of attachment. It's a way of integrating your brain and empowering your life.

The Ways We Attach

There are four broad ways we become attached to our parents or others who care for us. For simplicity, I will usually use the term "parent," even though you may have had a number of caregivers, be they your mother and father, relatives, friends, or others who took care of you and to whom you turned when you needed comfort and protection. As we've seen, our brains are capable of maintaining several different models of attachment, one for each relationship to a given attachment figure. So as we explore these four ways of being attached to our caregivers, keep in mind that you, like many of us, may actually have more than one of these models inside you shaping your inner sense of self and how you relate to others. The setting you are in, how people respond to you, and how people remind you of one of your attachment figures can all directly influence which of these models becomes activated at a particular time.

The Secure Model

If you had a relationship with a parent who in a somewhat consistent way provided you with a sense of being seen, feeling safe, and being soothed, then you will have a model of secure attachment. This secure model lets you balance your emotions, understand yourself well, and engage with others in mutually rewarding ways. Attachment continues across the life span, but to give you a sense of how the fundamental research is done, here's a brief summary of how attachment is assessed during infancy: After about a three-minute separation from the caregiver, the one-year-old infant seeks contact with the caregiver during their reunion, touches base for comfort, and then readily returns to exploring a room filled with toys. The researchers view this interactive behavior as evidence of a secure attachment model in the child that is activated in the presence of this

particular parent. The idea is that the parent has provided both a safe haven and a launching pad; the child feels seen, safe, soothed, and secure with this parent. This learned model is then activated so that the child makes contact, feels secure, and launches out to explore the world of new toys in the room.

From infancy on, we carry these models forward as they help us organize our approach to relationships throughout the life span.

The Avoidant Model

If you had a similar experience growing up to about 20 percent of the general population, you had a relationship with one or both parents that was filled with repeated experiences of your not being seen or soothed. Here the form of insecure relationship is called "avoidant attachment." This term comes from research findings in which investigators observed one-year-old infants who were separated from their father or mother later avoiding that parent when he or she returned, rather than reconnecting and seeking comfort from the parent, as happened in the secure relationships. Here the notion is that the child's experience of not being seen or soothed over the first year of life with this parent has led to the development of a non-secure model of attachment—in this case, an avoidant model. In the presence of that parent, the child activates a model of avoidance. This is a learned response quite adaptive for the child's survival.

It's important to note that in these studies it was also seen that several of the infants who avoided one parent actually sought comfort and closeness with the other parent. In other words, if you have an avoidant attachment model as a result of your relationship with one parent, this doesn't mean that you can't have a secure attachment with your other parent, enabling you to go through life knowing what a truly secure relationship feels like. But with avoidant models and the avoidant relationships they grow from, you've learned something very different. With a repeated set of experiences where interacting with that parent, say your father, is not soothing when you are distressed, and not connecting when you feel unseen, then the model you develop says something like, "I don't need this person for anything, because I have learned that he gives me nothing when I need connection or comfort." You learned to minimize your attachment needs. Having this avoidant model as your model for close relationships can potentially lead you to feel disconnected from others and also from your own emotions and needs. That's the disconnected self of avoidant attachment.

Let's highlight again here that your attachment model is a summary of how you've adapted to the relationships you've had with important people in your life. It's not, however, a sign of some problem you have inside you—it's merely a reflection of a learned response to real-life events, to your actual relationship in your early days. Furthermore, it does not mean you are now devoid of a need for closeness and comfort. While these models may be cortical adaptations that shape our external behaviors and our awareness, studies reveal that the limbic area that mediates attachment still retains a deep drive for connection with others. We all need to feel close to the people around us and know that we can rely on them for comfort. That's just being human. In this respect, the self-knowledge that comes from realizing you may have been living your life following an avoidant model can be very empowering. It can allow you to search the quiet, often hidden signals inside you that you may want closer connection with others. Sensing these signals may help you release your avoidant model so you can seek out from others what you need in life as you mature and age. The avoidant model was good and useful during your early years; now it needs updating. Reflecting on these patterns can be one important step in enabling you to transform your non-secure attachment models toward security.

The Ambivalent Model

A third type of relationship is when a child experiences inconsistency or intrusiveness with a parent, as occurs in around 15 percent of the general population. Being seen, safe, and soothed does not happen in a reliable way. When the parent returns after a separation, you go to her, but you cling to her because you are uncertain whether she'll meet your needs for comfort. Maybe she will, but maybe she won't. Better hold on! Your ambivalent model of attachment does not allow you to become soothed as you never know what to expect—she is not a reliable safe harbor. And her feelings and emotions flood your own inner world as well. For example, if you feel hungry, instead of your mom just figuring that out and feeding you, she gets flooded with her own anxiety and fears about whether she will be an effective mother for you. Since the human brain is composed of "mirror neurons" that soak up the feelings of others around us, you naturally sponge up her anxiety and fear. All you were feeling was hunger, but after interacting with your mom you now also feel fearful and anxious. Whose feelings are whose? That's the confused self created within ambivalent attachment relationships. You amplify your attachment needs with ambivalence because of the history of intrusiveness and inconsistency. Maybe this time she can soothe you, but maybe not, but maybe so, but maybe . . . That's ambivalence.

The Disorganized Model

The fourth kind of attachment can occur within the setting of the other three—secure, avoidant, or ambivalent. Besides those baseline experiences of attachment, something else is going on. For a variety of reasons, your parent, say your mom, is terrifying to you. This could be because she is depressed and irritable and runs after you, yelling at you when you get home from school. This could be because she is screaming at your father or your siblings and not at you. And this could be because she just looks terrified herself and you *sponge* her terror up inside you. The problem with being terrified of an attachment figure is that it activates two different circuits in your brain that just don't work together. One is the ancient brain stem circuit that mediates a survival reaction. This circuit gets you to flee or freeze in reaction to being terrified. Get away from this source of terror! But the second circuit is the limbic-based attachment system that motivates you if you are terrified to go toward your attachment figure to be protected and soothed. The problem is you cannot go both toward and away from the same person. After separation, the infant shows behaviors of attempting to both approach and withdraw from the parent, a very disorganized approach to the reconnection.

So when an attachment figure is the source of terror, we become fragmented. This disorganized attachment makes us vulnerable in many ways. We can have a tough time balancing our emotions, having good relationships with others, and even thinking clearly under stress. Even more, a disorganized attachment makes it likely that we'll have a fragmentation of the continuity of consciousness, called "dissociation." Found in about 5 to 15 percent of the general population even without a history of abuse, and in about 80 percent of children in high-risk families with trauma and neglect, disorganized attachment and the dissociation that accompanies it can be very challenging to our well-being. When we dissociate, we dis-associate different aspects of ourselves, such as separating feelings from memories, thoughts from actions. We can feel unreal and broken apart. This is the source of a fragmented self that emerges with a disorganized model of attachment.

Reactive Attachment

When a secure attachment is not available, we can experience a range of ways that we adapt and do the best we can, including avoidance, ambivalence, and disorganization. But there are a number of situations in which our attachment may not be simply secure or insecure. At one extreme of our human spectrum of experiences is the complete absence of attachment, in which there is no consistent figure that we can attach to. In this case, a dysfunctional condition called reactive attachment may arise and we may have trouble with our emotions and relationships, establishing rapid connections with a wide array of individuals in childhood, in adolescence, and into our adulthood. Reactive attachment can be thought of as the best a child can do with the absence of any attachment figure—not a response to forms of security or insecurity. This absence and the "disorder" that emerges with it are distinct from the variety of insecure forms of attachment we are exploring here. If you know individuals who've experienced this absence of attachment, or if you've been through this yourself, please refer to some of the important work in the professional literature on this situation as helpful resources for healthy growth.

Earning Secure Attachment and
Integrating the Brain

When Gail's son, Steven, was leaving home for college after his eighteenth birthday, he was excited to begin this next phase of his life. Many of his friends were leaving California for the East Coast, but he decided to stay in the West and attend a school about five hours away from his home in Los Angeles. His mother had gotten ill in his last year of high school, and he wanted to be able to return home and see her more frequently than a cross-country college would have enabled him to do. He felt close to his mother, and like his brother and sister, he was very distressed with her diagnosis of cancer. He did his best to support her during her radiation and chemotherapy, but she insisted he continue to go out with his friends during that senior year and get ready for this new time of his life. It was Steven's decision to stay close—but not that close. In fact he felt completely supported by his mother in his decision not to attend UCLA, a wonderful option for him just a few miles from his family's home.

Gail had herself been through a lot in her own childhood. Her mother died when she was fifteen, and her father had been an actively drinking alcoholic during much of her childhood. The death of Gail's mother "woke her father up," and he began a life of sobriety after that time and has stayed sober ever since. Her family seemed to get closer in the face of that tragedy of her mother's passing. For much of her adolescence, Gail was in turmoil about how she could leave her two sisters and her father when it was time to graduate from high school. She decided to go to a community college near home and help out her father, a decision she was glad to make then. But before she got married to Steven's dad, she spent a lot of time thinking about how upsetting her father's alcoholism had been in her childhood. When he'd come home drunk, he was terrifying. His fits of rage and drunken stupors led everyone to scramble for cover—everyone except her mother, who would take him on. Gail would witness her father berating her mom, and sometimes physically abusing her. She didn't know then but knows now that witnessing abuse is itself a form of abuse, a form of trauma. You might imagine that Gail's early attachment experiences with her dad being filled with terror led her to have a disorganized attachment to him. His drunken states were terrifying. His berating and beating her mom were terrifying. And her feeling of being unable to protect her two younger sisters made her feel terrified and helpless.

During Gail's later adolescence in her early twenties, she decided to try psychotherapy. This is when I first met her. We worked on her history of insecure attachments, including a disorganized attachment model and the accompanying tendency of her mind to fragment in dissociative states. These dis-associations of usually connected processes could come out when she was upset and felt like she was "not put together" and "unraveling at the seams." She'd go down the low road frequently with her boyfriend and her father, yelling at them, feeling intense and "overblown" emotional reactions to small things they'd do. Or these dissociative moments could emerge and she would feel blank and a have a difficult time remembering things or paying attention. When she was a teen, for example, there were times when she couldn't seem to hold on to her memories of her mother after she died, the loss being overwhelming and her relationship with her father still terrifying. We gathered from her attachment assessment that she had what is called an ambivalent history with her mom, who had been preoccupied about her competence as a mother and a wife. Her mom had been warm and caring, but it was a relationship that Gail said was "loving but a confusing mess." Dealing with her feelings toward this confusion was challenging in the face of her grief about

her mother's passing. In some ways, there were elements of unresolved loss around her mother, too. Reflecting on that important loss
in her life could help her resolve that grief and gain more access to
her feelings about their complicated relationship.

Gail generally did pretty well in her emotional and social life as
therapy went on, and she was grateful for these changes. Because she
had an ambivalent pattern of insecurity with her primary caregiver—
her mother—she needed to do some basic work on sensing her own
integrity, clarifying from the confusion who she was, what she felt,
and how she could hold on to her own inner compass in the face of
interacting with others. This transformation from her insecure ambivalent attachment model toward security meant that she could feel
her feelings and balance them well. And that meant that she could
have mutually rewarding relationships with friends and romantic
partners. Our attachment models contain the important ways we've
learned to connect to others and know ourselves. When we make
sense of our lives, we can move these models from non-security to
security.

When Gail met her husband, fell in love, and started her family
in her late twenties, some of the paternally related issues of disorganization began to emerge in her life and in their relationship. When
they'd have arguments, as most couples do, she would flip out and
feel terrified. Instead of standing her ground and expressing her
needs, she'd sink into a hole that to her felt like quicksand, and as she
struggled to get out she'd dissolve away. This repeating pattern revealed the rigidity of Gail's being stuck and the chaos of her falling
apart that were aspects of her non-integrated models of attachment.
Some of this pattern may have been a result of her ambivalent history
and sense of loss with her mom, and perhaps a fear of losing her present attachment figure, her husband. But in the setting in which these
experiences arose, they also seemed to have elements of a response to

being terrified and to be related to the dissociation from her disorganized attachment with her dad. Fortunately, these times of becoming fragmented were infrequent, and they emerged only in the close connection she had with her husband. Gail would find herself simply withdrawing from him in ways that dismissed her own needs for closeness. This pattern of disconnecting had the quality of an avoidant model, one that was clearly a part of her relationship with her father. With friends and her work colleagues, such disconnection and such dissociation never occurred. We can see this as her avoidant and disorganized models of attachment being activated only in the setting of her relationship with her husband. Such state-dependent activation of an attachment model is just how our human brain works. What was a problem, though, was that such disconnection and dissociation made her unable to have a solid sense of herself in connection with her husband. Whichever models were being activated, they were preventing her from having the kind of integrated relationship in which differences could be honored and compassionate connections created that would make her life more fulfilling and at ease with her husband.

Through making sense of her past and working on being present even in the face of her terrifying feelings—with her loss of her mom, with her memories of her dad, and with her fear of her husband's anger when they'd fight—Gail gained the integrative ability to simply hold in awareness whatever she was experiencing. She went through the painful process of reflecting on her relationship with her drunken father, about the terror, about her sense of helplessness. And in that process, she came to make sense of what had been non-sense at that time in her life. What this meant was that she could now see the impact that those terrifying experiences with no solution had on her at that time and how they'd continued to affect her now.

Gail would also practice a way of being mindful, of being curious and open about her own internal experiences without judgment. In the face of a fragmented consciousness with disorganized attachment, it became essential that we work to integrate consciousness itself. We did many of the practices you can learn in this book, like the Wheel of Awareness and breath practice, which strengthened her mind and integrated her brain. With this new sense of clarity, she could feel her own needs for closeness, her attachment needs, with openness and acceptance rather than the earlier confusion or dismissal. With the empowerment of these practices, too, her dissociation became less frequent and less intense and transformed into her ability to simply be aware of a sense of "wanting to fall apart" but able to resist that impulse. All of this reflective work enabled her to transform these non-secure attachment models into one of security.

By the time Steven was a young boy, Gail had taken the time to develop what researchers call "earned security." We could also call this "learned security." Over the years since Gail was initially in therapy, she'd come in for check-ins periodically and I'd hear about Steven's development. When Gail was diagnosed with cancer, I also saw her to support how she could deal with her fears during this terrifying time. With her earned security, she was in a new integrative position not to withdraw, become confused, or fragment her mind.

And with this earned security, over these years she could also be a source of secure attachment for Steven. She was able to be a soothing safe harbor for him and a solid launching pad.

So as Steven approached his own time to leave the nest, he came to this adolescent turning point with the integrative resilience of a secure attachment model with his mom. Research has shown clearly that no matter our challenging past, if we make sense of how our early experiences have shaped us and learn our new models of security, we can offer our children security of attachment. Steven happened to have security with his dad, too, so he was feeling solidly ready to leave home. His closeness with his mother in the face of her illness made him feel the need to stay close enough to home to come back whenever she might need him to be there, but not so close that he didn't realize the deep inner drive to explore the world that he could now launch into with security.

Reflecting on Your Attachments and Making Sense of Your Life

Whether you are an adolescent or an adult, it is important to make sense of what your early attachment relationships were like in your childhood. Given the nature of memory development before the age of five or so, it can be hard to recall in any continuous way from this very early period in our lives. This said, even the faintest impressions can be quite helpful. And research shows, too, that a set of questions that support your exploration of what you can recall can help reveal certain patterns that are helpful in your journey to get a broad sense of the attachment models you may have now in your life. The fantastic news is that if you can make sense of your childhood experiences—especially your relationships with your parents—you can transform your attachment models toward security. The reason this is important is that your relationships—with friends, with romantic partners, with present or possible future offspring—will be profoundly enhanced. And you'll feel better with yourself, too!

In science we use a formal Attachment Interview to figure out how a person has made sense of his or her attachment experiences. Hundreds of studies reveal that these patterns are helpful to gain insight into our attachment models. My own work in that field led me to develop a way to help people make sense of their lives and propose how this process may integrate their brains in psychotherapy, and I

figuring it out...

MY Life

...One piece at a time.

published that approach in a couple of books, including *Mindsight* and *Parenting from the Inside Out*. The latter book includes a set of questions that I've adapted here for you to use as a guide for reflecting on your own experience, whether you are an adolescent or an adult. Let me invite you to read over these questions, and afterward we'll go through each of the models of attachment and the kinds of responses they tend to include, and then we'll see how you can understand them and move them toward security. Remember, you may have many models of attachment, one for each relationship you have had with your caregivers. You may want to write your responses down in a journal, or simply reflect on them in your own way. Because you may still be living with your attachment figures, your parents or others, or you may have moved away from them, the questions are both in the present tense and in the past tense. Just focus on whichever one applies to your situation now.

Understanding yourself is a basic mindsight tool for integrating your life. Self-understanding is how you connect your past from memory with your present experience. This is an important step in learning how to have secure attachment models in our lives. When we create a narrative of who we are, we link past and present so we can become the active author of a possible future, too. So self-understanding helps us with "mental time travel" as we create a coherent view and integration of ourselves across the past, present, and future.

Questions for Reflection on Attachment

Background

What is (was) it like growing up in your family?

Who is (was) in your family?

What is (was) your parents' philosophy about raising children?

What do (did) or don't (didn't) you like about being raised in your family?

Would you raise (Are you raising) your own children in a similar way, or differently?

Relationships

Do (Did) you get along well with your parents and others in your family?

How do (did) your family members get along with one another?

How have your relationships in your family changed over
time?

If you have two parents, how are (were) your relationships
with each parent similar or different?

State a few words that reflect your relationship with each
parent from your earliest years.

Are there ways you have tried to be like or not like each
of your parents?

Are there any others in your life who have served as
parenting figures to whom you feel attached? If so,
please answer the above questions regarding that person
or those persons.

Separation

Can you remember your first time being separated from
your parents? What was that like and how did it affect
you and your parents?

Did you ever experience a long separation from your
parents in your childhood? What was that like for you
and for your parents?

Discipline

What ways do (did) your parents respond to your
behaviors to teach you how to behave?

Do (Did) your parents use punishment in their discipline?

How have these strategies of being disciplined influenced
your development?

Fear and Threat

Have you ever felt threatened by your parents?

Have you ever felt rejected by your parents?

Have there been any other experiences that may have been overwhelming in your life? What were these, and how do you feel they have influenced your life?

Do any of these experiences feel like they are still very much alive now in your life?

Loss

Has anyone significant in your life died?

Has anyone significant in your life left?

What impact have these losses had on you and your family?

How do these losses affect you now in your life?

Emotional Communication

How do (did) your parents communicate with you when you are (were) happy and excited?

What happens (would happen) when you are (were) distressed, unhappy, injured, or ill?

Does (Did) each parent respond with different patterns of connecting to you when your emotions are intense?

How do you communicate with others now when emotions run high?

Safe Harbor

Are (Were) there relationships you can (could) turn to, or places you can (could) go, that you can (could) rely on to help you feel comforted at difficult times? Did such a safe harbor exist when you were a child?

How do you feel those sources of a safe haven affect (affected) your life?

Do (Did) you feel seen, safe, and soothed by your parents?

Launching Pad

How do (did) your parents support your explorations
away from them or outside the home?

How are (were) your interests supported by your parents?

Did you feel secure as a child to go out and explore the
world?

Now

What is your relationship like now with your parents?

Why do you think your parents act (acted) the way
they do?

Do you try to not do things because of how your parents
treat (treated) you?

As you reflect on all of these experiences, how do you
think they influence the ways you relate to other
people?

How do you feel all of these things we have been
exploring have influenced who you are now as a person
and how you have come to be the way you are?

Future

What would you wish for yourself in your future
relationships?

How do you imagine the experiences from your
attachment relationships and early childhood may shape
the person you can become?

Are there any factors from your past that are restricting
you in the present and limiting who you can be in the
future?

What do you see as your "growth edge" for things you'd
like to change in yourself so that you can become freed

up to be the person you would like to be in the
future?

Any other questions we should have covered or that
you may have now?

You're worth figuring out.

How was responding to these questions for you? Sometimes reflecting on these questions can be quite draining. Sometimes what
comes up can be surprising, even shocking. And sometimes you already know how you will respond and it is not a big deal.

Interestingly, researchers who collectively have studied over ten
thousand formal Attachment Interviews featuring questions and topics similar to those above uncovered universal patterns. I'll present
you with the general findings next so you can get a feel for what may
be going on with you. Please keep in mind, however, as you read
these broad groupings and their narrative patterns, that the key to
reflecting on them is not to lump yourself in one category or an-

other, but rather to find helpful insights into your own life that you can weave together into a coherent narrative of your own. Research reveals that the more coherent a narrative we have of our own attachment issues in childhood, the more we've made sense of how our early life experiences have shaped us, the more likely our children will have a secure attachment to us and the more rewarding in general our interpersonal relationships will be. With our own coherent life story, we'll be more likely to consistently provide the four S's of attachment. And as securely attached children grow up, they'll be more likely, too, to have a way of making sense of their lives and creating a coherent life narrative. They'll have a coherent sense of who they've been, of who they are now, and of who they'd like to become. And they'll have a coherent way of being themselves while also having close, meaningful relationships with others. That's what making sense of your life can help bring into your world. That's what secure attachment can offer—whatever age you are when you develop that integrated way of making sense of your life.

Our Attachment Narratives and the Two Sides of the Brain

While the details of each of the Attachment Interviews scientists have conducted vary from person to person, when looked at as a whole across individuals, patterns emerge. Attachment Interviews are tape recorded and then transcribed. The written document is then analyzed for its language use and the ways in which the interviewee communicates with the interviewer (the researcher). In this way, the "narrative analysis" is really a discourse analysis that looks at how one person is communicating with another. The interview findings reveal that individuals with secure attachment models generally reflect in a coherent way on the good and bad parts of what may have happened during childhood. We can't know the accuracy of the facts that are recalled, of course, but we can assess how the responses fit together in a coherent manner—how they make sense, how they are open and flexible in reflecting on various aspects of the past, and how they are reflective and in the present moment with the questions and not just offered as a pre-programmed set of responses.

Even when experiences may have been difficult, or even frightening, a *secure narrative* reveals this quality of the person being present for whatever comes up in the interview. This state of presence is the hallmark of secure attachment, both in how we connect with others and how we connect with our own life story. We are present, meaning we are open and accepting to whatever is happening as it is happening. And this presence in our life story, this attachment security, comes along with narrative coherence, how we've come to terms with the positive and negative of our early relationships, and how we've made sense of our lives.

In others with avoidant attachment histories, or the parents of those with avoidant attachments, the narrative is quite different. The hallmark of these *avoidant narrative* reflections is that the individuals insist that they do not recall anything about family life and that their family life did not influence how they developed. That is a form of incoherence in that if you don't remember something, how do you know that this something did not affect you? The adults with this narrative are said to have a "dismissing" state of mind—they dismiss the idea that their past relationships may have had an impact on who they are. In short, they appear to "avoid" placing importance on the relationships in their lives possibly because this is the best adaptation they could come up with in the face of the emotional desert that is an avoidant attachment relationship.

To understand what may be going on in the pathway from specific forms of attachment relationships in childhood to corresponding attachment narratives in adolescence and adulthood, it is helpful to turn to studies of the brain in creating a working framework. In this view, non-secure attachment models emerge from non-integrated states of brain functioning. In many ways, the communication between parent and child that does not honor differences and promote linkage—that is, patterns of communicating in non-integrated relationships—leads to blocked integration in the child's developing brain. Simply put, this view suggests that integrated communication stimulates the growth of integration in the brain. Non-integrated communication leads to non-integrated brain development.

My proposal, drawn from clinical work and scientific reasoning, suggests that there is an underdevelopment of the right hemisphere of the brain in individuals with avoidant attachment. It is the right side that stores autobiographical memory and holds our raw emotional needs and feelings. In this way, the avoidant model enables us to not feel our needs, and we also don't recall our lived experiences of family life. That explains not only the narrative findings, but also the way avoidant models shape our behavior in relationships where we ignore the non-verbal communication from others, signals that are both sent and received by the right side of the brain.

Personal reflection in the cortex is a process that draws on autobiographical mappings in the brain's cortical region, dominant on the right side of the brain. Such autobiographical reflection is the way we look inward to the meanings and events of our lived experience. Interestingly, even our gut reactions and heartfelt sensations, signals arising from the intestines and the neural circuitry around the heart, arise and end up primarily on the right side of the brain, as it is the right prefrontal cortex that receives such bodily input. These

sources of knowing are generally not experienced much by individuals with avoidant attachment.

While both sides of the brain usually work together, they do have
differentiated functions. These functions influence not so much what
we do as the ways we perceive the world and our ways of being in
the world.

The left side of the cortex is dominant for language, logic, linear
and literal thinking, and even making lists, like this one! Notice, too,
that in English this is a convenient and easy-to-remember list because
each word starts with an *l*, as in "left-sided." Many studies also suggest that facts are dominant on the left side, while our autobiographical recollections of episodes of experience are right-side dominant.

(I'd like to ask you to focus on using your left hemisphere's skills
to take in some of these scientific details we're about to dive into.
The reason to do this is that when we understand some of the fasci-

nating and relevant brain facts in a logical, linear way, we actually can then use that knowledge to hyperdrive the ways we can transform our non-secure attachment models toward security. You'll need your right hemisphere's talents, too, in order to fully grasp the context and personal meaning of some of these brain notions. You can feel the sense of what we're about to explore, and you can track its logic as well. So at this very moment, we'll be calling on both sides of your brain to take in the details of what we're about to explore. In the following three sections, we'll use the gist of all this foundation to examine how each of the non-secure attachment models can be transformed by focusing the mind to integrate the brain and your relationships. Don't worry about recalling every detail, they're all here and you can review them whenever you want. The key is that soon we'll explore how we'll apply them in your own life. Just let the sense of these logical connections fill both sides of your brain and get ready for some continuing integrative work!)

The right side of the cortex is not only a primary source of our autobiographical knowledge; it is also dominant for receiving more direct input from the lower subcortical areas in addition to the body as a whole. And yes, you may have guessed that the right side is often considered "more emotional" in that subcortical and bodily input shape our emotional life more directly and perhaps more spontaneously and robustly. The right side of the cortex maps out the whole of the interior of the body; but the left does not do this. This means that intuition, how we receive the wisdom of the body's input from our muscles, our hearts, our intestines, likely first influences our right cortex. The left side of the cortex has emotion, too, but it may be experienced in a different way, as that side is not so powerfully influenced by the subcortical regions as the right is.

So you can see how different the two sides are in how they focus our attention and how they enable us to be in the world. They differ in other fundamental ways, too, as we'll see now.

The left side of the brain has one frontal region that when activated creates an "approach state" that empowers us to go out in the world and face challenges. In contrast, the right side has areas that create a withdrawal response to new things. This approach to the world goes along with what some summarize in this general way: The left looks outward to the world, while the right looks inward, in the self and others. For this reason, it shouldn't be such a surprise that the left side of the brain specializes not only in language but also in keeping track of our "social display rules," the culturally sanctioned ways we are supposed to communicate with one another. In this way, the left can track what others expect and govern what words are spoken to meet those expectations.

Let's pause for a moment and just sense what this means for our lives. One side, the left, has an outward focus of what it is concerned about, what it is interested in, what it enables us to do in terms of interacting with others. What does the right side help us with in connecting with others?

The right side of the cortex also communicates, but it specializes in non-verbal communication. What is this? This includes the following signals, which my left cortex would like to list for you here in a logical, linear, literal, linguistic fashion. Here's the list—thank you, left—of the right-sided dominant non-verbal signals that are both sent from and perceived and made sense of by the right side of the brain:

1. Eye contact

2. Facial expressions

3. Tone of voice

4. Posture

5. Gestures and touch

6. Timing of signals

7. Intensity of signals

In our narratives, the left side of the brain is thought to be the drive for telling our story. But the autobiographical goods are on the right. So in a nutshell, the coherent narrative of security is reflected in the way that the left and right are differentiated well and then linked.

The two sides can work together, or they can be functioning somewhat in isolation. When I first read about all this, I began to wonder how it might be a foundation for understanding the different attachment patterns of behaving and of telling our life story. What was amazing was that by understanding the brain, by taking on some of these basic brain facts, you could explain a huge amount of the research-established psychological and relational findings. Then you could use that information to catalyze more effective interventions to help people move toward security. It wasn't only helpful to understand the data, it was effective in helping people change.

Recall that the ambivalent attachment model has an amplification of attachment needs. How might that relate to right-left brain findings? Could it be seen as an overreliance on the right side of the brain rather than being balanced with the left? When the two hemispheres do not work in a coordinated fashion, one may become excessively dominant in the absence of the other because the two sides of the brain balance each other. In this case, the characteristic finding of the *ambivalent narrative* output is a flood of autobiographical details that are not directly related to the questions asked. This intrusion of images and emotions has the quality of an excess of right-sided activation without the balancing of the left side's role in keeping track of the language output. The left side is thought to be the source of the narrative drive, using words in a linear, logical way that explains the cause–effect relationship among events. But when those events are autobiographical, the left needs the cooperation of the right to tell a coherent story.

With ambivalent attachment narratives, it is as if the right is overwhelming the left's answering of the questions. In the research literature on adults and adolescents, this is called "preoccupied" attachment and a person is simply assigned one category of attachment. But in actual life we can have many models that shape our narratives in different ways, so we'll just stick with the baseline term of "ambivalent" model of attachment to permit us to realize that we have many models across all the categories of the basic childhood attachment groupings, not just one model. In other words, we are not just preoccupied or dismissing; as individuals, we can have ambivalent models and we can have avoidant models.

Okay. Avoidance seems to rely on the left mode of being in the world as a way of adapting to a disconnected emotional life. This explains the findings in the narrative of a lack of access to autobiographical memories and an insistence that relational matters don't matter. Ambivalence draws more heavily on the right side with a flood of feelings and memories that emerge in the attachment narrative, and in life. What if your attachment model is also disorganized? How can we understand that?

For the disorganized model of attachment we see times in the *disorganized narrative* when the responses become disorganized or disoriented. This disorientation usually occurs when addressing the questions of loss or of threat. If someone has died, for example, the person may lapse into talking about that person as if she were still alive. In the case of threat, a sense of terror may emerge in the person's responses as if he were being terrified right then. For example, I might say about my drunk father, "Well, he wasn't really terrifying, no, I mean, he would drink, and I guess at those times he would come home and, well, you can smell the alcohol in the room, and he comes in and I run, but he's too fast and I . . ." Notice how the discourse moves from the past tense to the present tense and gets disoriented, even disorganized. These features can be subtle or severe, but they reveal a non-integrated brain's functioning. As the left tries to tell the story, it becomes disoriented and loses track of the topic or the focus of time. The right side of the brain may send elements of the lived past over to the left in a jumbled fashion that cannot be easily decoded by the left. A sense of time, mediated by the prefrontal cortex that works with both left and right, gets lost and the past merges with the present. Raw forms of what are called "implicit memories" may pound my consciousness with a sense of my body and emotions, images, and even behavioral impulses that feel as if they are happening in the present. These are each the outcomes of overwhelming experiences that may be unresolved in our lives. This non-integrated state happens when the narrative focuses on loss or trauma. In these moments, the individual is filled with a blockage across many systems, including left working with right, the linkage of layers of memory, and prefrontal coordination and balance. The research term for this is "unresolved trauma or loss—disorganization," but we'll simply call it a "disorganized" model of attachment.

The great news is that unresolved trauma or loss can be resolved through integrating the processes of memory and narrative, and the person can move from non-secure to secure models of attachment. In terms of the left and right brain, disorganization may occur when the flood of bodily sensation and autobiographical memories of the right are not easily taken in and sorted through by the linear left trying to tell its story with words. So at a minimum, disorganization and the unresolved loss or trauma it reveals can be seen as an impaired coordination of the two hemispheres. With reflection, we can transform raw implicit memories into explicit memories of facts in the left and autobiographical memory in the right so that they do not enter our minds in various forms of intrusive emotions or memories and instead become part of a coherent narrative of who we are. Ambivalence likewise can be transformed into security as the left and right hemispheres are brought into balance by developing more of the left hemisphere's role in the person's inner life. Avoidant models can be moved to security by developing more of the right hemisphere's role, accessing those important healthy needs for connection that have been shut down in the past.

At a baseline level, then, we look to the notion of integration in the brain to gain insights into how to move toward security. Understanding how the left and right hemispheres each contribute important but different ways of being and seeing can help guide you in making sense of your life and moving toward a more integrated way of living.

Avoidance, Emotional Distance, and the Left Side of the Brain

If your responses to the reflection questions revealed a sense of disconnection from the experiences with your caregivers, there may be elements of avoidance in your history. Let's dive into what that may have been like, and what you can do about that now.

A parent with whom a child has an avoidant attachment often

does not perceive—or at least does not readily respond to—the non-verbal signals of distress, such as crying or facial expressions. There is a sense in the interaction between parent and child that the internal world of the mind of the child is just not important, or at least not seen. This is a lack of well-developed mindsight and reveals that life for this parent-child relationship is more about managing behaviors rather than empathically feeling another's feelings.

If your sense is that you had an avoidant attachment, you may have had experiences in which attention was repeatedly paid to the physical nature of life but not much of a focus was put on the life of the mind. Reflect on your relationship then, or now, and see if "mentalese," or mind language, was or is a part of your relationship. This would be conversations that lacked words and phrases such as "I was feeling . . . ," "That must have felt for you like . . . ," "I wonder what he was thinking at that moment . . . ," "I imagine that he viewed this as . . . ," "From her point of view it may have seemed . . . ," and "Her belief doesn't make sense to me, but I can understand why she thinks that way. . . ." Each of these phrases reveals an individual who has enough mindsight to communicate either his or her own internal mental state, or to take on, and ask about, the internal mental state of another.

If you were raised by caregivers who were not only missing in their use of mindsight but somewhat distant emotionally in their ways of being with you, it may be that mindsight was not something that these attachment figures helped you develop. In studies of attachment, the teachers of kids with avoidant attachment—who didn't even know the child's attachment history—treated them as if they didn't need help even when they did. Does this sound familiar in your life? For many with avoidant attachment, there seems to be difficulty expressing inner needs, or of reaching out to depend on others to meet those needs. As one person said to me, "I needed to be autonomous from a very young age given how disconnected my mother was. Why would I ever allow myself to need help from anyone?"

If we did an attachment interview on the parent with whom you had this avoidant attachment, we'd be very likely to find a narrative that reveals a lack of access to autobiographical memory and an insistence that relationships are not important in shaping who they are. If that is the way you've come to make sense of your own life, then relationships will not be high on your priority list. It isn't that the parent doesn't love the child, it's just that the adaptation the parent had to make in his or her own childhood minimized attachment needs then, and that adaptation continues now. If you are an adolescent still living with your parents reflecting on this, please keep in mind that parents often do what they do because of how they've adapted to their own childhood experiences. Finding ways to connect more fully can happen, but it just takes time, understanding, patience, and intention. This non-secure model of attachment that helped the individual survive is one of being disconnected from others. So if this is your relationship, please don't measure this as a lack of love. It is really a lack of skills to connect. And in many ways, it is a survival mechanism from the past to disconnect from the need for closeness that simply needs to be updated now in the present.

Another part of this journey for you is to realize that parental presence may seem in short supply in avoidant attachment, that the surface of behaviors is the focus of attention, and that attuning to the internal world of the mind, of the child or even of the self, is simply not often engaged. In this setting, you may have developed with a minimal sense of your own mind, too. The effective strategy to begin with is for you to get in touch with the side of your brain that lets you focus on the internal world—of yourself and of others. That is the right side of the brain.

Since emotions and our bodily sensations fill us with the vitality that makes life rich and meaningful, this avoidant pattern of relating from the left side may have created a disconnected sense of self that is short on the internal joie de vivre, that spirit of being alive, that gives life its zest. This lack of experiential nurturance leads, I believe, to an underdevelopment of the right side of the brain.

So here's a strategy. Integration is about honoring differences and promoting linkages. If you've had a hefty dose of avoidance, the left hemisphere may be in charge because it allowed you to develop in the face of an emotional desert. That was a great adaptation for your past. But what about now? What does that mean for your mental life?

Hold on to your hat as we slowly take in the science-established notion of what "being in the left" is like. When only the left is activated and dominant, then our ways of being tend to be externally focused, logical, "de-contextualized," and characterized by what is called a "linear way" of being in the world. "Linear" means one thing following another. "De-contextualized" means missing the big picture into which something fits. So rather than flowing with the context of a situation as it emerges, moment by moment, a left dominant way of being is to expect things to unfold in a linear sequence, in a specified order, that can be contained, predicted, understood, taken apart and dissected, analyzed, and, ultimately, logically understood. If that was a starting place for you as a child raised with primarily an avoidant attachment history, then adolescence might be particularly challenging with its fill of bodily, emotionally, and interpersonally intense experiences. These components of life—the body, the emotions, and the interpersonal world of other minds—each have a dominant role in right hemisphere ways of being. If you've been given the relationship setting to develop primarily the left and not the right, this would be a great time to balance yourself and develop both sides of the brain well. That's what integration is all about.

The great news is that whatever your age, it is never too late to bring both hemispheres into development and activity. Take a look at the story of Stuart earlier in the book (p. 49) and you'll find a ninety-two-year-old man with avoidant attachment history who made great strides integrating the two sides of his brain after nearly a century without it. With an emotionally and a bodily distant mode of living, he had to learn to develop his right side and then link these new capacities with his well-developed left. If Stuart can do this, it's very likely you can, too.

Just because parents didn't offer secure attachment does not mean you are doomed to stay with a non-secure model of attachment. In the case of an avoidant history, if you find that you have been "leaning to the left" in your experience of avoidant attachment with your caregiver, then the exercises within the tools sections on mindsight, time-in, and the Wheel of Awareness will be useful in integrating your two sides so that you can overcome whatever unbalanced adaptations you need to.

Here are some basic practices if you've had a history of avoidant attachment:

1. Practice becoming aware of your internal bodily states. The Wheel of Awareness rim review on the sixth sense, the bodily sensations, can be a very helpful place to start. If focusing attention on both limbs at the same time is difficult, try to first focus on the right side and then on the left.

2. Become aware of non-verbal signals. Try watching television shows with the sound off or foreign language films without subtitles in a language you don't understand. These experiences will enable you to let your left-sided language centers take a break and your right-sided non-

verbal signal perceiving circuits become more active. Recall that these signals include eye contact, facial expressions,
tone of voice, gestures, posture, and the timing and intensity of responses.

3. Learn to use non-verbal expressions. Try looking in a
   mirror or taking a video of yourself and watching the
   recording. Try to exaggerate the sending of these important right-sided signals.

4. Autobiographical memory is also a specialty of the right
   side of the brain. Begin by simply writing down the details of what you did today. Start with the specifics of
   how you got out of bed, what you did with your body as
   you got dressed, how your ate your breakfast. See if you
   can sense those experiences as you are recalling them.
   After these recent memories have been recounted, try
   more distant autobiographical reflections, also with details. Don't worry if you can't recall childhood experiences, as these may be quite difficult to access, and some
   may not have been encoded into your memory as well.

5. Emotions are felt on both sides of the brain, but they may
   be more direct or spontaneous on the right. When you
   are ready, you can find a friend who can partner with you
   in sending and receiving non-verbal expressions of differing emotions. Try out these basic nine: joy, excitement,
   surprise, sadness, fear, anger, disgust, guilt, and shame.
   See also if you can simply notice the emotions as they rise
   up, even fleetingly. Let the sensation of emotion fill you,
   and don't try to analyze it or even name it.

6. Context is something that the right hemisphere specializes in as well. Context means reading between the lines.
   It is like the spirit of the law rather than the letter of the
   law. It is context, rather than text. Context has a texture
   to it that is more subtle than the clearly demarcated definitions of things that the left hemisphere loves. Some
   compare the left hemisphere to a digital processor, with
   zeroes and ones, and clearly demarcated definitions such
   as up versus down, right versus wrong, in versus out. In
   contrast, the right is analogic, with a wide spectrum of
   values not separated into clearly boxed meanings as on
   the left side. So here you are simply letting yourself get an
   initial glimmer of the meaning behind words and their
   non-verbal components. An exercise you can perform is
   simply to say a neutral sentence with differing contexts
   embedded in the tone of your voice and the timing of the
   words. Here are two of an infinite variety of sentences
   you can try using this technique: "I expected you to
   come to my party on time," or "You always do what you
   say you will do." Try emphasizing each word in turn
   with different tones of voice, and see if you can sense how
   this changes the meaning of the message.

7. Recall that studies have shown that even if there is an
   outer focus on independence, there is often an inner sense
   of needing closeness that is beneath awareness. With this
   in mind, consider trying to tune in to any inner hints,
   however subtle, that you may feel a desire to be closer to
   people in your life. Being aware that avoidance was an
   important adaptation for you, go slow. Reaching out to
   another person to express your feelings in a gesture of

wanting more time to connect can be an important starting place. Since we each participate in creating our relational worlds, you can have a say in how to form new kinds of relationships in your life now.

As you develop a more integrated way of being, you may find that things begin to feel different inside you. Even the way that you sense how you are connecting with others may change as you find yourself sponging up their inner lives through their non-verbal signals. The presence that emerges now may seem overwhelming at times, filled with an enriched sense of being alive. While this new way of being in the world can seem unfamiliar at first, see if you can rest at ease with the knowledge that integration brings a new way of simply experiencing being alive.

In many ways, integration creates more integration.

In development we call this a "recursive" aspect of something—a reinforcing set of recursively influencing factors that continually reinstate the initial state of mind. In the case of insecure attachment and non-secure attachment models, we wince and the world winces back at us, we disconnect and the world disconnects from us. In the case of security and integration, we smile and the world smiles back at us.

Ambivalence, Emotional Confusion, and the Right Side of the Brain

Your responses to the reflection questions may have revealed that your attachment history involves the polar opposite of the frozen emotional distance that produces the avoidance of attachment. For you, childhood was more like a hot cauldron of emotional confusion. If avoidance is living in an emotional desert, ambivalence can be like living in an emotional fog if not at times an outright storm.

If this form of ambivalent attachment is in your history, then emotional inconsistency and intrusion by your parents may have been frequent. Keep in mind that your parents likely were doing the best they could, and that this way of being is most helpfully seen as their adaptations to challenges in their own childhood relationships or to other aspects of their lives. The leftover issues of their own parents (your grandparents) may have flooded their ability to be present and open in a clear and receptive way to what was happening within you. If this was the case, it is important to know that your own inner sense of self may be in need of strengthening.

In many ways, children can become an unintended receptacle for their parents' flooding emotions. The confusion that arises for the child is that at the same time he feels he is not being seen clearly for who he is, that he is in some ways invisible, he is also having to absorb emotions that have nothing to do with what he is actually feeling. It's a double challenge. And it's just plain confusing.

In responding to the self-reflection questions, you may have found that certain topics brought up a sense of something being raw or unfinished. In the formal interview, an individual with a history of ambivalent attachment may seem preoccupied with certain experiences from the past; for instance, the leftover emotional issue of a sibling favored by a parent may feel fresh and quite alive. It isn't disorienting as in unresolved trauma or loss, but it is preoccupying and upsetting. As ambivalent attachment amplifies attachment needs, there may be a sense of feeling alone or unseen that remains from childhood and gets experienced often in the here and now in ongoing relationships as a sense of anxiety and uncertainty. There may be a feeling that one's needs may never be met, and that if they are met, they can vanish in an instant. That's the amped-up attachment system that finds no relief, no security, with the ambivalent model. There is no reliable internal sense that things will work out in relationships.

As we take our attachment models with us when we move out into the world and recursively reinforce the very models we used to adapt to our earliest relationships, our learned adaptations evoke from the world similar patterns of interaction that we've grown up with. Studies reveal, for example, that if we've had ambivalent attachment at home, our teachers likely perceive us as less competent than we might really be, offering help when we may not have needed it and, in turn, stifling our independence. What we've acquired at home we carry forward out into the world. This is how the synaptic changes in the brain that developed in childhood as adaptations and models of attachment can persist and perpetuate in adolescence and adulthood, revealing themselves as a specific environment (like school or a new romantic relationship) evokes our unfulfilled attachment needs.

If you have experience with this self-reinforcing cycle of ambivalent attachment, it is important that you gain an understanding of how your brain works so that you can explore new ways of seeing and experiencing your relationships and your life in general.

If you often find yourself flooded by your own emotions without left-sided balance, you may have been struck by your emotional state when you were responding to the reflection questions. Research findings show that individuals with the ambivalent attachment model often respond to attachment interview questions by appearing to feel "intruded upon" by the narrative reflections they inspire. This can be explained on the level of brain science by the additional finding that these individuals display what could be seen as a right-sided excess without the calming effect of the left. The left portion of the brain cannot sort through the bombardments from the excessively active right hemisphere, and as a result, images, feelings, bodily sensations, and fragments of unsorted autobiographical recollections may inhibit the left's attempt to provide some kind of linear, language-based, logical telling of their personal narrative. The right hemisphere's autobiographical memory of your mother favoring your sibling intrudes on your left's keeping track of the question at hand, your body fills with tension, and your emotions influence the clarity and coherence of what you say. Beyond the scope of the research laboratory, what this means in real life is that individuals with the ambivalent attachment model often feel overwhelmed by interpersonal interactions that they experience as "flooding" or "stressful." Fear and anger mingle with the need for security and comfort.

Here are some simple practices if you've had a history of ambivalent attachment:

1. Cultivate the ability to name your internal emotional states. "Name it to tame it" is a starting place for building your left hemisphere's important language abilities and linking them to the more raw and spontaneous emotions of the right side of the brain. You can simply describe what you feel; you don't need to explain it.

2. Journal writing can be an incredibly valuable activity for you. Using your left hemisphere's drive to tell a linear, logical, language-based story will build this important narrative skill. Narrating your life can become an important integrative tool to build the connections between your two hemispheres.

3. Practice the Wheel of Awareness. Integrating consciousness will enable you to strengthen the hub of your mind.

It is in this strengthened hub that you may find the mental space in which to sort through your sensations, images, feelings, and thoughts before you choose to express them to others. This is how you can use your left hemisphere to actively participate in the SIFTing of your internal mindscape.

4. Know your emotions. For many, knowing that feelings are not facts helps to sort through the sometimes intense and rapid internal emotional world that may arise, especially in the face of relationship challenges. Feeling rejected, for example, can activate the same neural circuitry in the right side of the brain that represents bodily pain. Knowing this, you can use your "Name it to tame it" skills to acknowledge the pain of a feeling of disconnection and recognize that it may feel overwhelming but actually is not—in fact, it is something you can learn to reflect upon and calm.

5. As you develop the ability to use your growing left hemisphere to work closely with your right, see how you can connect with others in close relationships in a more satisfying way for all of you. Keep in the front of your mind whatever feelings arise, knowing that feelings are indeed not facts. You may at times have sensitivity to others' signals that makes their feelings enter you more fully and flood your sense of being a differentiated individual. There may be other moments when an internal sensation in you makes you feel that you can't rely on others. While these may be accurate assessments, they may also be clouded by an attachment system on "overdrive," based

on vigilance for connection in order to be safe. Working on the mindsight practices in the first two tools sections of this book may help bring an internal state of calm as you focus on observing these patterns of emotional response with others.

6. Attachment can feel like a life-or-death matter. When we are very small, we rely on our parents or other caregivers for everything—for food, for water, for protection. If we were cared for by unpredictable caretakers, we may still feel, as adolescents or adults, incredibly frightened and unprotected when something stressful happens in our lives. The increased attachment needs of this form of ambivalent attachment can feel, literally, like a matter of life or death. Knowing this can greatly help you to name this sensation, see it for the attachment-based emotional reactive state it is, and then not take it so personally as you acknowledge the emotion without allowing it to swallow you up.

7. Strengthen your internal observer. Developing a part of your mind that can observe, witness, and narrate your experiences can be a powerful way to "own" what you are going through within relationships. When you realize that your past experiences may have been foggy or stormy not because of something "wrong" with you, but simply a reflection of the kinds of emotional communications with your caregivers, then you can see how such emotional weather patterns now may simply be echoes from the past. Having your observing mind narrate how this is all unfolding can give you the emotional space to

calm your internal state and see what is happening in your ongoing relationships with more clarity.

You can grow the integrative circuits of the brain throughout life. As you move through this process of developing greater integration, you may find that your newfound sense of balance and equilibrium, even in the face of stresses that used to make you feel confused, can become a kind of safe harbor for you. As well, your growing inner security can become a solid launching pad from which you can draw strength as you interact with others and explore the world.

Disorganized Attachment and a Dissociating Brain

As a baseline, we have one or some combination of the three "organized" attachment models including security with its integrative functioning, avoidance with its overemphasis on left-sided functioning and the minimization of attachment needs, and ambivalence with its right-sided development and the maximization of attachment needs. For some of us, terrifying experiences with our caregivers can result in disorganized attachment and the tendency to fragment our minds in dissociation. Just as in our childhood these terrifying experiences could find no resolution and we have a disorganized model, so, too, in the present moment our behaviors and language output can become disorganized. In the narrative responses, we've seen that when disorientation occurs, it reveals a state of unresolved trauma or loss. If this is part of your experience, there is help ahead. Fortunately, the challenges of dissociating, balancing your emotions, maintaining clear thinking in the face of stress, and having mutually rewarding relationships, which are each a part of the disorganized model, can be healed.

The research is quite clear. When we make sense of events in our lives that made no sense, the mind can become coherent, our relationships more fulfilling, and our brains function in a more integrated manner. That's the movement from disorganized attachment with its unresolved states to resolution and security.

One way to think about unresolved trauma or loss is this. The brain first embeds experience in those implicit layers of memory that form the foundation of how we remember things. These building blocks include our emotions, our perceptions, our bodily sensations, and even our behavioral responses. We summarize these foundations as schema or mental models that help us get ready to respond to future events in a process called "priming."

Under normal conditions, these building blocks of implicit memory become integrated by a limbic region, the hippocampus, into the two forms of explicit memory of facts and autobiographical recollections. Dominant on the left, factual memory lets us know that something happened even though we may not know when or have the feeling of being in that experience. Autobiographical memory is dominant on the right and has the qualities of a sense of self at some point in time in the past.

I've proposed that one aspect of dissociation and unresolved trauma or loss is that the movement from implicit memory to explicit is blocked. When this blockage occurs, implicit memory in its pure, un-integrated state has the important characteristic of not being labeled as coming from some time in the past. So when a person with disorganized attachment and unresolved trauma or loss is trying to respond to questions about those experiences, the raw implicit memories are retrieved and the individual is flooded with sensations, emotions, images, or behavioral impulses that feel as if they are happening now. There is no sense that these are images or feelings from the past. That is what unresolved trauma or loss can create, and it feels intrusive, confusing, and even terrifying. Sometimes it may feel like a full-on flashback of the event without a sense that it is from the past, but more often it may simply be an intense image or emotion, bodily sensation, or impulse. These are each part of what can cause disorientation during the narrative responses. Simply living life, too, can recall elements of those times of loss or trauma—like someone getting mad at you as your parent perhaps used to—and that trigger evokes not only these intense implicit emotions and sensations, but also that fragmentation of your own inner experience, or dissociation.

Knowing about these processes of implicit and explicit memory, of unresolved trauma and loss, and of disorganized attachment and dissociation can be an essential starting place in the road to healing. Since these forms of non-integrated memory can be in fact inte-

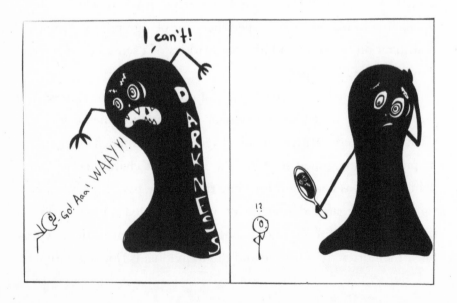

grated, the brain can move from unresolved states to resolution and healing. Here are some suggestions of steps you may consider in helping yourself transform disorganized attachment toward security.

Following are some simple practices to develop greater security and resolution if you have had a history of disorganized attachment in your life:

1. Keep a journal and be sure to write about times when your internal world may have felt it was fragmenting. What were the triggers that preceded such dissociation? How did you first know you were beginning to "unravel"? What enabled you to go from this state into a more integrated return to your usual functioning? The journal entries will be of great value as you reflect on what the common triggers were across different episodes in your life.

2. Knowing that disorganized attachment is a model that you may have had in response to terrifying and disorienting experience of trauma or loss in your life, it can be quite helpful to review those attachment questions that evoked particularly strong reactions from you in the process of reflection. Returning to those questions and diving more deeply into your present and past responses can illuminate which areas may be left unresolved. SIFT your mind for sensations, images, feelings, and thoughts that may arise as you ask yourself about any times you felt terrified in your childhood, any times you felt rejected or abandoned, and any losses you experienced. Focusing on the breath for a few minutes can help you as you explore these in her experiences.

3. RAIN heals the pain: Psychologists Tara Brach and Jack Kornfield use a wonderful acronym about being open to our internal experience that can help in bringing unresolved issues to resolution. We *recognize* the trauma or loss, *accept* that it has occurred and may be in a state of not being resolved, *investigate* the nature of the experience on our past and present lives, and have *non-identification* with the experiences, meaning that we don't let those events define our identity. Bringing a RAIN approach to those internal sensations, images, feelings, and thoughts that reveal unresolved trauma or grief is a helpful stance to take in healing your mind and moving toward resolution and integration in your life.

4. In SIFTing through your internal experience, there may be times when you feel that you are getting overwhelmed and are moving toward chaotic states of flooding of emotions or images, or shutting down in a rigid state of disconnection. Various approaches may be helpful at these times when you move out of the more flexible flow of integration. In Part I's Mindsight Practice F, we explored how putting one hand on your chest and another on your abdomen can be soothing for many. You can also try a research-established approach of putting a hand on each shoulder, left to right, then right to left, and then alternately tapping each shoulder in what is called a "butterfly hug," used effectively in helping those who have experienced the trauma of natural disasters. Another science-proven strategy that might be of help is the time-in with the breath practice (Part II's Mindsight

Practice A), which can also help bring calm to your mind as you explore distressful memories of the past.

5. If you find that particular areas in your explorations continue to be terrifying, sometimes seeking professional support can be helpful to move from unresolved to resolved trauma and loss. Think of it this way: A loss or trauma can be like a splinter in your foot during a hike. Once there, it becomes difficult to walk and the splinter becomes more irritated. The longer you try to simply ignore the situation and adjust to the splinter, the more you may limp along the trail. Taking the time to remove the splinter, either by yourself if you can reach it, or with someone's assistance if it is out of your reach, can greatly help your journey. Sometimes a trauma or loss is simply not so easy to reach with your own reflections. Having a supportive professional help you remove that unresolved splinter can empower you to begin the healing process.

6. If you are still living with or interacting with someone with whom you feel you have unresolved issues, when you feel strong and clear inside yourself, it can be very healing to go to that person and attempt to make a repair. Please keep in mind that the other person may not be in the same state of mind to make a reconnection with you, and being rebuffed because of this may lead to even more painful rejection or anger. Nevertheless, simply knowing that repair can be quite healing, just imagine that this may someday be possible when you and the other person

are feeling able to carry out such a reconnecting and healing process.

7. Whether or not the other person is able to communicate with you about these issues of terror and loss, the growth really begins and ends with your own internal work. If you find that implicit memories of past experiences of loss or trauma still intrude on your life, you can work on your journal writing, in conversations with close and trusted friends, or with a therapist to help bring these unresolved issues toward resolution. I will share with you this knowledge from working over the last thirty years with people who have lacked resolution: Healing is possible no matter what happened to you. Though all forms of insecure attachment may be accompanied by a sense of shame, that painful feeling that there is something wrong with you, please know that shame is an emotion that can arise especially with being disconnected and terrified. We all heal in different ways and in our own time, but beginning the process by seeing what happened and acknowledging how it has influenced your life, including any senses of shame that might be present, is a huge and important starting place on the journey to integrate your life and create the relationships with yourself and others that will be fulfilling and further support your healing and growth!

8. Disorganized attachment and its unresolved trauma and loss, like the other non-secure models of attachment, can be transformed through your relationships and your reflections. If you are a parent and have had the opportu-

nity to reflect on how such experiences in your own past may have led to some terrifying behaviors that frightened your offspring, it is never too late to make a repair. Begin with your own internal work, and then move to make a reconnection with your teen or older adolescent. I've even worked with adult children whose parents have had the courage to reconnect with them after decades following such disconnecting experiences. Sooner is better than later, but making the move when you are ready to acknowledge what has happened and bring the issue into the dialogue with your offspring can be a crucial step toward healing for everyone involved in what is often a cross-generational passage of disorganized attachment. You can end that legacy now with your own reflections and reflective conversations.

Creating a Safe Harbor and Launching Pad for Adolescents

The mind is shaped by changes in our relationships and in our brains throughout the life span. As adolescence involves so much exploration and change—of different interests, compatibilities and types of relationships—it is an extremely vital and formative time of life. If we add to these changes and challenges the attachment models that are non-secure, we can see how what could have been just rocky waters sometimes turns into overwhelming tempests.

Working on the impact of attachment during the adolescent period, for both adolescent and adult, is essential. Navigating the shifting needs for attunement and attachment as adolescence unfolds, riding the changing tides of the relationships between parent and adolescent and peer with peer can be a tricky challenge. Ideally, the adult will have the presence of mind to create the mental space so that he or she can continue to serve as a secure home base, a refuge in the storm that can be life, so that the adolescent knows that a safe harbor always exists. It is essential for both the adult and adolescent to "always keep the channels of communication open"—a statement that can apply as much to your relationship with others as it does to your relationship with yourself.

As I watched my eighteen-year-old daughter getting ready to leave for college, I felt the echoes of my own childhood—the attachment models I formed based on the manner in which I was raised and how these models have evolved as I strove to become a secure attachment figure for my son and daughter. Letting the transitions unfold as my children got older has somehow required that I care for a younger part of me, that collection of states of mind of all the various attachment models I have had from my own youth, so that I can feel clear in having her, our last child, leave home. The mind works to help us assimilate the many brain states, our states of mind, that we have developed in various ways and at various stages as we grow and go through life. The challenge is to find a way to connect with those brain states and take care of their various needs. That's a form of "state integration," which is a healthy part of living. And right now, I need to differentiate that younger state of mind, that younger me, and weave that inner aspect of myself more fully into my life, to prepare to no longer be the father with a child at home, and yet continue to care for my own inner needs for nurturance and connection.

I have had to take the meanings of parenting from the inside out on two levels. I have had to make sense of my own childhood so I can provide the kinds of connections needed to create secure attachments for my children. And I have had to parent myself from the inside out, meaning I have had to acknowledge that a younger part of me with states of mind that needed to be seen, safe, soothed, and secure in my own childhood is still alive and well inside me. Taking care of the needs of that part of me came naturally while caring for my son and daughter as they grew up in our home. That part of me somehow felt comforted by an older part of me caring for my own kids. But to get ready to see each of them go, to serve not just as a safe harbor but as a launching pad, I have had to be sure to directly nurture that inner place of my own attachment needs that is my birthright as a human being. We all have needs for connection. And as we move through life we have the opportunity to both receive that care in our youth and to receive and give that care as we move through adolescence and adulthood.

Watching our adolescents get ready to leave home brings up all these issues of nurturance and care, of attachment and connection. This is the "empty nest" period that we as parents hear so much about. I like to think of it as the "freedom phase," but I have to admit that when our daughter first left for college, it felt sad, overwhelming, and exhilarating all at once. I try to simply be present with all of this life, aware and accepting of all these layers of experience, letting these days unfold while taking in the majesty of it all.

MINDSIGHT TOOLS #3

∎

Time-Between and
Reflective Conversation

In this entry we'll be focusing on the reflective skill of mapping the inner worlds of others and the nature of our communications with one another. Such a tuning in to another's feelings, thoughts, memories, beliefs, attitudes, and intentions will enable others to "feel felt" by you. And this feeling, this sense of joining, which I call "time-between" is the key starting place to make close relationships work well. As we also focus on how we are communicating, we are attending to the quality of connection we have with other people and making it possible to improve our relationships.

For adolescents, the self is naturally changing a lot as they encounter and become adept at navigating more and more differing facets of life. Finding a strong inner sense of who you are in your connection with others is one of the major goals for this time of life. This is perhaps why friendship is so incredibly important to adolescents: It becomes a means for self-awareness and self-invention.

Relationships in which you feel felt by another person—when you sense that your internal world, your mind, is taken in by another and respected—are the building blocks of health. You may find that some of your connections with your friends feel this way and are wonderful in your life. You may find other relationships are rarely like that, or worse, they make you feel bad about who you are.

When we reflect on the inner life of others, when we participate in reflective conversations and attune to another person's mind beneath behaviors, we join with others and our sense of self is expanded. Life feels full. A positive sense of love and caring emerges between us, and within us. Feeling felt is the fundamental experience of a secure relationship, whether it is between friends, romantic partners, teachers and students, or parents and their offspring, older adolescents included. It is reflection that enables us to create that crucial feeling-felt experience in our lives.

A primary way we can connect with others in an integrative way can be called a "reflective conversation" or "reflective dialogue." Much of what happens in schools, and even in the busy lives of many modern families, does not offer an opportunity for such important conversations. Whether you are an adolescent or an adult, having these reflective skills in your life's tool kit is a great addition. Let's first examine how the patterns of relating to our attachment figures from early on may have shaped how we connect with others now.

Making Sense of How
Our Models Shape Our Present

Our attachment experiences with our own parents create a starting place where we learn the first lessons on how to be with our own emotions, how to reflect on our inner life, and how to have reflective conversations with others. In many ways, these attachment relationships shape the initial direction of how we'll sail out on our journeys. With these earlier lessons having shaped the deeper parts of the brain, our emotional circuitry, we set our course as adolescents into the wider world. Reflecting on those relationships can free us, at whatever age, to make the life we choose rather than live a life that has been chosen for us.

It makes sense for you as an adult and as an adolescent to make sense of your life history so you can be as fully present as possible in your relationships. What this means is reflecting on your relationships in the past in your own family life and asking yourself how those experiences influenced your development. How you've come to understand who you are and how you got to be that way is important not only for your own well-being but for how the well-being of your relationships with others, including with your own children, present or future, will unfold in your life.

For someone with an avoidant model of attachment, depending upon others may make him or her feel like a weak person. This model creates an inner stance of isolated thinking, of being analytical without feeling very much. If the adults around us have been ignoring our inner life—if they don't show interest or kindness for what we are going through—it can be very painful and even induce a feeling of shame. As with each of the attachment models, shame may arise when we don't have connections to our caregivers in a reliable way. While shame can shut down our freedom to connect, we can move past that, knowing that it may simply be an emotional response to misconnections in the past.

In many ways, reflecting on our own journey gives us a chance to do things differently with our own children. Without these important reflective conversations, people can simply feel alone and disconnected. Emotions can serve as our compass on life's journey— letting us know when to turn and, ultimately, where to go. Whether they flood us in the moment of interacting with an adolescent home from school for the holidays and moping about, or flood us as an adolescent trying to get our parents to agree to an adventure we are eager to embark upon, these internal measures of what has meaning can come from places we may not even be aware of. Sometimes we have major blocks to knowing what these emotions are. If we've used an adaptation to block feelings, as about one-fifth of the population does with an avoidant history, it has a big impact on how we can know our own internal worlds— and the worlds of others.

For others with a history of ambivalent attachment, we've seen that the flood of feelings from the lower regions of the nervous system moving up into the non-verbal right hemisphere can create a sense of being overwhelmed. If this is your history, we've seen that reflecting on your past and building the balance of the left hemisphere's more distant, analytical approach to weaving your life story can be an important and life-changing strategy. The amplified attachment system with an ambivalent history can at times make interacting with others filled with intense anxiety about how reliable this present connection will be. Taking the time to reflect on this model and how it is an adaptation from your own intrusive or inconsistent past relationships can help give you the internal ballast to engage openly in reflective conversations now.

Having a history of disorganized attachment experiences in which you may have felt terrified of your attachment figure may have left you with a tendency to dissociate—to disassociate your usually fluid flow of thoughts, feelings, and memories as you interact with others and reflect inwardly within yourself. Be patient with yourself. Dissociation is a developmental outcome of being terrified, and it can itself be terrifying. Journal writing, reflection, and being open about what is happening internally can all be helpful starting places on the journey to heal and to connect with others. Knowing that the brain continues to change across the life span and that healing relationships of all sorts, including the one you have with yourself, can support the growth of new integration can help give you a sense of strength, hope, and direction. If you need time to simply collect yourself when things get intense, find a way to request that with a mutual understanding that this is simply what you need while engaging in reflective conversation.

In avoidance, we can't just block out one kind of feeling: When we shut off a feeling, we usually shut off all our feelings. And with ambivalence and being flooded by feelings, we also become unable to connect with others and be fully present with them as well. If we have a tendency to fragment in response to intense interactions, to dissociate with a history of disorganized attachment, then learning how to befriend our own internal emotional world is an important starting place for being open to the feelings of others. Clearly, each of these non-secure attachment models has emotions at its core. And emotion itself is a process that happens not only within us, but also between and among us. So don't be surprised if having a non-secure attachment model, or models, makes reflective conversations challenging. That's okay! The key is kindness and patience. Reflecting on feelings in ourselves guides our decisions and even lets us know what things mean in our lives. Reflecting on feelings with others helps us to join minds, to connect with others in deeply meaningful ways.

The questions for self-reflection in Part III will be an important review in finding a way to enhance your time-between skills. How we have learned to relate to our own emotional life is a crucial starting place to having deep understanding and the possibility for growth.

MINDSIGHT PRACTICE A: Reflecting on How Your Attachment Models Shape Your Reflective Conversations

For this practice, let's return to the mindsight questions on your attachment experiences from Part III (see pp. 163–167). Consider the attachment model or models that you have experienced in your life, be they secure, avoidant, ambivalent, or disorganized. You may have had mostly one, or some of all four. Whatever your set of attachment models, I invite you now to consider how those attachment experiences and the models you developed in response shape how you now connect with others. How have these attachment models influenced your ability to be present for yourself or others? How do these models influence your skills of attuning to your own inner world—or the inner worlds of others? Do you have the experience of feeling felt? Do you feel connected to others in a way that supports the feeling of trust emerging?

These reflections can be an important exercise to heighten your awareness of the contribution you may be making to the quality of communication with others. I'll invite you to now consider that you have the knowledge to play a more vital role in your relationships than perhaps you had up to this point. Remember, your attachment models may shape how you connect and communicate with others, but these models are changeable! So the great news is that with your new self-awareness, you can develop the tools to have more fulfilling ways of connecting with others, and with yourself.

Reflection, Integration, and the Origins of Empathy

Time-in promotes internal integration. And time-between catalyzes interpersonal integration. As we've seen, one of the major experiences during adolescence is that the brain becomes more integrated. The key is that while such integrative changes seem to develop in their own time and we may not be able to alter this timing much, we can in fact stimulate the brain as it is undergoing these genetically programmed and experientially shaped changes to actually grow in more richly integrative ways! A similar process is possible in terms of interpersonal integration.

What happens in a family, with friends, at school, and even in the culture of our communities and larger society can shape the way the brain develops.

But how do you create more integration in your relation-ships with others?

By now you know one important strategy: reflection.

Reflection may not change the timing of integrative growth, but it can change the depth and richness of that growth.

And the great thing is that, as with internal integration, whether you are a teen or in your nineties, these time-between practices reinforce integration in your relationships no matter what your age.

When you take time-in, you are reflecting on your inner mental life. That means you sense and are aware of the sensa-tions of the body, you feel your feelings, think your thoughts, remember your memories. Whatever arises in your subjective experience, you let it enter awareness and simply be present as it emerges. That's inner reflection. When you did the time-in practices of breath awareness and the Wheel of Awareness ear-lier, you got a feeling of how focusing the mind on its internal subjective experiences can feel.

Now we'll explore how we can reflect on the inner world

of others, and on our connections with them. One of the principal means for creating time-between is engaging in a reflective dialogue or conversation that focuses on the inner experience of everyone in the communication. In reflective conversations each person can share what they are feeling, thinking, remembering, hoping, dreaming, believing, or perceiving. These conversations connect us to one another so that we can feel felt and seen—so that we can feel authentic and real. Reflective conversations make life meaningful and enable us to feel a part of something larger than our isolated sense of self.

Is there anything off-limits in a reflective conversation? I believe that anything from the inner worlds of the people in conversation brought out in a respectful and kind way is fair game. Why respectful and kind? Respect entails that we honor differences between ourselves and others. And respect means that we do not push people who are different from us away but instead work to promote linkage despite differences. With kindness we honor and support one another's vulnerabilities, creating a safe space where we can open up in an authentic way. Showing respect for one another and being kind are two essential ingredients in effective reflective conversations.

Another important aspect of reflective conversation is that we observe patterns in how we are communicating and connecting with one another. Studies of the brain clearly show that reflection, inward or in communication with others, stimulates the activation and development of the prefrontal cortex toward its integrative growth. When we study the mechanisms at work for such inner self-knowing awareness and other-directed awareness, we find that what is activated are the integrative prefrontal regions and related areas, including the mirror neuron system that let us sponge up the feelings of others inside ourselves and enable us to resonate with someone else.

When we attune to another person and allow our own internal sensations to be shaped by that other person's feelings, we create "resonance." When we resonate with someone, we come to feel their feelings at the same time as we become more aware of our own. This awareness includes our bodily sensations as well as our own emotions. We become more self-aware. When we tune in to the inner life of another, we can create compassionate communication, one filled with empathy and caring. This connection is the essence of a healthy, supportive relationship filled with mutual respect, kindness, and compassion. Reflective conversations make it possible to join with others from the inside out.

Learning to be more reflective can help anyone, regardless of age, develop a more integrated brain. For adolescents going through these important years when the brain is influenced by experience to lay the foundations of integration, working on these skills can be especially beneficial. Learning how to relate to others in meaningful ways using time-between reflective conversations can help adolescents become more resilient to life's changes and challenges—and resilient is a good thing to become as early on in life as possible! So let us now explore a mindsight practice that can help adolescents and adults alike develop the skills to be reflective conversationalists and mindsight mavens.

MINDSIGHT PRACTICE B: Reflective Conversations

Think of a person in your life who you feel brings out the best in you. Let the way you two interact fill your awareness. Now think of another person who brings out the worst in you. Reflect on the nature of your communication with that person. And now compare the two patterns you have in each of these relationships. How do reflective conversations play a role, or not play a role, in each relationship? How has honoring differences and cultivating connections been a part—or not been a part—of your relationship with each of these two people in your life.

In the first part of this practice, reach out to the person who brings out the best in you. See if you can find some time to simply express to them your gratitude for your relationship. You can SIFT your mind and let this person know how you feel and what your connection means for you. Let the positive sense of connection just fill you by taking time to soak in this sense of closeness. Being grateful is a powerful source of reinforcing the positive experiences we have in life. Sharing that gratitude with another person is a powerful way of amplifying the positive interpersonal connection.

Now imagine how you might try to improve the relationship with the person who brings out the worst in you. What would you do differently? How might you communicate with this person in a way that would be more in line with reflective conversation and integration? Do you think you could try to initiate such a new approach to your relationship? For your first go at this, try picking someone with whom you've perhaps had a long-standing relationship, one that in the past may have been filled with trust but recently has had some change that needs an attempt at course correction. It might be a misunderstanding or a missed opportunity to connect. Keep in mind that sometimes reaching out can be hard. But while making a change in how you communicate can be helpful, sometimes it just doesn't work well. So be prepared by embracing the uncertainty inherent in any relationship: We just don't know exactly how another person may respond. But time-between gives you a focus on the process, and that is an important place to begin. Consider writing down some of the thoughts that occur to you before and after you do this exercise. And remember, you can always choose how to be in your relationships with others. It's never too late to make improvements.

The PART We Play in Creating Ourselves in Relationships

We all have a role, or part, we play in creating the quality of our interpersonal relationships. Here's an acronym that can help us remember the essential role or part we play in cultivating healthy relationships with others. PART means that we are present, attune, resonate, and create trust. This is the PART we play in helping create the most balanced mental life for ourselves and the others with whom we are connecting.

Our mental lives will thrive if we take this PART we play seriously. This doesn't mean in a heavy-handed way but playfully and with intention! When adolescents are treated with this respectful PART we play as adults, they are given an invitation to enable their own minds to thrive. And when adults are treated by us adolescents with presence and attunement, when we are open to resonating with what is being communicated by the adults in our lives, then trust can be created across the generations. It is a two-way experience.

Being a PART of others' lives may not come easily at first if this was not a part of your own early life experience. Not only does learning to be present in this way help relationships with others; recent studies show that being present improves our own physiological health, too. This may sound more like science fiction than science fact, but carefully conducted research reveals that if we can be present for our experience, if we can be aware of what is happening as it is happening, then we'll improve our subjective sense of well-being and enhance the way our immune system functions and even make our cells live longer! Learning to be present reduces stress and even reduces the effects of aging on those caps at the ends of our chromosomes, our telomeres. Another aspect of these studies amazingly finds that learning to be present makes us not only healthier but happier. Our cells will thank us as we learn to be more present in life!

So this is a win-win situation. Not only will our bodies and minds be in better shape with presence, but this way of being open and reflective to others in the PART we play in communicating will also make our relationships thrive as well. Body, mind, and relationships are enhanced with presence— that's the win-win nature of learning to be present in life.

Reflection is the key to creating presence and connection.

MINDSIGHT PRACTICE C: Repairing Ruptures

If you have an argument with a friend or family member, it can be extremely helpful to reflect on what happened and then make an attempt to make a repair. In this practice, reflect on your ongoing relationships and think of one in which a rupture has recently occurred. It may be subtle or intense, but this disconnection between you and the other person may be in need of repair. Let me walk you through some basic ideas about repair, and I invite you then to reach out to this person to engage in a reflective conversation to reconnect.

When you repair a rupture in a relationship, it means making a move toward the person and reconnecting with them. If you have an open rupture with friends or family members, think of ways you might go back and reconnect with them. Before you share your own experience, see if you can imagine a way to explore their experience. One effective way to begin is by making a statement about your interest in connecting again; this can break the ice and set things in motion.

Sometimes as parents we do things that create a rupture in our otherwise close connection with our child or adolescent. It is our duty to reflect on such ruptures and make the effort to repair and reconnect after we've apologized for our contribution to the conflict. Another lesson is that sometimes we do things that we don't really want to do. The brain has its higher, prefrontal part that helps us be aware of things. But sometimes the lower limbic, brain stem, and bodily areas directly influence our behaviors without the intervening prefrontal filtering or calming influences. We can flip our lids and go down the low road. In the Low Road section in my book *Parenting from the Inside Out*, I discuss the importance of rupture and repair with regard to younger kids. Let me say that being reflective is essential to repair ruptures with those we care about at any age. In fact, during adolescence, because there can be so many challenges, it should be a central theme to maintain open lines of communication, especially when the inevitable ruptures in that connection occur.

Looking upon ruptures as an opportunity to connect again and not just a burden or a problem in life can help us approach these challenging moments as occasions to create integration when integration is broken. I know with my own two adolescents, doing so has allowed our connections to stay really strong. And it has also taught them through our interactions to develop mindsight in their own lives. Having the power of reflective conversation gives us a basic tool, an essential way to connect around things that really matter, that makes the way we relate to one another have a deep and authentic quality to it.

So here's the idea. When you are ready, you can check in with the other person and see if this is a good time to speak with him or her about what is going on. You can state that

A Tuning In

you'd like to reconnect and when it's time, you can find a quiet place to engage in a reflective dialogue. Listen to what is being said, don't judge. Being open to the other person is essential to let the person feel felt and for you to truly understand what might be going on. One of the hardest elements may be to let go of the notion that you are right, and the other person is wrong. Listen, take in the other person's perspective, and realize that understanding each other is the road to reconnection. When it's time, you can share in a non-judgmental way your own experience, using "I" language like "I felt that . . ." or "I thought that . . ." rather than "You made me feel . . ." or "You didn't do . . ." Letting each person in the dialogue have space to express and be heard fully is essential.

Though repair is not easy—and further rupturing can feel painful—it is worth trying. Be sure you are in that receptive hub of your mind before you start, so you can be open to whatever arises in the conversation. There are no rights and wrongs in repair, simply a sharing of each person's experience.

PART IV

■

Staying Present Through Changes and Challenges

In this fourth part we will explore various ways that as an adolescent or as an adult we can stay open and accepting to the changes and challenges of adolescence. This period of life is filled with new ways of seeing the world, interacting with others, experiencing the body, making decisions, and taking responsibility. All of these changes mean it can be a challenge for adolescents to maintain internal balance. And as adults supporting adolescents, such changes may challenge us to be open to what is happening, to be receptive and responsive instead of reactive, to connect rather than correct.

If I had to summarize in one word all of the research on what kind of parenting helps create the best conditions for a child's and adolescent's growth and development, it would be the term "presence." As we've discussed throughout our conversation together, being present means being open to what is. Presence involves being aware of what is happening as it is happening, being receptive to our own inner mental sea, and attuning to the inner life of another person. Being present for others means we resonate with what is going on in their inner worlds, creating the essential way we feel their feelings. This feeling felt sensation is at the heart of how we can help one another feel seen, safe, soothed, and secure. Feeling felt is the basis for secure attachment. It is also the essence of healthy relationships in all domains of our lives.

So often we want to help the people we love fix their problems. We want to show them how to solve a dilemma, resolve a conflict, or get rid of painful emotions. But in order to give them what they need most of all, which is to make them feel felt and connected with us, we need to *not* do these well-intended things first and instead simply be present for our loved one. If we can stay attuned to this person and allow the SIFTing that emerges to enter us, we can truly resonate with what this other person is sharing about their experience. This is the part that may be the most challenging, especially for adolescents and parents who are experiencing different feelings about all the changes that are occurring in the adolescent's life and perhaps not seeing eye to eye. Resonance requires that we let someone's internal feelings enter us and change us. If, for example, the feeling that arises is something we cannot handle, then we'll automatically, without conscious intent, shut down the attunement process. If I am unable to be open to a sense of excitement about my daughter's plan to go on an adventure and travel to another country with friends, it becomes quite difficult for me to simply take in her feelings about her plan and sense what is happening in her world in that moment.

In an attempt to problem-solve about how she might avoid any danger in her travels, I might fail to simply be present to her experience and, in so doing, miss a great opportunity to connect. Understanding does not mean going along with every idea or plan; it means starting with connection and then exploring together what might be the steps she could take to remain safe on her journey to see the world.

The problem with putting up such initial blockades to presence is that trust between adolescent and adult will likely be damaged. Presence, attunement, and resonance, on the other hand, create trust. Remember our mindsight tools on time-between (see pp. 201–216)? This is the PART we play in helpful communication. PART means that we are *present*, *attune*, *resonate*, and create *trust*.

In any close relationship, connection means becoming a PART of the communication in that moment.

Honoring the Person an Adolescent Is Becoming

As parents we cannot control the people our adolescents are becoming. As adolescents, we can try to be open to the many internal and interpersonal experiences that emerge in our lives as our teens and early twenties unfold. This adolescent period is by definition one of intense change, and the potential for intense challenge—for adolescent and adult—is great. The key for both generations is to be open to what is unfolding, to honor the person an adolescent is becoming through all of the many unpredictable stages and experiences this time entails.

Honoring means being present for what is happening and being open and accepting so that we can play an important PART in our adolescent's life. And honoring our own changes as an adolescent means, too, that we can be present for what is happening as it

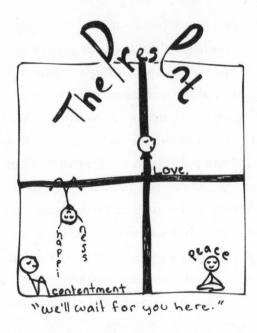

"we'll wait for you here."

happens. I cannot control my life, but I can be present for it in my teens and twenties so that I can best support my own emerging development.

In many ways, the essence of adolescence can serve as our guide to knowing how this becoming process is working. The emotional spark of adolescence means that the feelings that arise will be intense and sometimes challenging, for ourselves and for others. While this passion can fuel a full life, sometimes wide swings in emotions can be exhausting and make life difficult. Social engagement means that our peers play a sometimes crucial role in how we feel and how we make decisions. Depending on who our friends are, sometimes those influences may be good for us, and sometimes they may not be in our best interest. Novelty seeking is a wonderful part of our adolescent journey, filling us with new experiences that are enriching and challenge our learning. But focusing in on one passion, having discipline to stick with difficult projects like learning a musical instrument, a foreign language, a sport, or an academic subject, can require singular focus of attention that may be challenging. Embracing this tension and realizing the need for focused efforts is part of the "work" of adolescence in addition to taking on new experiences. Finally, our creative explorations that are fueled by new ways of seeing life can often be an exhilarating journey into exciting new ways of approaching the world. Not every exploration is easy to understand or accept, but for adolescent and adult alike, focusing on this internal drive for creativity can be an important way of staying present on the journey itself.

In the sections that follow, we'll explore a number of specific changes and challenges that confront us through the adolescent period, such as romance, sex, drug use and abuse, and the experiences of leaving the family and returning home. Naturally there are an endless number of challenges that can arise during adolescence, such as dealing with divorce, the demands of school, the distractions of an increasingly "online, all the time" world, and finding employment. The selected examples we'll explore here offer us an opportunity to build on our earlier conversations and mindsight tools to illuminate how staying present for whatever arises, as an adolescent or an adult, is the essential foundation for a healthy and productive journey through adolescence no matter what issues we are experiencing. What follows are stories blended with science that offer us ideas and facts about how to stay present and maintain an open relationship as we move through these important times.

Leaving Home

I first met Sara when she was twelve. She came in for therapy to discuss her anxiety about being at a new school and making new friends. She ended up making the transition well but came back to therapy several years later as a senior in high school because she was anxious about starting college across the country. She was excited to study biology at a challenging school but was nervous about being far away from her parents. She would be the first to leave home, leaving two brothers back with her parents, who were happy she had found a passion in her life. In therapy this time Sara learned to do some basic time-in practices, such as breath awareness and the reflective exercise of the Wheel of Awareness (see pp. 131–136). With some practice she soon was able to calm her anxiety: She made space in her mind to hold in awareness whatever feelings arose and then just to accept them for what they were. She used the acronym RAIN to remind herself to *r*ecognize, *a*ccept, *i*nvestigate, and *n*ot identify with her anxiety when defining who she was. From a Wheel of Awareness point of view, she came to sense her anxiety as simply a point on the rim, a feeling she could be aware of but was not completely immersed in. She was able to center herself in the now more spacious and strong hub of her mind. These time-in practices strengthened her mind and empowered her to approach this moment of leaving home with more ease and enthusiasm.

I am finding
the antidote to "overwhelm"
not by completing more
or doing less
but by falling *madly*
in
Love
with
Stillness

When we move from the comfort and familiarity of our family home out into the unknown of the wider world, it is quite natural for anxiety to emerge. When the mind tries to predict what will happen next and everything is new and unfamiliar, it is natural to feel nervous and uncertain. However, depending on how one responds to these natural feelings, either they can move to the background and be stabilized or they can take center stage and be amplified, absorbing us in the intensity of feeling worried and concerned.

Ironically, when we fight what we feel, the feeling gets bigger, not smaller. When Sara came in for therapy, she was understandably in the midst of trying not to feel anxious. But that effort only intensified her anxiety. Acceptance of what is, being present for life as it emerges, moment by moment, is the key to mindfulness and the essence of presence. With such mindful practice on the breath and immersion in the Wheel of Awareness exercise, Sara learned to transform her anxiety into a sense of openness to what was.

During this time at the close of her last year in high school, we also explored what her relationships with friends and family were like. She was close to her parents, and felt that they supported her and understood who she was for the most part. Though her mother never went to college, and her father, an accountant, was not interested in science and initially thought she should go into business, both her parents were open to her getting a college education in biology if that was what she wanted. With her younger brothers, one a freshman in high school and the other just beginning middle school, Sara felt annoyed at times, but mostly she felt close to them, and even proud and protective of them when they weren't "invading" her life with their joking around.

Sara had a close social support network, with an extended group of classmates she would hang out with on the weekends and with a few very close friends she considered her best friends. Sara had dated a lot in her last two years of high school but had no ongoing intimate relationship, no romantic interests, during her senior year.

Nothing stuck out in Sara's history to make me worry about a major psychiatric illness like depression or an anxiety disorder. We all have a temperament, which means the innate predisposition of our nervous system to react in certain ways. Temperament includes our sensitivity to input from the environment, the intensity with which we react to inner or outer stimuli—like our own feelings from the inside or sounds or sights from the outside world. These inborn characteristics also include the qualities of having a generally positive attitude toward life and whether we enjoy or react negatively to change and novelty. One way to describe personality is that we can have a general tendency to activate one of three major emotional states of distress: fear and anticipatory anxiety, sadness and separation distress, and anger and rage. For much of Sara's life, she described a tendency to lean toward fear and anticipatory anxiety when she felt stressed, rather than to the other two modes.

We could see, especially after Sara's parents came in with her for a few sessions, that her reactions to leaving home for school likely were related to her temperament, not to her specific attachment to her parents. Attachment, as we've seen in Part III, is how a child connects with parents, a form of relationship that shapes us in many ways. According to her parents, Sara was "always," for as long as they could remember, a person who had an intense reaction to the world, especially toward changes in her routine, but she also had a generally positive demeanor. She was an upbeat child and now seemed to be the same way as an adolescent.

Sara was very sensitive to things, meaning that small amounts of input (sounds, sights, smells) would get a significant response from her, and that response would be big. Another temperament characteristic was that Sara generally did not like new things. Perhaps *like* is not the right word. Sara had a big, negative, automatic reaction to novelty and change such that new things seemed to evoke a feeling of anxiety and fear at first. After a while, when she could figure out what was happening, she'd warm up and dive into the new activity with some reserve but ultimately with gusto. Some would call Sara "shy," and that would be a fair term; others might prefer to use the phrase "slow to warm up."

We all have a temperament, an inborn propensity of how we respond. And this was simply Sara's way of being in the world. With adolescence, the changes that emerge may intensify some of those earlier characteristics from our childhood as we face the challenges that arise. But for many of us, in fact for the majority, our childhood temperament does not predict how we'll be in our teenage years or beyond. It's a fascinating issue, but realizing that we change and evolve based on our experiences as well as our temperaments is important as we create the life we want to have.

Attachment experiences and temperament interact to form our personality. And personality is what is being shaped during our childhood and adolescence. If we are open as adults, we can even create changes in who we are throughout our lives.

While attachment is based on our interactions with our caregivers and is not related in a significant way to our genes, temperament is inborn and is related to our genetic factors or other issues unrelated to experience. For the majority of us, the externally observable features of our temperament, when not in the extreme, in fact do not predict how we become later on. For about 80 percent of children, their temperamental characteristics are in the "middle range" of values, and experience plays a larger role in shaping their paths. For 20 percent, 10 on either end of a spectrum of typical temperamental characteristics, the extremes of their temperament seem to be associated with the persistence of nervous system tendencies such as sensitivity or aversion to novelty. Experience plays a role in the development of these individuals as well, but the unfolding of personality for this 20 percent is shaped in a greater way by the propensities of the nervous system based on inborn temperament.

For Sara, if her nervous system had an intense degree of reactivity, sensitivity, and withdrawal from novelty (she is slow to warm up), then her internal experience would be intense as she went through life. Fortunately, her attachments appeared to be secure as a child, so her ability to regulate her own internal state—her emotions and reactivity—would be optimized because those integrated relationships would have cultivated integration in Sara's brain. And integration is the basis for flexible regulation. That's what attachment does: Our parents provide the scaffolding when they attune to us with their presence, which shapes how we learn to calm our own reactivity and soothe our own distress and balance our own emotions. Interactive attunement in attachment leads to internal regulation.

So Sara had started life with the secure relational world to optimize her self-regulation. That's a great start. But she also had a temperament at the extreme, suggesting that these propensities toward fear and anxiety might persist and might intensify as she approached the adolescent challenge of leaving home.

Sara did not seem to have a disorder of her mood, her thinking, or her bodily image and eating. She also did not have the clinical presentation of someone with an anxiety disorder, such as panic or obsessive-compulsive disorder. Like the majority of adolescents, Sara was experiencing the common challenges of moving from childhood to adulthood but did not have a formal psychiatric disorder. She was experiencing the challenges of adolescence, not the emergence of a disorder in need of specific treatment interventions such as medications or intensive psychotherapy.

But if you have an inborn proclivity to be reactive, sensitive, and novelty-distressed, then even with a history of secure attachment, life will continue to be distressful and challenging. You may not have a formal disorder, but you may be experiencing significant and real distress. So using the mindsight tools (in the form of mindfulness of the breath and the Wheel of Awareness practices) to help her learn for herself how to calm her innate nervous system reactions worked well for Sara, and off to school she went.

The lesson for Sara was that even if you have a temperament that is inborn, a particular personality propensity you are living with, you can still use ways to strengthen your mind to improve your life. Rather than trying to ignore her internal experience, Sara could learn to be present with her propensities so that she could become more resilient in life.

Now here we were in her first year of college. She loved her classes. She loved being at the dorm even if the first few weeks were filled with the unavoidable feelings of loneliness and homesickness. Sara had learned to create a space in her mind, the strengthened hub of her Wheel of Awareness, to reflect on her feelings so that she did not let her feelings take over, so that she was not lost on her rim. She could give her emotions the space to arise, fill her awareness, and then just float away as other feelings came up.

Remember that after ninety seconds an unimpeded emotion will begin to transform on its own. It is often how we fret over a feeling that creates suffering and maintains the intensity and duration of that feeling in our lives. Fretting can involve attempting to avoid a feeling and it can mean vigilantly clinging to that feeling out of fear. Fretting can involve us saying, "I should not feel that feeling—go away!"but the feeling just gets stronger. And fretting can also involve a rapid shutting down of being aware of a feeling even though the emotion remains beneath our consciousness. Just giving space to a feeling without fretting about it lets us make it "mentionable and manageable," as Fred Rogers used to say. Mister Rogers was so right.

As Sara learned to name her internal state of worry as a natural human concern about newness and uncertainty, she could simply be present for this initially uncomfortable feeling and then let it lessen in intensity so that she could move on to live her life. That's the power of presence to bring freedom and vitality to how we live.

Puberty, Sexuality, and Identity

When Sara first came in as a sixth-grader and just turning twelve, she had entered puberty. Puberty is marked by the development of the body and its changes in secondary sexual characteristics (growing genitals and larger muscles in boys; widening hips and budding breasts in girls). This sexual maturation anatomically is associated with increases in chemicals that are distributed throughout the body, hormones of various sorts that help regulate growth and activation of the sexual regions of the body. Changes in the brain itself may not correlate directly with the timing of these changes in the body, so we can't state that mental changes necessarily go along with these sexual changes. But the increase in circulating sex hormones following the onset of puberty creates new and intense sexual drives, feelings of attraction, and erotic arousal.

This increase in pubertal sexuality in the setting of sometimes later brain maturation with delayed impulse inhibition and other executive cognitive functions becomes an important issue in modern times. Many studies suggest that adolescents' sexual maturation used to be much later, in the later teen years, sixteen or seventeen. In earlier cultures adolescents becoming sexually mature at that age would then be very near the time when they'd become not only sexually active but domestically ready to settle down to raise a family. For a variety of reasons, including nutritional intake, children are sexually maturing at earlier ages, especially girls—sometimes before hitting their double digits—but their brains are not maturing at this same rate. Sara was typical of this trend, entering puberty before she was a teenager.

On top of this earlier onset of puberty in modern culture, establishing an independent home life and reaching sexual maturation associated with bearing children will not generally occur for another decade or two after puberty. That is a long transition period to be sexually mature but domestically non-responsible, a duration that has never existed, as far as we can tell, in our human history. This is the modern experience of a substantially longer adolescent period of time between childhood and adulthood.

To understand the changes of sexuality and romance and the challenges they present to both adolescent and adult, we need to explore how these physiological factors influence both our internal experiences and our relationships during this time. Being present for these issues as they arise is greatly aided by understanding what is happening in the body and in our social worlds. Brain changes are rarely demonstrated directly to the visible eye, but parents and teachers can tell when the mind's capacity for abstract thinking begins during this period of early adolescence. As teens, we begin to see the world with conceptual patterns beyond the concrete facts we've been learning throughout elementary school. As we've discussed, such abstract reasoning and thinking include seeing ourselves and others from a bit of a distance, seeing general patterns about life set out in stories within novels and films, and beginning to wrestle with issues about life and death and the meaning and purpose of why we are here on Earth. The notion of personal identity—who we are and what really matters to us—will begin to become a central theme in our inner thoughts, in our journal writing, in our conversations with friends, and in our academic work.

At this age, too, adolescents begin to act in very distinct ways with different groups of people. They may have one "persona" or way of being with fellow teammates in soccer club, another with friends from school, and another with siblings or with parents. During this early adolescent period, studies show, there is often little awareness of these distinct "ways of being" or "states of mind" that can dominate and distress teen and adult alike. It can seem that people have many divided states that they are not even aware of having. I know for myself, as a fourteen-year-old, when I moved past this early adolescent time into mid-adolescence, I felt as if I were split up, as if I had many personalities that seemed to be activated in different ways depending on whom I was with. Those shifts were confusing at best. Who was I really if I could be feeling and acting in such different ways?

In addition to these experiences of changing identity and its various manifestations internally and interpersonally, the impact of increased levels of sexual hormones in both boys and girls has an effect on an adolescent's overall physiology and neurological functioning such that feelings of sexual attraction and arousal begin to arise within awareness. Now we develop a sexual self, a new identity filled with novel and powerful sensations. Some of these feelings may have been present earlier in life, but they were usually less intense, less persistent, and less available to conscious reflection during those years. For many reasons, then, adolescence is marked by an increased awareness of sexual sensations.

For some individuals, this new awareness is exciting; for some, feeling sexually aroused in general or attracted to one person in particular may feel very uncomfortable and "out of control"; for others, awareness of these new sensations can be outright terrifying.

Sara did not share with me much of her inner experience of attraction to some of the boys at school, perhaps because I am a male therapist. She would mention them to me in passing, and then move on to other issues, often about her finding new girlfriends at school. By the time she felt acclimated to her new middle school experience, she was ready to stop therapy.

For any adolescent, the new sensations of romantic interest and sexual arousal can be uncomfortable. When they first arise, their newness and their intensity can be confusing. These feelings can be powerful and exciting but also overwhelming. And when sexual feelings intensify, they can feel like just too much to handle. Given Sara's extreme of temperament toward sensitivity and novelty, we can imagine that these new feelings might be especially overwhelming. Feeling out of control, feeling helpless, feeling that something is "taking over" are all natural responses to the hormonal and neurological alterations that emerge during this period.

Let's think about this for any of us as adolescents: We've gone from an intense interest in the world *around* us—people, activities— to a new state of huge feelings *inside* us. That change alone is a major shift in the origin of both the quantity of sensations and the specific quality of them. Now add to this the reality that these emotional sensations are doing exactly what emotions do, they are getting us to "evoke motion," e-motion. They create a state of mind in which our whole system, our brain and whole body, is being readied to take action. And the action that sexual feelings prime us to take is to move toward the persons to whom we are attracted and connect with them. That's a drive, an impulse, a deep motivation. It fills our awareness automatically, it activates our behaviors automatically, and it colors the way we feel automatically.

When the emotional state is attraction, the drive is to connect. Talking to that person is a start. Getting to know them, holding their hand, kissing them, fondling them, engaging with them sexually, having intercourse are all sometimes hidden (and sometimes not so hidden) desires and images of what may unfold. The kinds of images and degrees of drive vary from person to person, dependent upon individual differences, maturation level, access to emotional states within consciousness, social settings, and culturally sanctioned norms of behavior. Sexual attraction captures our imagination too, weaving the content of our attraction into the daydream-like quality of fantasies. Sexual drives, sexual fantasies, sexual behaviors, these are all a part of what we mean when we say that following puberty as adolescents we experience the maturation of our sexuality. We become sexual beings.

Emotions drive us to move, to take action, to satisfy a need, and adolescence is filled with these new emotions that drive us to fulfill these new needs. It's a lot of new feelings, images, and impulses. And if cultural practices inhibit those internal sensations from being expressed as actions, there may be a lot of gestures without engagement. But in cultures where engaging in sexual behaviors is permitted, or even encouraged as in the modern cultural practice of "hooking up," such sexual activities may be frequent. Our biological legacy is to move from sexual immaturity during the pre-adolescent years to sexual maturity in the adolescent and adult years. How we experience and express those sexual feelings will be shaped by our temperament, our family, our friends, and our culture.

Let's remember, too, that in our evolutionary past, there was a much quicker transition that bridged the divide between sexual immaturity and adult responsibility. By the time physiological sexual maturity happened in the middle to late teens, we were socially set up to make sexual connections with others and ready to make babies.

Now we have a prolonged period of adolescence in which sexual feelings emerge with maturation but pair bonding (finding a mate and creating a new family home) does not occur until much, much later. In modern cultures today, these informal sexual connections sometimes shape how an adolescent first realizes his or her sexual life.

Hooking Up

The last two years of high school for Sara had been filled with learning about her sexuality by experimenting through "hooking up" with boys at parties and after school in casual encounters that felt good to her body but hard on her mind. Sara would find herself wanting more from these boys, at least most of them, and would then feel rejected when a boy she had hooked up with would not reach out to spend more time with her in the days and weeks after or, sometimes, even completely ignore her when they crossed paths at school. In some settings, there is an implied if not outright stated rule that two people hooking up should in fact not get involved with each other emotionally. That can work for some people but not others. And when that doesn't work out for only one member of a pair, it can be painful for either or both of them.

If you are in your adolescence now, you may feel a social pressure to hook up, as if it is an expected way of behaving in social settings. But remember, times are always changing, and your parents may remember feeling quite the opposite societal pressures: that casual sex was unacceptable or taboo. Even if the adults in your life don't seem to "get" what you're going through, keep in mind that getting sexually involved outside the context of a trusting relationship can have significant challenges. Sex without commitment can feel less rich, and even if neither party is looking for a lasting relationship, it can lessen the deep, intimate connection that is a component of any sexual encounter.

As we'll explore in the next section on romance, there are three major ways we can connect with others in deep ways. One is as friends in an attachment-based connection where we feel close and connected, receiving and giving care, creating a sense of security through seeing the inner life of a friend and soothing them when they are distressed. Another is simply being erotically aroused and feeling physically attracted to someone. And a third way of connecting is through romance, feelings of being "in love" and wanting to be around a person as much as we can.

One challenge of hooking up is that sometimes there can be an imbalance in what each person expects. If two people simply want the sexual activity, assuming that pregnancy and diseases are being prevented, then it can be straightforward. The fact that sex without commitment can lessen the deep, intimate connection is something to consider, for sure, as we'll discuss in the next section. Sometimes, however, the falling-in-love circuits become active only in one person and then it's painful for both. If this is happening with a friend, then the friendship may become in jeopardy because one of you wants more of a commitment than the other. Then even the friendship may not be able to survive.

During her senior year, Sara's parents were more concerned about the possibility of her getting pregnant or contracting a sexually transmitted disease than Sara becoming frustrated in her romantic interests. As for Sara, even though she was nervous about her future of leaving home, she would get swept up in her sexual feelings of attraction for boys and lose her concerns and sometimes her caution.

The culture in which Sara was growing up made these informal sexual liaisons an expected part of her teen life. From kissing and fondling to oral sex and sexual intercourse, over her junior and senior year Sara learned a lot about being erotically involved with boys but not much about romance or long-term relationships. She would learn of these things later. Many of her friends had boyfriends, but she said it was "a little ridiculous" because those same boys would be hooking up with other girls at parties all the time. That was a betrayal Sara said she did not want to experience in her life, so she had no interest in such a "fake" setup.

For Sara, there were times when her hooking up at parties was enjoyable for her; at other times she felt it was simply her "duty" to be a part of her clique at school and a way to feel attractive. While she mostly enjoyed her sexual experiences, by the end of her senior year her conflicting feelings were making her think that she'd like to try something different. When she went off to college, I was able to keep in touch with her by phone for that first year. I'd see her in person on breaks from school and was happy to see how well she adjusted to her new life. After her first year of college, though, things changed.

Romance and First Love

Sara's tears slowly welled from her reddened eyes and trickled down her cheeks as she told me how horrible her situation was during her summer break after her freshman year. At the end of her first semester, she had fallen in love with a sophomore at school and they decided to spend their summer together, working at jobs during the week that they were fortunate enough to get in town, and then being with each other and friends on the weekends. It had been an ideal summer and Sara could not believe it was over. So what was the problem?

Jared, her boyfriend, was going to South America for his junior year abroad. He'd be living in the dormitory there with other ex-change students from around the world. Sara was worried that Jared would find another love.

Sara's relationship with Jared began at the end of her first semes-ter. I was relieved that she hadn't met him earlier, as I had hoped she would be able to experience the strength of her newfound ability to soothe her own innate reactivity without the assistance of a boy-friend. Her last year of high school enabled her to move away from her emotional dependence on her parents as she relied more and more on friends for support. That's part of the adolescent journey, to connect more with peers than parents. During her high school senior year "freak-out" about leaving home, it was a natural state, given her temperament, to feel that leaving her friends and leaving her parents was just "too much." Now she had learned, with some internal edu-cation, that she could calm herself. That was a great step in strength-ening her mind.

Jared entered the scene at a school party one weekend. The two met and Sara began to feel feelings she had heard about from friends and movies and books, but in all of her dating and hooking up had never experienced. When she saw Jared at the dorm event, she felt an immediate sense of attraction to him. Jared was a sweet and sensitive person. Unlike Sara, he seemed not to be reactive in the ways that she was, fortunately, so he could approach her and the newness of her with calm and focus. They made a "great pair," Sara told me. The end of that semester was fun for them both. They got closer and closer, and soon their dancing and talking and going out together became "romantic."

Sara told me that though she had hooked up with other boys in college as she had in high school, they never really meant that much to her. Jared was the first guy who she really liked, who she really cared about. It somehow seemed different to her than the informal sexual encounters she had had in high school. This really mattered to her, she said, and she wanted to wait until she knew Jared for a while before things became sexual. And Jared, too, was patient enough to wait until things happened naturally.

Throughout the second semester of her freshman year, Sara and Jared were sexually intimate with each other. Sara went to the college health clinic and started birth control pills, and both of them got checked for AIDS and other sexually transmitted diseases before engaging even in condom-protected sexual intercourse. I was surprised by their conscientious approach to such an important issue that Sara would have treated before with casual disregard. Somehow a more reflective and thoughtful part of her was being engaged with her sexual life now that these new feelings were emerging.

When Sara's parents found out that she had a steady boyfriend, her mother was overjoyed, but her father was nervous, Sara said. Not until her dad met Jared in person did he seem to relax. "He just needed to see who Jared is so he could know I wasn't being hurt by this guy." As a father I know that feeling of wanting to be protective while also wanting to support. It's the parental challenge of being a safe harbor and a launching pad all at once. It's not so easy sometimes.

In many ways, this was an ideal way to get into the experience of romance for Sara. She learned that she could have intense feelings of attraction that were mutually shared by her partner. She learned that her timing for moving from feelings of attraction to getting to know Jared to becoming sexually involved with him could be discussed openly and respectfully. This was the longest lasting relationship Jared had had, too, so he was also learning a lot of new things about romance and emotional involvement.

And now it was August.

I said to Sara that I imagined she might be feeling a very intense sense of loss over what was going on right now. She had become very attached to Jared, I explained, and that was beautiful. Our romantic life is intimately interwoven with our attachments. Some researchers, like Helen Fisher, suggest that at least three kinds of love exist, which I mentioned briefly in the last section.

When we are romantic we "fall in love" and have a deep sense of longing to be with someone, think about the person when he or she is not around, and feel a deep sense of loss when they leave. When the committed relationship ends, or threatens to end, we can feel absolutely bereft. It's like a part of us is being amputated. We are ripped apart. We become not whole. Something is missing.

That's the "addiction" part of love that drives poets and songwriters to devote so much time and energy to trying to express the pain and pleasure of romance. Like other forms of addiction, scientists think dopamine may be the main neurochemical involved in this aspect of love. On one level, this is a "healthy addiction" that creates happiness in our lives. On another level, when the relationship is ending or uncertain, it can create huge pain within us. The very parts of the brain that register bodily pain also represent the pain of a severed relationship. It can feel like we are being stabbed and are dying.

Then there's the sexual or erotic aspect of love, the attraction and arousal. This libido or sexual energy is a natural part of our experience. It doesn't always come along with romance, so these two feelings can be somewhat independent. This form of love may be primarily mediated by androgens, a form of hormone associated with increases in sex drive. In fact, hooking up, as Sara had learned, often involves sexual arousal and not romantic engagement. "One-night stands" are good examples of the passionate engagement of this erotic form of a "loving" experience.

For some, sexual intercourse involves not only the androgens that help mediate arousal but also the secretion of oxytocin, the hormone that generally intensifies our feelings. Some of this intensification can be to enhance a sense of bonding and connection. But be aware that this intensification can be, especially for males, an intensification of jealousy and aggression. For others, especially intense for females, sexual intercourse is associated with oxytocin release; the person one is with becomes the person of one's bonding. This bonding can be in the form of romance. In this case, sexual involvement can create an intensification of romantic dopamine-driven obsession. At times, that obsession may not be shared, and such imbalance may be quite distressing.

Oxytocin release can also be a part of the next form of love, attachment.

Attachment, the third form of love, is what we feel in our close friendships and it is what we feel toward our parents and may involve primarily the serotonin system. Attachment is the kind of love in which we want to offer the nurturance that others need to help them feel safe, seen, soothed, and secure. When we are distressed, going to an attachment figure soothed us. Being around a secure attachment figure calms our inner turmoil and gives us a feeling of being "home" and at ease. This is why children can be soothed by an attachment figure with whom they have a secure attachment. And this is why connecting with a close friend is soothing. This is why even our romantic partner and our sexual companion who is *also* our attachment figure can be so soothing. It is possible to have all three forms of love shared with one person.

When one individual is your romantic partner (you are in love with someone), your sexual companion (you love making love together), and your attachment figure (you love being around this person and go to him or her at times of distress or when you want to share something positive), it's a relationship jackpot.

Not all romantic, sexual, and attachment relationships work out like this. We can imagine all the combinations that can exist: having

relation ships.

all three, just two, or only one form of love present. When it's not balanced between two people, it can be really upsetting for one person who wants more, and even for the person who wants less. But when the balance is all there, it's one of the most rewarding experiences we can have. Jared was all three for Sara. And Sara was all three for Jared. Jackpot.

For me, Sara began to look much like she did her senior year of high school just a year and a half earlier. She was filled with sadness and separation distress, the emotional state that was her "go-to" default mode of temperament when she was upset. What had happened to all of the growth and progress she had made? Why was she now so "dependent" on Jared?

Yes, you may say, she is in love with him and doesn't want to leave him. Maybe she should take off and go down to South America with him? Well, I can understand the romantic sensibility of that suggestion, but I don't agree. At this age, during the important adolescent period of time of growing into who you are becoming, I believe that it makes more sense to find your own equilibrium and direction without changing plans to maintain a romantic relationship. And believe me, I'm a pretty romantic guy. It's like what an older adolescent in her twenties recently suggested: "Tell your reader not to get committed too early. If it is going to work out, it will work out."

If you've seen the films *Before Sunrise* and *Before Sunset,* by the director Richard Linklater, you've seen up close and personal the dilemma someone in his adolescent years has when he meets up with a "soul mate" with whom he feels so aligned, so connected, so bonded. I know from personal experience how the timing of such connections makes a huge difference. I know, too, many people who meet up at this age and don't give themselves the space to create their own identity, and then years and sometimes decades pass by and it comes back to haunt them. There is an important maturation during adolescence that requires a freedom of emotional life, thinking, planning, and plain old self-discovery that committed relationships can sometimes curtail.

Please don't get me wrong: I would not be surprised if Jared and Sara ultimately find a lifelong commitment to each other. It's very possible. I just don't think they should make that serious commitment right now at this time in their journeys. I think they both would come to resent that decision and each other.

But how could I help Sara get through this period? In therapy I don't tell people what to do, I try to be present with them to help them figure out how to figure out what to do. The following sections offer examples of a few steps parents and other adults attempting to offer encouragement to adolescents can take to help support them through the intensity of first love and the endings of relationships.

First Be Present

What seemed to help Sara a lot was for me to first connect with exactly where she was. What this means is that I focused on just what was going on inside Sara, helping her to SIFT her mind by sensing, observing, and describing her sensations (what she feels in her body), her images (what she hears and sees in her mind's eye), her feelings (what emotions she is aware of), and her thoughts (in the form of ideas or concepts and word-based thinking). When we help others to SIFT their minds, we are helping them create a focused space in which they can explore their own inner sea. This mindsight skill is by no means the domain only of therapists such as me. Anyone who is willing to stay present for another person can do it.

In any close relationship, connection means becoming a PART of the communication in that moment. By being present for what is happening as it is happening, attuning to the inner experience of what is going on with the other person—not just to their external behaviors but actually resonating with their internal experience—a trust is born. That state of trust between us turns on what Steve Porges calls the "social engagement system." This system calms the internal storms, relaxes a state of distress, and creates a sense of openness to new experience. This is a fundamental way in which being present not only allows us to understand another person, but also allows that connection to create clarity and calmness inside that person.

Once Sara could share the sensations of heaviness in her chest and the empty pit in her stomach, the images of being alone in her sophomore year and of Jared with other women in Argentina, her feelings of fear and rejection, and her thoughts that she'd never find another love like him, we had SIFTed through the contents of her mind at this moment in her life and she was able to feel truly felt.

Repairing Ruptures

You might ask what words I said, if any, during our connection. Mostly my words were aimed at showing her that I understood her feelings, that I could imagine what she might be feeling because I had experienced some of these feelings myself. I said that I understood what she was saying and could feel how painful this was, and how it seemed there was no solution to this situation but loss. After we spoke for a while about this sense of being stuck, and of how ironic it was that an experience so powerfully good could change and create such powerfully painful feelings, I said something about our common human predicament. To feel such elation means we sometimes will feel intense loss. They go hand in hand.

A common and parallel metaphor I shared with Sara seemed to

help and goes like this. If you take a teaspoon of salt and put it into a small cup of water, that water will taste too salty to drink. But if you imagine putting that same teaspoon of salt into a lake, the water will remain clear to the taste. That's like the difference between getting lost on the rim of the Wheel of Awareness and experiencing life from the hub. Opening the hub of the wheel enables whatever feelings that arise to be experienced within a deep reservoir that gives us resilience. That's the clear taste of diluting the salt in the larger body of water. We can feel whatever feelings arise, not fret over them, and stay fully present as we embrace a wider awareness of knowing beyond only the one feeling or thought or idea. That's how the wheel practice strengthens the mind to be present as we open the hub and become empowered to embrace our experiences with more clarity.

This kind of presence is at the heart of what it means to be your own best friend. You are available to yourself as an attachment figure, as a close companion, as a support, and as a guide. Anything that comes up, you can share. This is what you do with your social best friend; this is what you do with yourself as best friend.

Presence enables us to develop resilience. I focused now with Sara on reinforcing this skill that we had worked on earlier when she was in high school and found the wheel practice to be so helpful and empowering. I also now wanted her to have the knowledge about the three forms of love. In particular, I wanted her to consider this possibility. Jared had become an attachment figure for her, alongside his being a romantic partner and a sexual companion. Three forms of love in one relationship—bingo. No wonder she loved being with him and didn't want to lose this relationship. But as an attachment figure, Jared may have become the person she now relied on for all of her soothing. So while she made the transition to college well, learning to rely on herself to soothe her intensely reactive temperament in an excellent way, perhaps her relationship with Jared after that first semester—being with him essentially all the time for the last nine months—had made her not practice being her own best friend. Perhaps Sara had given up her own inner resilience for the compelling nature of her new love.

Changes and Challenges to Integration

I described to Sara how integration is the linkage of differentiated parts—like connecting the different aspects of ourselves, or like honoring differences with another person in a relationship and then connecting with that person. And well-being emerges from integration. When our inner mental experience and our interpersonal relationships are integrated, harmony emerges. Without integration we move toward chaos or toward rigidity. Sara's "stuck" response to the prospect of Jared being away for a year was, in a sense, rigid and inflexible. What was not being integrated in Sara's life now? What was not being differentiated and linked? Sara was not letting Jared differentiate himself from her. He had his own ideas for the next step in his life journey to fully experience a year abroad, and she was fantasizing about how to join him and not allow him to have that individualized journey unfold. Sara and Jared had been very linked. Now, so early in their lives, it was time to allow more differentiation between them.

Sara had her own work to do, too. She had given up some of her friendships in order to spend more and more time with Jared. Relationships, I told Sara, are like a garden. They need tending to keep growing and thriving across time. Close relationships need devotion and dedication, yes. But they also thrive if they have the balance of differentiation and linkage. Too much of one over the other and integration is not created. You can always tell a relationship that is out of balance because one or both people appear in a repeated state

of chaos, with fits of rage. And they can reveal rigidity, too, and sometimes display a sense of enveloping boredom and loss of vitality. While all relationships meander at times toward chaos or, the seeming opposite, boredom, with integration there is a feeling of harmony and energy, openness and vitality.

I told Sara that at this stage perhaps she feared too much differentiation and losing Jared. And I explained why at their young age, the old adage "If you love someone, set them free" had special relevance.

The other issue for Sara was that her attachment system was triggered by her relationship with Jared. To a certain extent, she had been relying on him as an attachment figure, as if he were a parent and she his young child. Of course this meant that his moving away for a year was absolutely terrifying. Sara needed to learn to soothe the "younger Sara" inside her by speaking directly to that young side of herself, that young state of mind, and letting that part of herself know that everything would be okay, that she would not be ignored or forgotten. As we've seen in Mindsight Practice F in Part I, for some people placing one hand on the chest and one hand on the abdomen, applying some gentle pressure and closing the eyes, can be comforting and a source of soothing as well. This helped Sara to find a way to comfort her feelings of longing and distress and find an inner sense of peace.

Fortunately, these ideas and suggestions, as well as her past experience with practices like the Wheel of Awareness when she was anxious about leaving home for college, helped Sara a lot. She was able to face her intense fears and distress head-on and to soothe herself. She also understood that she could feel whatever she was feeling and just let that be where she was at that very moment. That's presence, and that's what created a pathway for Sara's sense of clarity and empowerment. She is currently missing Jared but not fretting over him as she has been able to find an internal balance and continues to cultivate integration in the garden of her life.

Acceptance, Letting Go of Expectations, and Sexual Orientation

As we have discussed, presence is the most fundamental gift that we can give our children in terms of creating a positive environment for them to develop and grow. One of the greatest challenges we may face in our work to stay present for our children, however, is our own expectations for them. Whether you are an outgoing parent who has a shy or introverted child, or an athletic parent who has an artistically inclined teen who steers clear of sports, this issue of how to be present for who your adolescent actually *is* creates the most important starting point for all of us as parents.

Fear and *anger* are words that don't quite describe the emotions that Andy's parents expressed to me on their first visit to my office after their fourteen-year-old son told them in our family session that he might be gay. I had been seeing Andy for issues related to anxiety and poor academic performance for over a year. Andy was a bright young eighth-grader who had come to psychotherapy at the suggestion of his school counselor and upon the insistence of his parents. Initially uninterested in being in an office with a stranger, Andy soon warmed up to the idea that he and I could just talk about whatever came to mind.

Andy and I initially spoke about his friends at school, many of whom he had known since preschool days. He, like virtually all of us, could not recall those times before elementary school very well but had a sense that he had been happy in those early years and that his life and his friendships had been "fine."

I was interested to see if Andy could tell me anything about his understanding of why he was so anxious at school. He recalled doing well in elementary school, recounting his interest in all his classes and sports and art after school. He had a love of drama and a fascination with science and seemed to be a Renaissance man, interested in many dimensions of life and excelling in lots of things. Andy was a person with deep passions about the world around him. During those earlier elementary school days, he told me, he "wasn't anxious, just happy."

When sixth grade came along, things began to change. He moved from a small local public elementary school to a much larger middle school farther from his home. He recalled making this transition without much problem, making new friends, and even continuing to do well with his classes in school. But by the middle of that year, he felt a pit in his stomach when Sunday night would come around. He began to dislike the idea of going to school, and on Monday mornings he often felt as if he was coming down with the flu or some kind of food poisoning. He felt sick to his stomach. His parents soon noticed this pattern of Monday distress, and after a few months of his grades falling and their trying to figure out with his teachers what might be going on, they followed his teachers' advice and brought him in to see me toward the end of that academic year.

My own experience of Andy during seventh grade was that his Monday morning anxiety was more about his social life than about his academics. He had continued to enjoy his classes, worked diligently to keep up with his homework and assignments, and committed himself perhaps to too many activities but ones he really enjoyed. He loved soccer, was excited about drama, loved his art classes after school, and enjoyed just being with his friends.

What slowly became clear during that seventh grade year, however, was that Andy was becoming aware of feelings inside him that were new. Like most adolescents, the physiological changes in his primary sexual organs—testicles for a boy and ovaries for a girl—gave rise to a number of secondary sexual changes. Andy's body was physically changing, and so were his internal sensations.

One day Andy described to me the feeling of being attracted to a particular player on his soccer team. While his teammates would be gawking at some of the girls' soccer team players down the field, Andy found his eyes turning toward his own teammates, and one in particular. When this direction of his attention kept happening, when feelings of interest and arousal arose inside him, he began to feel scared. He said to me that he "knew that wasn't right" but that it was simply what he felt.

Emotion is a deep process that not only gives us the subjective sense of our feelings, but also orients our attention and lets us have a felt sense of "This is important." In this way, Andy was having an emotional experience that let him know what mattered to him. He did not intentionally create this emotional response, he did not choose to focus his attention on boys or on that one boy, it was simply what his body's brain was creating inside him.

For me to help Andy's parents learn to be present for him, I needed to help them be open to what Andy was going through. While Andy's sexual maturation was happening at the same time as the majority of young people in our society, Andy was in the minority of individuals whose sexual orientation was not toward someone of the opposite gender. Andy was having sexual and romantic fantasies about other males. Decades ago, this orientation would have erroneously been called an "illness," but now we know that homosexuality is not a disorder. Just as people who are left-handed are in the minority and this is (usually nowadays) not seen as evidence of a "problem," having a sexual orientation that is in the minority does not make homosexuality a dysfunction. There are still some individuals who view homosexuality as a condition that should be altered clinically or otherwise, but these are mistaken views from a not-so-distant past. Being sexually attracted to people of your own gender is not a "condition" to be treated professionally.

So let's keep track of that as we see how Andy's parents could be present with him and who he truly is so that they can support him living as an authentic self.

Being present is what Andy's parents needed to become. Presence is a way of keeping trust alive and keeping connections strong and communication wide open. That doesn't mean becoming permissive parents, where anything goes. Authoritative parenting where structure is apparent but connection and communication are equally valued is the goal.

But Judy and Peter, Andy's parents, though they claimed to be open-minded people, were each in their own way not open to Andy's sexual orientation. As the majority of individuals in the population are heterosexual, it is understandable that, by simple statistics of probability, no parents would expect that their child would have a homosexual orientation. And this is exactly the point: To be present we need to be open to life, to be open to things occurring that are beyond what our expectations created for us. Being present enables us to become freed from the "shoulds" of life, letting go of expectations and being open to what is actually happening. In mindful awareness, we let go of expectations and are open to what is. Remember the COAL combination of curiosity, openness, acceptance, and love from our time-in practices in Mindsight Tools #2? This COAL state is the stance we take when we are present.

Presence cultivates authenticity in how we live.

Naturally we come to life with expectations. This is just the way the brain works. It is an anticipation machine, setting up from prior experiences a neurological filter that enables us to get ready for the next thing. We survive in the world because of these filters. We make sense of the world and then get ready for what the world is likely to dish up for us. That's what expectations empower us to do. But the downside of such expectations is that they can make it difficult for us to clearly see what is in front of us, or even inside us.

In simple terms, there is no such thing as "immaculate perception."

We can work on being present in an approach that lets go of our expectational mind-sets, our previously created judgments or "prejudgments," and we bring into perceptions a more direct, unfiltered input of what is. In this way, being present, learning to intentionally let go of expectations, enables us to become mindfully aware of what is happening. This is the receptive perceptual stance we can take when we are present in life.

The mind-set that a child will have a heterosexual orientation is understandable given the statistics (that is, it's more likely to be the case), but it is an innate bias, an expectation, that made it difficult for Andy's parents to see Andy for who he is. If this mental model inside them of what is expected turned into a rigid model of what "should" happen, then presence would be impaired. When we have fixed expectations, we cannot see clearly. Our prior learning (what the society and our family and our own individual experiences have taught us) can create mental models that are the perceptual filters that skew our view of present experience through a lens that biases what we see in the moment. Expectations become fixed, and mental "shoulds" distort what we are open to seeing and accepting.

Even if we think we don't have these biases and expectations, our facial expressions and tone of voice may reveal disappointment and disapproval. We as parents need to be very conscious of the depths of our responses to unexpected developments with our children so that we don't unwittingly make them feel judged, condemned, or even invisible. All of these things can inhibit our ability to be present and can threaten trust in our relationship with our child.

Studies of temperament, for example, reveal that the ultimate developmental outcome for children is not in what temperament the child has, but how accepting the parent is to that child's individual characteristics. If you feel loved for who you are as a child or adolescent by your parent (or for any of us in all of our relationships!),

you will have the foundation you need to thrive. Being seen and accepted for who you are makes you feel good about yourself and helps give you a resilient mind. Your home base is strong as a safe harbor, and your home base serves as a solid launching pad from which to move out and explore the world.

When I joined the girls' modern dance class in high school, my father was very upset. He told me that he was worried "everyone would think you are a homosexual." I asked him why that mattered, and he could only look at me with a frightened and angry look on his face. For myself, I knew that joining the class was what I wanted to do. I loved to dance, and found the activities in the boys' physical education program uninteresting. I didn't really enjoy being shoved around on the football field, even though I was one of the fastest runners at my high school and usually didn't get caught as a wide receiver. And I was short, so basketball was forever frustrating. Dance was a way to feel free, and I loved girls, and many of them were in that dance class, so it was a "no brainer" for me to transfer into that activity for my physical education requirement. It was physical, and wow, was that a great education.

I felt a deep sense of being real, of being truly myself, of being authentically there in that class. It was a powerful and life-changing step to ignore my father's reaction and my peers' expectations and simply be me.

Like my father, Andy's parents were afraid that his peers would humiliate him. But also like my father, there was something more. I asked Andy's parents what they felt about Andy's feelings of being attracted to boys, and Peter, Andy's father, had a terrified look on his face. "Being a homosexual just isn't right. There must be something wrong here . . . (long silence) . . . Those feelings just aren't okay. . . . What happened to you?" he asked Andy with a stern voice and terrified look on his face.

What "isn't okay" about having a feeling that you authentically have? Peter wasn't alone when it comes to men having what generically can be termed "homophobia"—not only a fear of others' being homosexual and of homosexuality in general, but also a fear that he himself might be gay. Some of that fear may arise from the spectrum of sexual feelings that are quite natural to have in mammalian life. Sexual urges awaken, genitals become engorged with blood, impulses and sensations emerge, behaviors to move toward individuals to whom we are attracted start to "take over" our external movements, sometimes even before we are aware of them. We can know what we feel by how our bodies behave. And for a young teen, sometimes those feelings surface for a wide range of people—same age, younger or older, same gender or different. Sexuality is a natural feeling, and the sense of attraction arises along a spectrum. Unlike our external genitals and chromosomes that are usually (there are some rare exceptions) either male or female, our sexual arousal can be generated from interacting with a wide array of individuals. That's just human nature.

Yet this uncertainty of the object of our sexual attraction can create anxiety for some people. Mindsight helps us see that this spectrum of sexual feelings is quite different from the internal—often hidden—mental model most of us have of a fixed sexual orientation. That is, many people have a belief that you should be attracted only to people of the opposite gender. The violation of this expectation can agitate some people. In fact, having sexual arousal toward someone of the same gender can create panic. And having sexual arousal toward people of both genders can be befuddling. I have met many patients whose natural spectrum of their own feelings freaks them out. They "clamp down" on their own inner experience in order to conform to the mental model they've learned from family and society that says boys like girls and girls like boys. No exceptions to this rule. Period.

We've seen that a violation of expectation can create profound anxiety and a cascade of internal and external reactions. The internal reactions to such a violation can include shutting down freedom of feeling, creating a cascade of thought processes that condemn such ambiguity of feelings in the self and others, and even a deep fear re-action that becomes a complex web of anger toward anyone else who may evoke such a spectrum of sexual feelings within the person. You can imagine perhaps how such internal reactions are an attempt of the mind to reduce the anxiety of uncertainty. But the irony is that the rigid response to such initial chaotic reactions to a natural spec-trum of feelings also shuts the individual into a prison of their own making.

Anger "projected outward" onto others who show a deviation from the societal norm is a primitive defense that is an ineffective and sometimes violent attempt to shut down awareness of the initial spectrum of internal feelings that created the now forgotten anxiety. That anxiety may have been about one's own internal experience and identity. For some, the initiating anxiety may be simply about not knowing what to do with those feelings. Fantasies, dreams, bodily sensations, and impulses directed toward same-gender people may evoke confusion, anxiety, and fear. Rather than simply feeling these feelings, there is a set of reactions against having them. These unexpected and therefore uncomfortable feelings can be "defended" against by being shifted into outward directed emotions and behav-iors: fear of others' homosexual feelings, not one's own; anger toward others' homosexuality, not one's own. These projected feelings and reactions are often so automatic that the projecting individual has no conscious idea that such homophobic reactivity is coming from their own inner sense of vulnerability. Quite the contrary, being aware of one's own vulnerability is often the last thing on the angry, fearful person's mind.

With all of these possibilities in mind, I gently tried to align myself with Peter's experience. I had to be present with him, to be open to what his experience was right at that moment in time. With Andy's permission (and relief), I took some time alone with Peter and Andy's mom, Judy, to help give them all the space away from one another they needed to explore some of these issues and whatever might be going on in each of them.

Judy was able to state that she herself was mostly frightened of AIDS and the social exclusion Andy might experience by being gay. Her fears were quite understandable, and as we discussed together the notion that "being gay" was not a choice but a biological reality, she was able to sense that the work she needed to do was to embrace these challenges of his new reality. She still felt scared, scared that he could get ill or be ostracized, but she was open to the fundamental idea that what Andy really needed was her love and support. This love could be expressed by her learning to be present for him—to be curious, open, accepting, and loving.

Peter listened to this discussion silently, his face appearing terrified as we spoke. As the conversation turned toward him, his fear quickly mutated into fury. At first he blamed Judy for being "too doting" over Andy when he was a baby. Then he turned his anger toward me, saying that "therapy brainwashes people" and that I failed to help Andy by making him "too soft" with this "therapy crap" and that I pushed him toward this "gay stuff." As Judy and I let him express his viewpoints, Peter said that this was the "worst thing that could have happened to him."

As a therapist, part of the challenge is to blend the need to give people the space to find out their own inner truths with the need to

A worthy distinction

—rusty wells

clarify what is scientifically known about how we develop. I acknowledged to Peter and Judy that there is indeed a "controversy" in this and many other fields. I let them know that some small group of therapists would try to convince Andy that he is not gay. I invited them to find such therapists if they wanted to. But in my scientific and clinical opinion, research and experience suggested instead the approach that people should be given the support to discover who they actually are. I talked to them about the spectrum of feelings and the need to explore those sensations in a safe way so that both the body and the mind remain healthy. When a family pushes for only one set of feelings or identities to be "permissible," authentic feelings and identifications simply go underground, they don't disappear. I talked to them more about presence and Andy's need to feel their acceptance and support. Knowing that Andy was my primary patient and that I wouldn't have much time with his parents beyond a session or two, I then brought up the possible source of Peter's fury.

What amazed me about that extended session was that by using mindsight skills of seeing the inner world of self and others with more stability, Peter's response was actually quite open. We did some breath-awareness practices to let them simply be with their own internal world. And then we let whatever feelings and concerns that were there simply be expressed and explored. Perhaps it was Judy's readiness to help him change, perhaps it was the sense of inevitability of Andy's identity, and perhaps it was his true love for his son and family that contributed to the opening of Peter's mind. Whatever elements, the time felt right and we dove in.

By examining the general issues—the ways the brain works and how relationships support the emergence of our minds—we could then focus on the specifics with a neutrality that was a crucial starting place. This was no longer just about Andy or their family, it was about being human. Embracing the universal is a part of self-compassion, as researchers like Kristin Neff define it. We see that we are not alone, that we are a part of a larger, universal human drama. Being compassionate to ourselves also comes along with being present and mindful of the moment, as well as being kind to ourselves and being gentle and caring.

As mentioned earlier, kindness can be seen as the way we are supportive and honoring of one another's vulnerability. So my whole inner intention was to be kind. Now in many ways, integration made visible is kindness and compassion. So to promote integration, I needed to empower Andy's parents to explore their own differentiated views, and then to help them link to Andy's experience.

To be supportive of Peter's mind, to let him be differentiated in our session, I needed to suspend my own judgments and expectations of "how a father should be" and instead embrace exactly where he was. I needed to know my own inner mental sea, to differentiate myself, and so I reflected within myself on the experiences I have had, including the journey through girls' dance and my father's fearful reactions to that, even before the days of AIDS. With that inner knowing open in myself, I could be ready to be open to Peter's inner mental sea.

I remembered then what you and I have been reviewing in our conversation of the fundamental stance we can take: Chaos and rigidity emerge from impairments to integration. When we are integrated, we are in harmony. When we are not integrated, we are in states of chaos (wild, unpredictable) or rigidity (stuck, paralyzed, unchanging). Peter's response to Andy's experience was to become both rigid and chaotic. He was clearly not in an open state of presence, not in a state of integration. My goal needed to be open to where he was, and then to help him see a way to move toward a more integrated way of being himself.

With all of this in mind, my intention was to simply use mindsight to be present with Peter, attune to his inner experience, resonate with those inner states within myself, and then allow trust to emerge naturally. Remember that mindsight has these three components of seeing inside yourself, seeing inside another, and promoting integration. Mindsight is what I could offer to Andy's family, and it is what any parent can cultivate with their adolescent. And naturally, it is what an adolescent can learn to do with others as well.

Peter struggled mightily with his own fears and his own memories of being a young boy in the competitive, sports-focused world of his family. His father had particularly emphasized his three sons' participation in contact sports, especially football. As we gave Peter the space in the session to speak the truth, his truth, of his own upbringing, he then could move toward finding a new way of approaching his son. The idea in my mind was to be present and enable differentiation to flourish before we might move on to the linkage that Andy so desperately needed at this vulnerable time with his family.

It was tentative at first, but you could see the love both parents had for Andy shining through when we had our next session with the three of them together. Peter told Andy that he was trying to be open to what he was saying, open to who he was, and that he understood Andy was just "being himself" and that he would stand by his side. There was a moment of silence that just hung in the air, unmoving, and then Peter got up and walked over to Andy's chair and without a pause Andy rose and the two hugged each other in an embrace that felt suspended in time. Peter told Andy that he would do his best to be the father Andy deserved.

None of us knew exactly where Andy's life would go, but setting up this presence of his parents was a crucial step for him to feel em-

Building Trust

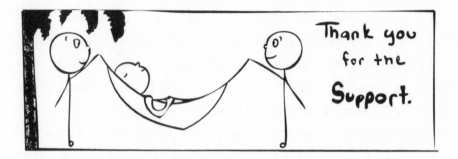

powered to become the most fulfilled and free, to become the most authentic Andy that he could become.

Time has unfolded well for Andy in the years since those initial sessions. I feel deeply grateful that Peter and Judy were able to open their minds to seeing Andy for who he was at that time and for his courage to continue to become the wonderful human being that he is. Andy is supported in his childhood home by his loving parents, and that has made all the difference in his rewarding and authentic life.

Drug Use or Abuse?

One of the greatest challenges for adolescents and their families can be the potential for the use of mind-altering chemicals, which include alcohol and other recreational drugs. Staying present as a parent in the face of an adolescent's drug involvement can be difficult, especially if you think that this use is a form of abuse or addiction. For adolescents, while it may feel very common and therefore "safe" to be involved with drugs, it is important to acknowledge that drug use can lead to powerful changes in your internal experience and social relationships. If your own activity with mind-altering substances feels like it is becoming something that is controlling you rather than your controlling it, understanding these issues can be essential. In order to stay fully present for the meaning of drugs in your life so that you can make decisions that are best for your own well-being, having some of the basic facts about the brain and drug use is crucial. While these facts could occupy an entire book, here I'll present a fundamental framework that I hope will put drug use in perspective.

As the drive to explore new ways of experiencing reality emerges during adolescence, the use of drugs that alter brain function can be very intriguing. We all have differing emotional reactions to drug use, from excitement and interest to fear and repulsion. Whatever the science or the laws are about using substances that alter our mental state, adults and adolescents alike may use various ingested and inhaled chemicals to alter their experience of consciousness, including alcohol and marijuana, psychedelic mushrooms and cocaine.

There are at least four fundamental drives that can motivate our increased use of drugs during the adolescent period. These include experimentation, social connection, self-medication, and addiction. Let's review each of these in turn so we can understand how the use of mind-altering substances may affect our adolescent growth and social life, now and for our life in the future.

Alcohol is a common drug used legally by adults and illegally by individuals under legislated minimum ages. For an adolescent whose dopamine release is already revved up, drugs, including alcohol, that directly increase the release of this transmitter create an especially challenging mix of drug-enhanced dopamine levels on top of an already activated adolescent dopamine system. In other words, adolescence is a period not only of drug experimentation to explore novelty, but also of vulnerability to becoming physiologically drawn to using and becoming addicted to alcohol and other drugs.

As discussed in Part II, the dopamine system is more reactive in a teen, with heightened release that drives our reward and sensation-seeking behaviors. Even in the face of this enhanced release, as mentioned earlier, the baseline levels of dopamine during adolescence are actually *lower.* What this means is that teens may be prone to feeling "bored" unless they are engaging in novelty-seeking behaviors. An adolescent's dopamine profile has lower troughs, higher peaks. That's the activated reward system of the adolescent brain and one source of the lows and highs of the adolescent mind. So when we realize that many drugs are chemicals that increase dopamine release, we can see how such substances would be attractive to raise ourselves out of the boredom of a trough. That's just the nature of adolescence that may make us especially prone at this time to use dopamine-enhancing substances.

We've seen that adolescence is a time of experimentation, of trying new things. So the drive to alter consciousness and experience new ways of perceiving and feeling and thinking is a natural outcome of a push for novelty and the experience of new sensations. Novelty itself is rewarding and also activates our dopamine release. One aspect of this experimentation is simply to try something new. Another dimension is to widen our understanding of reality by altering the usual patterns of perception that shape our commonly held views of reality. This is sometimes referred to as an exploration of consciousness or a spiritual search and may involve psychedelic drugs such as peyote or psilocybin, which have been used for thousands of years in various cultures. Some drugs used for the purpose of altering consciousness do not involve dopamine, and because of this they may influence a person's life but not be addictive. This drive to expand consciousness and see life with new eyes is important for some drug users, adolescent or adults, but for others it is merely a drive to experience something new without a search to understanding new meanings of life.

Experimentation with novelty is likely a prime reason why a majority of teens have been found to use mind-altering substances no matter what their parents may think or have as rules of the house. Parents of high school students are often surprised at surveys revealing that the majority of the juniors and seniors in high school have used alcohol and marijuana. It is important for adults to realize that this "norm" of teenage life does not make it right or permissible; it does not make it safe or legal; it simply makes it very likely that it is happening. To deny such a reality as parents is to put our heads in the sand. It's also important to remember that how we approach this aspect of our teen's life will shape our relationship with our child for the years ahead.

The experimental aspect of the use of alcohol can be an important dimension that drives an initial interest in drinking and getting drunk. For some, there can be the emergence of an intense interest in using alcohol in one's social life. Recall from the story of Katey, in Part II, that drinking alcohol became an important part of her life and motivated her to make decisions that got her expelled from high school. Katey's drinking had also become a central part of her social life, a way she connected with friends and organized her relationships. But in the setting of group alcohol use, the tendency to engage in binge drinking, consuming large amounts of alcohol in short amounts of time, is an especially risky behavior adolescents may be prone to engage in. From the social point of view, it is a group activity, done with a sense of camaraderie and of accomplishment—who can consume the most booze? From the mind point of view, the decision to limit intake depends on executive functions that become suspended after a couple of drinks. And from the brain development perspective, alcohol poisoning has been clearly demonstrated to kill brain cells and their connections, especially in regions that control attention and memory. Repeated bingeing damages the brain.

Group binge behavior reveals the second major reason people use drugs: to be part of a common social fabric, part of a shared experience. In some social circles and in certain social settings such as parties or concerts, drinking alcohol or smoking marijuana may be an expected behavior. The lowering of social anxiety and the lowering of defenses make many people feel more at ease in social settings, and so these drugs are used as a "social lubricant" that facilitates communication. While Katey didn't feel nervous in social situations, she did enjoy the "fun in getting smashed" with her friends. She enjoyed the shared experience and always drank with someone, never by herself. At least that was true while she was in high school.

A third drive for drug use is in its role as self-medication for a primary psychiatric condition or a painful situation. For example, someone with depression may feel so down in the dumps that she wants to "go numb" by frequently using alcohol or she may get herself "revved up" by using amphetamines. Someone with mania as a part of manic-depressive or bipolar illness might use alcohol or barbiturates to slow himself down. A person with schizophrenia might use alcohol to quiet the hallucinations and delusions that are terrifying for him. For others with attention deficit difficulties, the use of stimulants may temporarily increase the focus of sustained attention. And for individuals with social anxiety, taking alcohol may decrease their concerns in social situations, whereas smoking marijuana may inadvertently lead to an increase in their panic. Katey did not have any of these underlying psychiatric conditions, and it did not appear that she was treating any post-traumatic symptoms with alcohol use. It's crucial to be sure that alcohol or street drugs are not being used to treat some underlying challenge to an individual's mental health. Katey was not self-medicating as far as I could tell.

A fourth drive involved in drug use, one that can emerge after drug use begins, is addiction. Katey showed some early signs that were of concern to me regarding her becoming addicted to alcohol, as she needed to use increasing amounts of alcohol to get a "buzz," a state of mind she began to crave. This need to increase the amount of an ingested substance to achieve a certain effect may have been a sign of her developing tolerance to the drug, possibly because her brain was getting used to it or her liver was more rapidly metabolizing it. Tolerance isn't necessary for addiction, but it can be present and be an important sign of a larger issue unfolding. Katey also became obsessed with the use of alcohol in ways that felt more like an addiction than just a pastime interest or a part of her social life. She seemed to have a craving that was more than simply an enjoyment; it had the quality of withdrawal from the alcohol. This made me concerned that an addiction was developing in her. We began to discuss whether her preoccupation with alcohol and bringing the liquor to the party that got her expelled from school was more than just "being a teenager," as she had suggested. When I asked her at the time she just shrugged her shoulders and said, "I don't know . . . but I don't think so."

Addictive substances and addictive behaviors, like shopping or gambling, involve the reward circuit's major transmitter, dopamine. As we've seen, this is the transmitter that is already revved up in its reactivity in adolescence. Dopamine is released from a brain stem– related area, the nucleus accumbens, and influences our limbic emotional, motivational, evaluative, and memory systems, and even pushes up into our cortex to influence our thinking, decision making, and behaviors. Alcohol can activate the dopamine system in anyone, leading to surges in this reward-based brain chemical.

Beyond stimulating a dopamine surge that is especially intense in adolescents, alcohol and other drugs have an impact on the way our minds see reality, as they dampen cortical functioning and alter our conscious experience of the world. Substances that alter our state of mind also alter our capacity to responsibly manage a large vehicle as it hurls through space, or manage our own body as our consciousness fails to keep us alert. Some substances, too, especially if taken in excess or in combination with other substances, can kill you. I have two friends who lost an adolescent son and daughter because of such experimental excesses, one in a fatal car accident, the other breathing in her vomit and dying alone in her college dormitory room.

So when adults get agitated about substance use, adolescents should keep in mind that the adults may naturally be concerned about their safety. One approach is to insist on total avoidance of such substances, a position many parents like Katey's and her high school took. From the adolescents' perspective, such a policy may make no sense and seem unrealistic, rigid, and unfair. Other parents take the position that if teens are going to participate in such activities, using substances that alter their state of mind, they should do so in a responsible way. The hopeful aim of such a policy is to save lives. "Call if you need a ride home, no questions asked." "Learn to use alcohol in moderation." "Avoid mixing substances." Helping kids manage their drug-related activities, so that when they are out of the house they don't' "go wild with the freedom they've been waiting to have" and drink themselves into oblivion, can be a crucial first step in helping adolescents navigate this challenging terrain.

Addressing the possibility of addiction at this time in life is important. Adolescence is a period of great risk for not only using mind-altering drugs but also abusing them and becoming addicted to them. As adolescents we begin to experiment with many drugs that activate the dopamine system, and it is during our adolescent period that the brain is most sensitive to becoming addicted to a substance. Our changing adolescent brain is especially vulnerable to respond to drug use with the onset of a cascade of behavioral and physiological responses that can contribute to addiction. Such vulnerability to addiction is due to both the activation of certain genes and the altering of neural functioning, making the dopamine release dependent on drug use. The earlier in adolescence we are exposed to alcohol and drugs, the more likely we are to develop an addiction.

Think of it this way. Addiction is where we get used to the dopamine surge an activity or substance creates in the brain stem and limbic regions that pushes our cortex to make decisions regarding our behavior to continue to do things that may be destructive to us. In fact, a simple way of defining an addiction is when people continue to do something that is destructive even after they know it is hurting their life. The boundary between drug abuse and addiction can be quite hazy.

In Katey's situation she was discovering that she could not stop drinking, even after that party and her expulsion. And she could not stop drinking after just one drink, either. It is true that once you are intoxicated, the very prefrontal regions that would help you decide to stop drinking go off-line. Even one drink, for some individuals, can create sudden and intense shifts in judgment—like the discerning judgment not to drive a car while intoxicated. For some, just one drink can change their personality, and they may not even remember what happened to them. Others can experience a blackout after a lot of drinking. This is different from passing out in that when you are in a blackout, you are aware, more or less, of what is happening. But while you were drinking, your limbic memory region, the hippocampus, had so shut down that, afterward you simply don't recall what happened to you.

Even when Katey was not actively under alcohol's direct effects, alcohol was still influencing her life during high school. She didn't have blackouts, she could "hold her liquor," and she didn't drink alone. Yet Katey's interest in alcohol felt like something more than just an interest in exploring other states of consciousness with her friends; it was more than experimental and more than social.

There was something in the way she talked about getting "smashed" that had the sense of some intense dopamine-driven-reward circuit speaking through her. She was intensely focused on alcohol and its effects on her life. For some individuals who experiment with drugs and alcohol to alter their state of mind temporarily, such dopamine-surge-driven behaviors lead to an alteration in their lives in long-term ways.

Some studies suggest that in those at risk, and especially during our adolescent period, a gene inside our brain's motivational circuitry is activated when a particular substance is ingested. Once this gene activation occurs, the dopamine circuit locks on to a certain "substance of choice" and an intense focus of attention, thought, energy, and behavior is directed to the substance. Alcohol, cocaine, amphetamines, barbiturates, and heroin can all activate that circuit. Rats given cocaine, for example, will choose that dopamine-stimulating drug over food and then die of starvation. With people, studies reveal that this dopamine surge is released not only when *taking* the substance but even when *planning* to take it, when *thinking* about it, when being around people with whom it has been taken, when in similar rooms where it was taken, when getting ready to take it. In short, the intense release of dopamine, which gives you the feeling of urge and the drive for reward, occurs both with the ingestion and with the intention behind use of that substance.

That's the cycle of addiction.

The broader story of the role dopamine plays in our lives goes like this. When we work hard at something and finally finish it, like writing an essay or a book, creating a painting, learning a piece of music, constructing a model airplane, practicing a sport, or going for a long hike, dopamine rises and that disciplined effort is rewarded. There is no sudden peak, no dopamine surge, but there is a gradual rise in dopamine levels above baseline that gives us a feeling of deep satisfaction, a fullness, a pride in our accomplishment. We get lost in the flow of something we love, and we get pleasure in doing it. That flow is how we lose ourselves in an activity and become at peace and content in our experience. Different people have flow in different activities. The key is to discover what our own particular passions are and cultivate them in our lives. We can enjoy an experience of flow and that feeling of a job well done, of hard work completed, of an accomplishment well earned.

When a substance or behavior of addiction happens in those at risk, then there is a surge in dopamine that feels thrilling and compelling and good and rewarding and something that needs to be repeated, and repeated soon. Not all of us may become addicted, but some of us will with exposure, especially with early exposure. With the precipitous drop from the surge's peak, we have a relative plummet in our dopamine levels, and after a while this drop feels really bad. We've gotten used to the dopamine thrill of the peak, and we've become bored with the dopamine trough. And boring becomes so dull and painful in contrast to the surging peak that we need to repeat the dopamine surge-releasing behavior soon, like very soon, like now. Given that the adolescent trough is already low, we can see how this period of time may be especially vulnerable to developing an addiction to the surging dopamine peaks.

Research reveals, as mentioned earlier, that even anticipating and planning for the act of ingesting a drug captures our intentions and focus on the addiction, and these mental processes themselves release the dopamine surge. It's not just the drug's ingestion. It's imagining the drug and the ingestion of it. What this means is that addiction is a life-consuming challenge, not just something we do because we are choosing it. Once a substance becomes an addiction and not just an experimentation we choose to do, the addiction is in charge. But even if we don't get addicted to a drug, studies show that chronic use of a substance like alcohol, for example, can damage the liver and damage the brain.

When we think of Katey's description of her planning, we realize that the excitement and the thrill that felt compelling to Katey may have been more than simply adolescent hyperrationality with dopamine-driven reward amplification. Naturally, Katey is a teen, and so these elements were there. But could it be that this focus on alcohol was also further amplifying the PROS of her dopamine drive because she had inherited her family's legacy of addiction, which included alcoholism?

There is no specific test for that possibility at this point, but I brought it up with Katey and we discussed the issue, and we discussed her lack of concern about it. All we could do at that moment was raise her awareness about addiction as a possibility beyond adolescent experimentation. And this awareness was exactly what she had been missing before her expulsion. That risk of addiction, like all the other cons her mind was minimizing, was just filed away as not that important even as we did our work at the end of high school. She continued to drink at parties during her senior year. All I could do was to help her become more and more aware of herself as the year went on. I was in the role of the non-parental adult who could support her during this period of her life, helping her get ready to carry this new self-awareness with her as she left the safe harbor of her home.

Katey was developing a new sense of herself, one with a great sense of humor, and one with an understanding of who she was and who she could become, even as her drinking continued. Knowing that those reflections emerge from the integrative prefrontal regions of her brain helped me feel as if we were building the important skills of self-awareness that could continue to develop in the months ahead.

Just before she went off to college, Katey was doing pretty well and was ready to stop therapy. At that point she was aware that her use of alcohol might become an issue in her life and what it might mean in the long run if she ended up being consumed by her drinking. I saw Katey periodically during her first year of college. It took several reminders in the course of her active social life, with its many forays into binge drinking during this freshman year, for Katey to discover and admit to herself that she likely had a serious problem with alcohol abuse, and possibly even addiction. When she told me she was having blackouts, that she could not remember things that happened at parties when she had been drinking, and that she had started drinking by herself before she went out, we both knew it was time to consider a different strategy for her life.

Katey is in the midst of trying to stop drinking, at least for now. I've told her that research suggests working with a twelve-step program, like Alcoholics Anonymous, would be the most helpful and effective way to support her efforts to stay sober. But at this point, she says she is reluctant to participate in "something as ridiculous as that." Even the notion of seeing alcohol as a food allergy, like something she just shouldn't eat, seemed "dumb." Time will tell how she'll hold out, and how she'll let her brain recover from the continual dopamine-surging alcohol bath that she's soaked it in over this past year and a half since her expulsion from school. That's a brain, Katey admitted to me, that's gotten "really used to partying hard." That's a brain, too, I told her, that needs a break to think clearly. We've talked to each other on and off over these last few months, and Katey told me recently that she feels challenged by not drinking but is trying to find new ways of focusing her mind during parties and when out with friends in other settings.

What I really needed to have Katey learn is a way to focus her attention to integrate her brain and give her the strength to calm her cravings and clear her mind. Those are skills she should learn to increase her self-awareness and reclaim her life. As with Sara, I've encouraged Katey to take on the mindsight tools we've been learning here. We'll see if she's open to strengthening her mind and integrating her life from the inside out. But with this particular challenge, if she could also find support in a group like Alcoholics Anonymous, it would be great—if she would just go. Let's keep our hopes up that she'll be open to these known ways to improve her life. I know her parents are trying their best to support her, but we all know that at this point it is up to Katey to take the initiative to empower her life.

Returning Home: Reflection, Realignment, and Repairing Ruptures

Moving out of the house is a change and challenge, a powerful transition for adolescent and adult alike. After moving away, many adolescents find themselves coming back home for extended periods of time before they establish their own financially independent lives. In the United States in recent times, one-third to one-half of "grown children" move back in with their parents. This trend is influenced by our stressful financial times, so living at home saves money. But this trend also has its emotional side, in which parents and the parental home provide needed support during this period of stressful transition and employment uncertainty. The emotional impact of older adolescents' returning home needs to be addressed directly and reflected upon internally for this period of time to go well for all concerned.

This returning home has its own challenges for all of us. Whichever side of the generational divide you may find yourself on now, I invite you to try applying your mindsight skills to understanding the experience of both the adult and the adolescent in the following story.

"If you don't like the rules of the house, you can go out and find a job, earn some money, and move into your own apartment."

How many times have these words been said from a frustrated parent to an assertive adolescent? When things arrive at this point in a relationship between a parent and an older adolescent, it doesn't feel good for anyone. I know because I said these very words to my son in a moment of intense frustration and irritation. My saying them was heavy-handed, and as they came out of my mouth I already felt bad in my heart. My son had just graduated from college. He, like many his age, had come back home following his four years away. His plans were uncertain: He might be with us for just a few months over the course of the summer and then start his career in Southern California, or he might move back up to Northern California where he'd gone to college and start his work there. We had all been getting along very well, having meals together, going for walks, watching television, going to concerts. It was, in so many ways, quite wonderful. But a number of times when my wife and I came home, the place was a bit of a mess. It was probably cleaner than his cooperative housing at school, but for us, it was a mess. Pots from morning breakfast were still on the stove, unmoved. Plates filled with food were strewn around the counter; pieces of vegetables and other reminders of earlier meals lay on the floor.

In all honesty, the place was cleaner than when I was there on my own, when my wife was traveling and I was a bachelor "empty nester," with our daughter away for her first year of college. But when I came in from walking the dogs and heard my son say to his mom that it wasn't a big deal to have some plates around, I immediately felt frustrated.

I had learned long ago that life goes well in our household when our cleanliness standards were based on the "highest" expectation of each individual sharing the space. My standards are quite low, I'll admit, and my wife's are high. And we've worked out that tension, or continue to try to work it out, in a way that I think works well for us in our partnership in life. So when our son was, in my view, talking back to my life partner, I found myself getting protective of her. A twenty-two-year-old male back at home can be like a young wolf returning to the pack he'd left, and my alpha male wolf hackles were raised when this young wolf was "threatening" the alpha female of our den. That's the backstory happening deep in my limbic-thumb and brain stem–palm areas. In my cortex-fingers I said to myself, "Don't gang up on him—she can state for herself the case for needing him to clean up after himself. Don't double up on him!"

However, that very morning my wife had given our son a polite but clear talk about our standards of clean and asked him to respect those values. So when we'd come home after a night out and found stuff still around from the morning, it was frustrating. Before I'd left to walk the dogs, my wife and I saw the mess and reflected with each other on what it was like to have a college graduate back at home, about how we'd have to work out some new rules, some new ways of all getting along after his years of living without our oversight. My son and his friends must have come in while I was out with the dogs. My wife and I had agreed earlier not to just blurt out demands but to take a more sensitive approach with our son. At that moment as I stood in the kitchen, it was like saying to myself "Don't think of a pink elephant" and being able to think only of that pink elephant. When the brain is given instructions to be sure *not* to do something, it keeps on checking that thing to keep an "eye" on it. That tracking just primes the thing, making it more likely to be activated. So out of my mouth came some words I shouldn't have said about his needing to clean up, and then when he said that it was not really a big deal to leave a few cups and plates around, I became frustrated. "Look," I told him, "you are back from college and this can happen. You've been living on your own, and with your own rules. And we have *our own* standards. So understandably you may see things differently than we do. But here's the deal: This is our house, not yours. And these are our rules. If you want to live here, you'll need to respect our requests." And then I said those words about his getting his own apartment.

Now, you may be thinking that all this sounds fine. If you are an adult reading this you may feel that way, but as an adolescent reading this you may not. I don't know. But *I* felt terrible right away. That evening I felt heavy and drained and irritated with myself. It wasn't so much about the issue of rules and cleanliness, it was the proclamation that this was not his home. That was just plain insensitive and over the top. It was just wrong. The economy is tough, unemployment is high, college graduates abound, he works hard, and the fact is, this is his home, too. The next morning and throughout the day at work, I couldn't stop thinking about what was really going on inside me that got me to say the part about this not being his home. Why had I gotten so mad *so* fast?

When I came home from work that next day, my son and I had a big discussion about what it was like to be at his stage of life, twenty-two years old and transitioning from college to working life, about going from being a kid at home to an adult in the world.

I apologized for what I had said: "This *is* in fact *your* home. I am sorry for what I said. Yes, you need to keep the place clean, but I was out of line to tell you to go out and get your own apartment. You may want to do that in the future, but you have just graduated after four long hardworking years at school, and I shouldn't have said something so harsh." He thanked me for the apology, and said that he felt that I was probably irritated by something else going on in my own life.

That's mindsight in action. He was right . . . and that something else is what I needed to reflect upon. Our experiences with our attachment figures, our parents, can affect us even as we are parents ourselves. Making sense of those experiences helps us become more present, more self-aware, and better able to connect with others. I had to reflect on my own internal meanings of this period of life so that I could remain present with him as we all moved along on this life journey.

This brief story brings up a number of issues at the heart of adolescence and life in general. One is that sometimes as parents we do things that create a rupture in a close connection. It is our duty to reflect on such ruptures and make the efforts to make a repair, to reconnect after we've apologized for our contribution to conflict. A second lesson is that sometimes we do things that we don't really want to do. The brain has the higher, prefrontal part that helps us be aware of things and creates conscious intentions. But sometimes the lower limbic, brain stem, and bodily areas directly influence our behaviors, motivating our actions and filling them with feelings that shape our non-verbal tone of voice, timings, and facial expressions without the intervening prefrontal inhibition or filtering.

In this case, the output of my using words with him was pretty mild, but sometimes, as we've seen, we can flip our lids and go down the low road with more force. In some of my other books (in *Mindsight*, the chapter "Crepes of Wrath," and in *Parenting from the Inside Out*, the section on the Low Road), the importance of rupture and repair is explored in detail regarding younger kids, including my own. So my son has grown up knowing that if there is a rupture, there ought to be a repair. That's how we can acknowledge that there is no such thing as a perfect way of behaving in a relationship, which is simply the mindsightful way of recognizing when a rupture has occurred and making efforts to reconnect in the repair. But let me say here that being reflective is essential to repair ruptures with those we care about at any age. We've practiced repair in the Mindsight Tools #3, and making a reconnection is crucial at any age. During adolescence, it is a central theme of this period to maintain open lines of communication, especially when the inevitable ruptures in that connection occur. The changes and challenges of this period make it imperative that we work on our own self-understanding as parents and work on repairing ruptures when they inevitably occur. I had to examine my protective stance toward my wife in response to what our son was doing. And I had to reflect on what went on at home when I was an older adolescent, too. So looking upon ruptures as opportunities to reflect internally and then connect interpersonally again, to create integration when integration is broken, is a helpful inner stance to take. My hope was that my son would be able to forgive me, and to experience my apology as an example of how to respond in the face of conflict.

Since this experience, our connection has been really strong. Mindsight gives us the way to be open to our inner lives and maintain an empathic connection with those we care about. Even when our outward behaviors make a rupture in our communication, mindsight can guide us back to connection. It is through the full spectrum of these mindsight moments that our relationships can truly be integrative, honoring differences and cultivating compassionate connections. I love the ways my son and I can communicate with each other now as he moves through his later adolescent years; our connection grows deeper and stronger the older he becomes. Having the notion of staying present through these many changes in his life and the challenges that they have raised has been a guiding principle for us all. Using the power of mindsight's reflective conversations also gives us a basic tool, an essential way to connect around things that really matter, that makes the way we relate to each other have a deep and authentic quality and makes these challenging moments truly opportunities to deepen our connections with one another.

MINDSIGHT TOOLS #4

■

The Mindsight Simple Seven

In this tools section, I'd like to introduce you to seven activities you can do on a daily basis that are scientifically proven to keep your body healthy, your mind strong, and your brain continuing to grow in integrative ways throughout your life. Research into the brain's ability to change and develop in response to experience, what is referred to as "neuroplasticity," reveals that regular practice of these activities can activate the growth of neural connections, and even new neurons. As you may have noticed by now, I like to enlist acronyms to help readers (and myself!) remember important concepts with regard to how our brains and emotional worlds work. In this spirit, I offer here SNAG—*stimulate neuronal activation and growth*. Scientific investigations have shown that when we do the seven activities that follow, we SNAG the brain toward growth, and that growth is often in the direction of integration. I put these seven processes in a visual image with a colleague, David Rock, at the time the United States Department of Agriculture was putting out a new set of suggestions in the form of a food plate revealing what were the recommended daily food groups to keep the body healthy. David and I thought it might be useful to make the same kind of plate for the mind, which we call "The Healthy Mind Platter," a set of seven activities that promote optimal brain matter.

The Healthy Mind Platter

The Healthy Mind Platter for Optimal Brain Matter™

MINDSIGHT PRACTICE A: Time-In

You'll see that these seven include time-in, which we've explored in depth in Mindsight Tools #2. Time-in is how we reflect on the inner nature of our mental lives and our bodily sensations. It enables us to perceive our feelings, thoughts, memories, and beliefs, and our intentions, hopes, dreams, attitudes, and longings. Time-in practiced on a regular basis has been shown to stimulate the growth of many fibers in the brain, especially the integrative ones that help regulate attention, emotion, and thinking. It also improves empathy and compassion.

Taking time-in means reflecting on your inner world. A simple way to do this is to SIFT the mind, paying attention to your sensations, images, feelings, and thoughts. You can go to my website, DrDanSiegel.com, and explore the breath awareness practice for a simple mindfulness exercise. And if after strengthening your ability to focus your attention for a few weeks, you are ready for something a little more comprehensive that integrates your consciousness, try out the Wheel of

I'm investing in myself.

Awareness practice, too. These are all various ways of giving yourself a time-in that supports the growth of your brain and the well-being of your mind. It's not bad for your relationships, either!

Amazingly, the mindful awareness of time-in that supports your being present for whatever arises in your life also helps to increase your levels of the enzyme telomerase, which repairs and maintains the ends of your chromosomes that help keep your individual cells alive and healthy. That's not a joke—taking time-in makes your cells healthier! In addition, your immune system will function better and you'll have more energy, and even develop a more resilient way of approaching life's challenges because of specific ways your brain will change. Not bad for a simple daily practice of taking time-in and reflecting on the inner world!

MINDSIGHT PRACTICE B: Sleep Time

Another daily activity that has been shown to increase the way your brain continues to grow in an integrative way is the time you sleep. In our modern times, digital displays and electrical lights keep us stimulated and awake long after we'd naturally be falling asleep. Since the time we need to wake up in the morning does not change much, this means that we will be getting less sleep than we may need for optimal brain growth. When you add to that the reality that the teenage brain's cycle of waking and sleeping is on a different schedule than adults or children, with staying up later being a natural outcome for many adolescents, the early time of school makes this setup a chronic source of not getting enough sleep.

Think of the following amounts as a ballpark starting point for thinking about your own sleep hygiene. According to the United States National Sleep Foundation, most teens need about eight and a half to nine and a quarter hours and most adults need seven to nine hours of sleep each night. When I write the word *need*, what I mean is that for optimal brain growth, for optimal memory consolidation of the day's learning, for optimal insulin function and food metabolism to keep fit, for optimal immune function to fight off disease, for optimal response to stress to deal with life's hassles, and for optimal mental functioning with effective abilities for focusing attention, thinking, remembering, problem solving, handling your emotions, and connecting with others in relationships, you need at least the lesser amount of your range of sleep. How much uninterrupted sleep a night are you getting?

Without adequate sleep, each of these important neural, physiological, and mental processes is in jeopardy of not functioning well. What's the outcome of inadequate amounts and quality of sleep? The brain doesn't grow well, memory is not consolidated and you don't remember what you learned, insulin doesn't work right and becoming overweight is more likely, stress hormones rise and make you feel lousy, immune functions don't work well and you can get sick more easily, and your mind won't be as sharp for paying attention, thinking, and problem solving. Plus you may simply have less energy, feel bad, become irritable more easily, and get frustrated with others more frequently. In short, you can become moody and not much fun to be around. You may come to feel out of sorts and not even realize that this state of being is because of your sleep habits.

The great news is that you are in control of your sleeping.

Here is a list of simple daily sleep habits you can practice that will help you get enough sleep soundly throughout the night:

1. Turn off digital objects and electronic screens at least an hour before you go to bed. These objects—computers, smartphones, televisions—keep your brain thinking it should be wide awake.

2. If you have trouble falling asleep, try turning down the lights a bit in the half-hour before you get into bed.

3. Try not to do work or homework in bed. The bed should be for restful activities, not associated with working.

4. Be mindful that caffeine in soda, coffee, or tea can keep some people up at night. This also includes chocolate, unfortunately. So watch when you drink and eat these substances, and make sure you are not consuming too much overall or too late in the day for you to easily fall asleep and maintain sleep through the night.

5. Some people like to take a warm bath before bed. Others like to drink a glass of milk or some other beverage containing calcium, which can help you sleep.

6. Some like to write out the day's events in a journal so that they are not worried about things when

they fall asleep. If that works for you, great! Keep in mind that journal writing has been shown to improve the immune system, and it helps resolve challenging issues in your life. Others find journal writing right before bed too stimulating. Naturally this is true if you are keeping a digital journal on a back-lit screen, so try using a paper journal for evening reflections. See what works for you.

7. The amount of continuous sleep you get matters. So set up the evening accordingly, keeping in mind when you need to get up the next morning. Eight to nine hours is a range to aim for. See what your natural needs are, no matter your age. Over a week's time, give yourself plenty of time to sleep.

MINDSIGHT PRACTICE C: Focus Time

The brain grows not only when we sleep but also when we focus our attention in a continuous way without frequent distractions. In fact, learning is the way our attention streams

energy through our brain's circuits, creating information in certain areas that become activated, and then linking those activated neurons with brain growth. That's neuroplasticity, how the brain changes in response to experience. The brain is built to focus on one thing at a time, processing it into more elaborated forms, connecting it to similar items, linking it to others, and then consolidating all of the neural firing into long-term structural changes.

Focus time refers to those periods of time when we focus intently on one thing at a time. Unlike when we are multitasking, such as reading a book while texting or surfing the Web while speaking on the phone, focus time means doing only one thing at a time.

Peace: | One. | Thing. | At. | A. | Time. |

. When we focus intensely, we do three things in the brain. One is that the part of the brain just above the brain stem—palm secretes an important chemical, acetylcholine, throughout the brain. A second thing is that paying close attention intensely activates specific circuits. When neurons fire together, they wire together. And this brings us to the third: When we pay close attention to one thing, the acetylcholine bathing those activating circuits works with the localized release of another neurochemical, brain-derived neurotrophic factor, or BDNF, to optimize how genes become expressed to produce the proteins necessary to strengthen the connections among those firing neurons. In short, when you pay close attention, you optimize neuroplastic changes that are the basis for learning.

I know of adolescents who say they are having trouble with schoolwork. They cannot remember, they tell me, what they read or what they studied. And, indeed, all of the homework and studying they are doing just doesn't seem to have a lasting impact on their test performance. When I ask how they study, they reveal that they are often involved in multitasking. So what happens is that the person sits with a book but her attention is constantly being divided. This division of attention toward non-school material, in the form of chatting, texting, blogging, and Web surfing, continually disrupts the neuroplastic conditions necessary to make those studies turn into synaptic change in the brain. Without the lasting structural changes in the brain, no long-term learning can occur. The exam comes and goes, just like the divided attention that prevented any synapse growth from occurring.

These digitally enhanced disruptions to paying close attention compromise long-term learning for both adolescents *and* adults. In fact, many adults who are not involved in some life-long learning program, like book clubs or discussion groups or adult educational courses, have a serious potential problem. If we don't have focus time on a regular basis, our brains stop doing what they were born to do—continue to learn and grow and make new connections throughout our lives. Adults without the projects that enable them to closely pay attention to something can begin to feel like life has become a rut, unchanging, and boring. Lifelong learning should be seen as an opportunity to keep challenged, to keep the brain growing, and to keep ourselves engaged in learning.

Sadly, school for many of us becomes a burden, not a pleasure. The emphasis on competition instead of collaboration, on achievement rather than creative exploration, makes many of us turn off to the learning experience. Focus time reminds us that we need to keep our minds well honed and to keep on learning throughout our lives.

MINDSIGHT PRACTICE D: Downtime

While focusing attention in an uninterrupted manner helps the brain grow, you may also be relieved to know that we don't need to do that all the time. In fact, giving yourself a break and varying what you do is the whole idea of these simple seven daily mind activities. Every day we can have some downtime to enable our minds to unwind and our brains to sort themselves out. Downtime is when we have no plans, nothing we are trying to accomplish, nothing that needs to be done. During this period the brain seems to recharge its batteries, allowing the mind to intentionally be given a break.

Downtime is quite different from unintentional mind wandering. If the task at hand is to focus on something, like a conversation with someone or an assignment or talk at school, letting our minds wander off task without the choice to do that can be pretty disruptive to what we're trying to achieve. Some studies even suggest it's not good for our health and happiness.

Instead, downtime means that we designate a time to just chill out, to have nothing on the calendar, to let our imaginations go wherever they will. Vacations are a great time to just hang out. But on a daily basis, it's also good to set aside some time to take a brain break, to relax and unwind. Give yourself permission to do this intentionally. That's the goal of downtime, when we intentionally have no set goal. Sounds ironic, I know, but research reveals that it's really important, even in limited amounts, each day.

MINDSIGHT PRACTICE E: Playtime

The term "play" may make you think of childhood experiences on the playground, but we're discovering that participating in the spontaneous exploration of life with others in engaging, pleasurable, and non-judgmental ways is actually crucial for a healthy and fulfilling life throughout our life span. Laughing is a serious matter when it comes to brain matter. When we are spontaneous and having fun, the brain grows. It's as good for adolescents as it is for the adults who less frequently engage in play or just hanging out or goofing around. Giving ourselves the time and the permission to engage in activities, by ourselves and with others, where we are simply creating new and unexpected ways of being—in how we feel, in things we say and things we do, in ways we interact with others—is great to let the mind feel free and accepted for whatever it comes up with. It also lets the brain become active in new and unpredictable ways that are good for it to grow and solidify new connections. That's the basis of creativity and innovation. That's the pleasure of presence and connection.

Sadly, kids in school are scheduled for mostly goal-directed activities in which they are being judged and evaluated, compared with others, and asked to compete and beat their rivals. Whether it's in the controlled setting of a didactic lesson or exam in a classroom, or being on a team on the athletic field, those structured times are not what we mean by playtime. Instead, imagine an interaction where there is no winner, an interactive activity where there are no rigid rules, a time when laughing and creating and goofing around are accepted and people are engaged and silly and having a great time, without judgment, without a winner or loser. That's playtime.

I never stop surprising myself

Playtime

Sadly, adults often forget how to play. The social engagement system of the brain, a set of circuits that make learning facilitated and fun, becomes rusty and out of shape and can shut down. Activities become routine, and the spontaneous exploration of life and the world becomes a thing of the long distant past. In fact, the kind of creative thinking that emerges with such open and accepting engagement decreases dramatically once we get into elementary school. That divergent thinking enables us to "think outside the box" because we see life with fresh eyes and are not worried about being punished or embarrassed for getting something wrong—because there is sharing and exploration, not control and humiliation. A young child in preschool will be filled with curiosity about life and the world. But once that child gets to elementary school, the standard approach is to say that there is a right or a wrong, and if you study well, you'll get the right answer on the test or book report or essay or lab assignment. Nothing is wrong with learning to spell well. But we don't need to shut our spontaneity into little boxes, imprisoned in the routine of studies and tests and studies and tests. Creativity is often out the elementary window, and the rest of our school experience too frequently becomes filled with a non-playful seriousness that can kill spontaneity. And it can stifle the courage to be creative, to take a chance and imagine something new. That's part of why people can come to feel that school life is oppressive and uninspiring. When that's not the case, teachers often may have found a way to instill the spirit of play in the daily life of the classroom.

When I came to realize that as an adult playtime was not a part of my life, I signed up for an improvisational acting class for non-actors to join with others in just cracking up and having a good time. I love it. And though it is only once a week, I try to bring the joy of that experience into my daily life. I also started roller blading around the neighborhood on my own, listening to music and rolling and rocking down the street. The odd thing for me was that not only did I have to give myself permission to have fun, but for the serious part of my adult mind, I had to convince myself that it was actually good for my brain to let myself goof off. It's a win-win situation—my brain grows and I have a good time.

Playtime corrects the usual seriousness trend of school and adult life, giving us a daily time for being spontaneous and creative, feeling accepted and connected, alive and joyful, and having a whole lot of laughter and fun.

MINDSIGHT PRACTICE F: Physical Time

Moving your body grows your brain.

Aerobic movement that involves getting your heart rate up for over thirty minutes, preferably closer to forty-five, is a great start. Lifting weights or doing other activities that strengthen muscles with, for instance, stretch bands also supports how our brains function.

In the school district where I live, the loss of school funds and the emphasis on pure academic achievement led to physical education being disbanded and recess time for kids being shortened. On top of those changes, art and music and drama and dance were cut down as well. Something is off in these priorities, especially when you simply look at this from a brain perspective. Art and music and drama and dance support the creative explorations that playtime facilitates. And physical activity supports all our learning. When we move our bodies, neuroplasticity is enhanced. We remember more, we grow more connections in the brain, and we solidify those connections. Moving the body is crucial for not only brain health but also mental health. Aerobic exercise enhances our mood even if we are prone to becoming depressed. I know many a friend whose moodiness was evened out when exercise became a daily part of their lives.

For adults and for adolescents, physical time, if medically possible, is an important part of your daily brain and mind health. Ask your doctor how intense you can be with your physical activity if there are any medical issues that may limit your movements. Working up a sweat can be great, and finding variation in what you do can be essential in creating fitness and avoiding injuries. The key is to warm up, stretch, work out, stretch, and cool down.

Remember that daily movement of your body is your choice. No one can make you do it but you. But it's a win-win situation. You'll feel better, your brain will grow better, and you'll become more fit and healthy. Not bad for a daily workout.

MINDSIGHT PRACTICE G: Connecting Time

Numerous research studies reveal that the way we connect with others makes our lives more meaningful, healthy, wise, and happy. In Mindsight Tools #3, we explored how time-between and reflective conversations help us connect with others in supportive ways that are mutually rewarding. When we have supportive relationships, we are not only happier, we are healthier and live longer! Other studies show that when we are out in nature, we feel more grounded and our moods are more stable. So connecting time is when we connect to other people and the planet.

I try to remember the qualities of connecting time with the strange term "3G-2P." I know that isn't so memorable, but at least it has the core features of this important daily practice. 3G stands for the gratitude we have for being alive on this precious planet, the generosity we can bring to others in connecting with them, and the giving back (or gifting back) we can practice each day as we serve the well-being of others. And the 2P? You may have guessed. We bring gratitude, generosity, and giving back to other people and to the planet.

People and the planet. When we connect with other people in these positive ways, when we wish others to be happy, to be successful at what they do, to have joy and health in their lives, we bring a compassionate stance that supports something called "empathic joy"—getting joy from another's well-being. I know that sounds quite different from the usual competitive environment that modern society cultivates. But just try it out and I think you'll see that it's a win–win situation again. Studies of how we function as people reveal that we are built to collaborate with one another. When we work together in these supportive ways, the collective intelligence created is much more powerful than the solo person trying to beat out others.

On a simple level, connecting time means taking time to be with friends or family, hopefully face-to-face. The signals we get from others that are non-verbal, like eye contact and facial expressions, tone of voice, posture, gestures, timing and intensity of responses, and the human act of friendly and appropriate touch, are unavoidably missing in our digital means of communicating. If we mostly communicate with others via texting or digital chatting, there is a whole lot of important brain real estate not being engaged. If you can, try to make a daily practice of connecting time in person so that you engage your friends face-to-face when possible.

And the planet? How we take time to be in nature can shape our mood, help us focus attention, and give us a feeling of renewal and pleasure. If you live in a city, it may seem hard to get out in nature on a daily basis. But getting to a park or looking out at trees and clouds and the sky and moon is a good start. We come from the planet, and nature is our original home. Connecting with the planet can also mean doing more than simply being in nature, it can mean taking care of our environment. Picking up litter when we see it, and not littering ourselves, is a great start. Finding ways to avoid waste by recycling and being mindful about how we use energy can all be important ways each of us can connect to our common home, this planet Earth.

Connecting time can help us feel the truth that we belong to a larger whole than the body we live in. We may walk with our own two feet on this planet, but we are not alone. The Earth is our common home, other people our tribe, and all living beings our relatives.

CONCLUSION

■

MWe and the
Integration of Identity

We have come a long way in our conversation about adolescence. I cannot know how you are feeling about this exploration coming to a close soon, but I myself am feeling sad it's ending
yet exhilarated by the territory we've covered.

Our adolescence is a time of great integration—integration of
the many aspects of ourselves. During this important period in our
lives, the second dozen years, we explore the very nature of who we
are. And as we weave the essence of adolescence—the emotional
spark, the intense social engagement, the novelty seeking, and the
drive toward creative exploration—into who we are becoming, we

are undergoing a fundamental life process that does not, by any means, end when we are twenty-four. Integration of identity is a lifelong journey of defining what has meaning in your life now and for all the years to come.

Some time ago I began to think about the great human need we are facing at this moment in our history to move our focus from "me" to "we." I believe that as inhabitants of this planet the world *needs* us to stop being so self-involved and to instead transform in a way that is giving back, or gifting back, to the planet. I believe it is our duty to help other people and to protect the Earth. Interestingly, numerous studies support this idea that the more we help others, the healthier and happier we ourselves become.

At a lecture I gave on this subject, one of my seminar students became quite upset with this notion of "me to we." She said she was working hard on the various aspects of her personal integration, like finding a way to make sense of her attachment history and create both integration of her memories and a coherent narrative of her early life experiences. She said that she didn't want to give up finding a way of making sense of her individual life and instead focus on a "we." I listened closely to her concerns, and realized that the phrase "me to we" might imply something more extreme than what was intended. So I suggested to her that this notion was more like moving "from only me to also we." While such a phrase may not rhyme so well, at least it embraced the integration intended at its core, one that could embrace the importance of our individual, personal life as well as our interdependent, connected life.

Still, I started wondering how this idea of a bodily-defined self, a "me," opening itself up to and becoming a part of a larger self beyond, a "we," might be described in one word. I offered this young woman the following term, which I'll share with you as well:

MWe.

This is a term I have come to use to succinctly describe the integration of identity. It embraces the notion of breathing across our individualized, bodily defined self and linking all of us together as members of a larger whole, a we-defined self. *MWe* as a word itself, and as a concept, is defined by me and we, so we don't need to give up the important differentiation of a personal self and of an interconnected self. Each is different, each is important. Linking them together in our lives is a key that may help in our journey toward the integration of identity.

But why do we need the notion of MWe in the world?

Studies show that the more individualized and isolated our sense of self is, the less happy and less healthy we'll be. When we define a "self" as limited to the boundaries of our skin-encased bodies, we limit our sense of belonging and meaning in life. Yet so much in our modern culture, on the Internet, in our busy contemporary lives, reinforces this view that the self is a bodily defined aspect of who we are. Studies reveal clearly that when we are in supportive relationships and engage in helping others, we are happier and we are healthier. Even research on people who are given money demonstrates that they will have more long-lasting happiness when they use that money to benefit others rather than keeping it all for themselves.

Embracing MWe also means that we experience the sense that we are a part of a larger whole, a part of a larger purpose in life than just our own personal journey. MWe embraces notions of spirituality and that there is a deeper meaning to life directly. But it is important to note that being connected to something larger than ourselves does not mean that we must discard our private self. We simply need to expand it to include an interconnected self as well. That's integration. That's MWe.

Another aspect of MWe is crucial to mention here. People and our planet are in a painful state of needing care. When we look at the increases in the human population and the challenges for healthy food, air, and water, and the ever-increasing need for medicine, clothing, and shelter for our human family, and when we realize how other living creatures are suffering and disappearing because of what we humans are doing to the planet, we realize that there are a lot of problems we need to try to collectively solve.

Adolescents have so much to offer our world in this regard with their drive and ingenuity to find new solutions to these important global problems. But to do this, younger people need the support of elders; they need to be honored for their emerging minds' drive to push back and find creative explorations that may just open our minds up to new ways of dealing with these challenging times.

Working creatively and collaboratively in their communities and with their families and schools, the emerging generation will have the vision to move away from the mere memorization of facts and figures to create more imaginative and meaningful ways to inspire their generation and the generations that follow. We will be able to create the necessary changes for this new era through education and through the important role of our family life, the message of adolescence then moving out into our communities and the larger society in which we live. There is plenty to tackle, but when we pit our wits against the complex problems of global hunger, disease, and violence, pollution, climate change, and the loss of plants and animals in our ecosystems, we will succeed. By collaborating rather than trying to only surpass or annihilate one another, we will prevail as a human society living in an interconnected world.

When we bring our individual skills and passion and knowledge for the benefit of the larger whole, we are maximizing our chances of solving the world's practical and moral problems. I say "moral" here because it is a moral imperative to find a way to work together to solve our collective challenges. We share the same air, the same water, the same home, our planet Earth. A good planet is hard to find, so let's collectively take care of this one now. It is time to find a new identity to face these crucial times together.

As an adolescent these may seem like lofty ideas, I know. They may even seem irrelevant. I say them as we get ready to say goodbye, because I believe so deeply that our individual needs for meaning and belonging in order to feel happy and fulfilled in life can actually be satisfied by expanding the way we define the self. This is a win-win situation. Developing toward a MWe will make us happier, and it will give the world a fighting chance to become healthier as well. I believe that the world's challenges can most effectively be addressed by helping expand our sense of identity beyond a separate self.

Albert Einstein once said that the notion of an isolated self was "an optical delusion" that leads to all sorts of problems in the world and in life. A delusion is a false belief, a view that is not consistent with reality. When we see ourselves as separate, we are not facing the reality of our interdependent, interconnected nature. We are not integrating our identity with the larger world that we are fundamentally a part of. It just may be that many of our biggest challenges individually and collectively are in fact revealed as the chaos and rigidity of such impaired integration, a state created by our human sense of a separate self that assumes happiness comes from material acquisitions alone and that infinite consumption is possible on our resource-limited planet.

Integrating our identity reminds us to differentiate our bodily self and our interconnected self, and then to link them. It reminds us that our minds emerge as much from our bodies and brains as from our relationships with one another and with our planet. Why would an adolescent or an adult really care about integrating identity? For all of us, these second dozen years of life—whether we are in them now or are learning to hold on to their essence in our lives—carry the core qualities that just may be what we need to move the course of our planet's health in a positive direction. The integration of MWe can draw upon the essence of adolescence to harness the emotional spark that fuels our vital sense of being alive in our journey of life, not just while we are teenagers but throughout our later adolescence and into our adult years. We can harness the power of our social engagements to brainstorm ideas and find deep, meaningful connections that sustain and enrich our lives. With our search for novelty, we can make life an adventure that transforms the ordinary into the extraordinary, finding the unique aspects of our experience within each day of our lives. And with the creative explorations that inspire our inquiring minds to think in new ways, perceive with new eyes, and innovate with original contributions to our world's basic challenges, we can confront the problems ahead with a new sense of potential, purpose, and possibility. So this small word, *MWe*, lets us see the power of differentiation and linkage. And it reminds us of where we can go together as we encourage and expand the essence of adolescence throughout our lives.

E. B. White wrote: "If the world were merely seductive, that would be easy. If it were merely challenging, that would be no problem. But I arise in the morning torn between a desire to improve the world and a desire to enjoy the world. This makes it hard to plan the day."

To improve the world is a great intention, but if we see that as a pressure to "save" the world, it can become too overwhelming, too distant a goal. Instead, perhaps we can simply think of *serving* the world, of helping the planet and other people one relationship and one interaction at a time. The potential outcome of improving or saving can be a broad intention, but cannot be guaranteed; the act of serving is a goal we can grasp, something we *can* achieve. The other urge White felt is equally important. We should honor our desire to create joy in life, and we must never stop *savoring* the world. And so perhaps a way to embrace these two natural drives side by side can be our integrated approach: *Savor and serve.* Integrating our lives is about differentiating and linking these two goals that, though in many ways are separate, contribute to a full life of enjoyment and connection, pleasure and purpose. We can enjoy ourselves and one another; we can have fun and explore this life, this world, these relationships. And we can find ways to help others, to reduce suffering, to heal our planet. Savor and serve. MWe can help us achieve this balance.

The poet Maya Angelou, paraphrasing an old Chinese proverb, reminds us that we don't have to wait to have all the solutions before we express ourselves, before we participate in sharing this collective story of our lives. "A bird doesn't sing because it has an answer, it sings because it has a song." As we develop into adolescence and beyond, it is time for us to connect with one another, to share our songs of life, as we move through this journey of MWe together.

How can we know as adolescents if we are succeeding in living our lives fully? How can we know as adults that we are successfully supporting the emerging minds of the new generation well—and even carrying the essence of adolescence forward in our own lives? A poem by Bessie Anderson Stanley offers insights into what a successful adolescence might look like, how the essence of adolescence can enrich the rest of our lives:

SUCCESS

To laugh often and love much;
To win the respect of intelligent persons and the affection of children;
To earn the approbation of honest critics and endure the betrayal of
    false friends;
To appreciate beauty;
To find the best in others;

To give of one's self;

To leave the world a bit better, whether by a healthy child, a garden patch or a redeemed social condition;

To have played and laughed with enthusiasm and sung with exultation;

To know even one life has breathed easier because you have lived—

This is to have succeeded.

As we come to our final moments together, I wish for you all the vitality and authenticity that adolescence offers to those still in this period of life and those who have passed through it but have the opportunity for the rest of their lives to embrace its essence. May you be successful in letting the essence of adolescence thrive throughout your life. May an emotional spark fuel your life; may social engagement encourage collective intelligence and collaborative action; may the drive for novelty let you hold on to the privilege and thrill of this adventure of life; and may your creative explorations empower you to imagine and construct a world of tomorrow that all of us will be proud to live in for generations to come. I hope you will find ways to savor and to serve, to share your life's songs, and to integrate yourselves in new and authentic ways in your life ahead. Enjoy!

Acknowledgments

A book is like life: it depends on so many to nurture its essence as it grows and develops. In the journey to come to life, this book has had many individuals who have contributed to its various ages and stages. The experiences working with the many teens and parents over the years as a child and adolescent psychiatrist has been invaluable in gaining insights about the inside-out experience of the adolescent period. I would like to thank the adolescents and adults who have read various drafts of *Brainstorm* and offered insightful comments, questions, and suggestions that have been important in making the messages as accessible and useful as possible. These thoughtful people include Kayla Abrams, Michele Chuban, Jonathan Fried, Lorna Gallant, Mahayla Galliford, Mike Galliford, Laura Hubber, Laura Kastner, Scott Kriens, Lynn Kutler, Maria LeRose, Sally Maslansky, Mike McKay, Mary Pipher, Ellen Ridgeway, Rebecca Shahmoon Shanok, Maddi Siegel, Rich Simon, and Jamie Zimmerman. I thank you all for your time, energy, and wisdom in helping with the creation of this work.

I have also been fortunate to have a team of wonderful people at the Mindsight Institute, including Eric Bergemann, Tina Bryson, Adriana Copeland, Stephanie Hamilton, Teresa Reilly, Ashish Soni, and Whitney Stambler, who work tirelessly to bring into the world these scientific and practical ideas about our relationships, minds, and brains and about compassion, connection, and community. Special thanks to Caroline Welch for her visionary leadership in guiding our institute and creating a culture of creativity. I am grateful for the professional and personal support of Douglas Abrams as the literary agent representing this work from the start.

Leah Pearlman of Dharmacomics.com was a dream to work with as we selected from her joyous and loving illustrations to illuminate the ideas and feelings of the book, finding parallel passions as we went along. It has also been a pleasure to work with my thoughtful and incisive editor at Tarcher/Penguin, Sara Carder, a wonderful companion in shepherding the ideas and their expression into their final form. Also part of the terrific team at Tarcher are Joanna Ng and Brianna Yamashita, who have worked hard to help this book see the light of day. I thank you all.

I could never be the person I am, or the person who put "pen to page" to help this book be born, without the support and inspiration of my family at home: Alex and Maddi Siegel and Caroline Welch. I do not have the words to express the gratitude and love I feel for the three of you. Thank you for our adventures and for being you.

Index

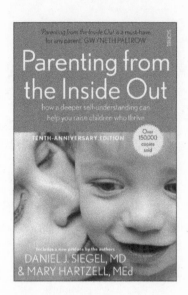

Parenting from the Inside Out
DANIEL J. SIEGEL, MD & MARY HARTZELL, MEd

**An updated edition — with a new foreword by
the authors — of the bestselling parenting classic**

'Dan Siegel and Mary Hartzell have quite deftly managed to translate
highly complex neuroscientific and psychological matters into lay
strategies for effective parenting.'
MARILYN B. BENOIT, MD, former president,
American Academy of Child and Adolescent Psychiatry

'*Parenting from the Inside Out* is a must-have for any parent.'
GWYNETH PALTROW

SCRIBE   Seriously good books.
scribepublications.co.uk